Jaguar Books on Latin America

Series Editors

WILLIAM H. BEEZLEY, Professor of History, University of Arizona
COLIN M. MACLACHLAN, John Christy Barr Distinguished Professor of
History, Tulane University

Volumes Published

John E. Kicza, ed., *The Indian in Latin American History: Resistance,
Resilience, and Acculturation* (1993; rev. ed., 2000).
Cloth ISBN 0-8420-2822-6   Paper ISBN 0-8420-2823-4

Susan E. Place, ed., *Tropical Rainforests: Latin American Nature and
Society in Transition* (1993; rev. and updated ed., 2001).
Cloth ISBN 0-8420-2907-9   Paper ISBN 0-8420-2908-7

Paul W. Drake, ed., *Money Doctors, Foreign Debts, and Economic
Reforms in Latin America from the 1890s to the Present* (1994).
Cloth ISBN 0-8420-2434-4   Paper ISBN 0-8420-2435-2

John A. Britton, ed., *Molding the Hearts and Minds: Education,
Communications, and Social Change in Latin America* (1994).
Cloth ISBN 0-8420-2489-1   Paper ISBN 0-8420-2490-5

David J. Weber and Jane M. Rausch, eds., *Where Cultures Meet: Frontiers
in Latin American History* (1994). Cloth ISBN 0-8420-2477-8
Paper ISBN 0-8420-2478-6

Gertrude M. Yeager, ed., *Confronting Change, Challenging Tradition:
Women in Latin American History* (1994). Cloth ISBN 0-8420-2479-4
Paper ISBN 0-8420-2480-8

Linda Alexander Rodríguez, ed., *Rank and Privilege: The Military and
Society in Latin America* (1994). Cloth ISBN 0-8420-2432-8
Paper ISBN 0-8420-2433-6

Darién J. Davis, ed., *Slavery and Beyond: The African Impact on Latin
America and the Caribbean* (1995). Cloth ISBN 0-8420-2484-0
Paper ISBN 0-8420-2485-9

Gilbert M. Joseph and Mark D. Szuchman, eds., *I Saw a City Invincible:
Urban Portraits of Latin America* (1996). Cloth ISBN 0-8420-2495-6
Paper ISBN 0-8420-2496-4

Roderic Ai Camp, ed., *Democracy in Latin America: Patterns and Cycles*
(1996). Cloth ISBN 0-8420-2512-X   Paper ISBN 0-8420-2513-8

Oscar J. Martínez, ed., *U.S.-Mexico Borderlan... Historical and
Contemporary Perspectives* (1996). Cloth I...
Paper ISBN 0-8420-2447-6

D1416570

William O. Walker III, ed., *Drugs in the Western Hemisphere: An Odyssey of Cultures in Conflict* (1996). Cloth ISBN 0-8420-2422-0
Paper ISBN 0-8420-2426-3

Richard R. Cole, ed., *Communication in Latin America: Journalism, Mass Media, and Society* (1996). Cloth ISBN 0-8420-2558-8
Paper ISBN 0-8420-2559-6

David G. Gutiérrez, ed., *Between Two Worlds: Mexican Immigrants in the United States* (1996). Cloth ISBN 0-8420-2473-5
Paper ISBN 0-8420-2474-3

Lynne Phillips, ed., *The Third Wave of Modernization in Latin America: Cultural Perspectives on Neoliberalism* (1998).
Cloth ISBN 0-8420-2606-1   Paper ISBN 0-8420-2608-8

Daniel Castro, ed., *Revolution and Revolutionaries: Guerrilla Movements in Latin America* (1999). Cloth ISBN 0-8420-2625-8
Paper ISBN 0-8420-2626-6

Virginia Garrard-Burnett, ed., *On Earth as It Is in Heaven: Religion in Modern Latin America* (2000). Cloth ISBN 0-8420-2584-7
Paper ISBN 0-8420-2585-5

Carlos A. Aguirre and Robert Buffington, eds., *Reconstructing Criminality in Latin America* (2000). Cloth ISBN 0-8420-2620-7
Paper ISBN 0-8420-2621-5

Christon I. Archer, ed., *The Wars of Independence in Spanish America* (2000). Cloth ISBN 0-8420-2468-9   Paper ISBN 0-8420-2469-7

John F. Schwaller, ed., *The Church in Colonial Latin America* (2000).
Cloth ISBN 0-8420-2703-3   Paper ISBN 0-8420-2704-1

Ingrid E. Fey and Karen Racine, eds., *Strange Pilgrimages: Exile, Travel, and National Identity in Latin America, 1800–1990s* (2000).
Cloth ISBN 0-8420-2693-2   Paper ISBN 0-8420-2694-0

Joseph L. Arbena and David G. LaFrance, eds., *Sport in Latin America and the Caribbean* (2002). Cloth ISBN 0-8420-2820-X
Paper ISBN 0-8420-2821-8

Samuel L. Baily and Eduardo José Míguez, eds., *Mass Migration to Modern Latin America* (2003). Cloth ISBN 0-8420-2830-7
Paper ISBN 0-8420-2831-5

Erick D. Langer with Elena Muñoz, eds., *Contemporary Indigenous Movements in Latin America* (2003). Cloth ISBN 0-8420-2679-7
Paper ISBN 0-8420-2680-0

Vincent C. Peloso, ed., *Work, Protest, and Identity in Twentieth-Century Latin America* (2003). Cloth ISBN 0-8420-2926-5
Paper ISBN 0-8420-2927-3

Contemporary Indigenous Movements in Latin America

Contemporary Indigenous Movements in Latin America

Edited by
Erick D. Langer with Elena Muñoz

Jaguar Books on Latin America
Number 25

A Scholarly Resources Inc. Imprint
Wilmington, Delaware

Scholarly Resources Inc.
104 Greenhill Avenue
Wilmington, DE 19805-1897
www.scholarly.com

Library of Congress Cataloging-in-Publication Data

Contemporary indigenous movements in Latin America / Erick D.
   Langer with Elena Muñoz, editors.
      p. cm. — (Jaguar books on Latin America ; no. 25)
   Includes index.
      ISBN 0-8420-2679-7 (alk. paper) — ISBN 0-8420-2680-0 (pbk. :
alk. paper)
      1. Indians—Social conditions. 2. Indians—Civil rights. 3. Indians—
Government relations. 4. Indians, Treatment of—Latin America.
5. Self-determination, National—Latin America. 6. Latin America—
Race relations. 7. Latin America—Politics and government. 8. Latin
America—Social policy. I. Langer, Erick Detlef. II. Muñoz, Elena.
III. Series.

E65.C66 2003
323.1'198—dc21   2002044513

∞ The paper used in this publication meets the minimum requirements of
the American National Standard for permanence of paper for printed library materials, Z39.48, 1984.

About the Editors

ERICK D. LANGER is professor of history in the School of Foreign Service at Georgetown University. He has done research and lectured extensively on indigenous affairs, especially on Indian rebellions in the Andes and on issues relating to frontiers.

ELENA MUÑOZ works for the International Rescue Committee in New York City. She is also a student at the School of International and Public Affairs at Columbia University.

Contents

ERICK D. LANGER, Introduction, **xi**

I   In the Defense of Land

1   EMILIENNE IRELAND, Neither Warriors nor Victims: The Wauja
     Peacefully Organize to Defend Their Land, **3**

2   MARIO SZNAJDER, Ethnodevelopment and Democratic
     Consolidation in Chile: The Mapuche Question, **17**

II   Indigenous Political Participation

3   LEON ZAMOSC, Agrarian Protest and the Indian Movement in the
     Ecuadorian Highlands, **37**

4   ERIN O'CONNOR, Indians and National Salvation: Placing Ecuador's
     Indigenous Coup of January 2000 in Historical Perspective, **65**

5   SILVIA MARÍA HIRSCH, The Emergence of Political Organizations
     among the Guaraní Indians of Bolivia and Argentina: A
     Comparative Perspective, **81**

6   RENÉ HARDER HORST, Consciousness and Contradiction:
     Indigenous Peoples and Paraguay's Transition to Democracy, **103**

III   Indians and Guerrillas

7   ORIN STARN, Villagers at Arms: War and Counterrevolution in the
     Central-South Andes, **135**

8   KAY B. WARREN, Pan-Maya Activism in Guatemala, **169**

IV   Indigenous Leaders Speak Out

9   Marta Silva Vito Guaraní (Brazil), **187**

10   Davi Kopenawa Yanomami (Brazil), **191**

11   Luis Macas (Ecuador), **195**

12   Nina Pacari (Ecuador), **201**

13   Felipe Quispe Huanca (Bolivia), **205**

14   R. Marhikewun (Chile), **211**

Selected Bibliography, **217**

Internet Sources, **219**

Introduction

Erick D. Langer

Indigenous peoples have become an important political factor in many Latin American countries, both in states where they represent a large proportion of the population, such as Bolivia and Guatemala, and in states where people who are defined as Indians constitute a tiny minority, such as Brazil and Chile. This phenomenon is a relatively recent one—mostly from the 1990s onward—although many indigenous organizations trace their roots back at least to the 1970s. Thus, this reader includes selections that deal with the origins of these organizations, with the emphasis on the most recent period.

A brief introduction to such a complex topic can only cover some of the most important issues of native movements in Latin America over the past decade or so. To do so, this chapter includes a brief analytical overview of types of indigenous actions since the European invasion in 1492, the diverse nature of the movements since 1992, and the connections between indigenous peoples and other groups, particularly on the international scene.

Some Historical Background

Indigenous peoples participated actively in politics long before the last decades of the twentieth century, in pre-Columbian states such as the Aztec empire in what is now Mexico and the Inca empire in the Andes.[1] Even "stateless societies" such as the Mapuche of Chile or the various tribal peoples of the Amazon were engaged in some sort of politics on the regional or village level. Likewise, when the Europeans invaded from 1492 onward, indigenous peoples acted within the new context, either defending their territories against the Spanish conquistadors or allying with the invaders for strategic reasons. A significant number, both indigenous leaders and common folk, continued to work with the invaders even after it became clear that the Europeans were there to stay. Others, however, refused to accept the Spaniards or Portuguese as overlords and launched revolts, often messianic in nature, to overthrow the new colonial regimes.

The Mixtec Revolt of the 1640s in Mexico and the Taqui Onkoy rebellion in the 1560s in the Andes merged Christian elements with native beliefs to create vibrant movements that threatened Spain's colonial dominance.[2] Large swaths of territory inhabited by such people as the Chiriguano in Bolivia, the Apache in northern Mexico, and the Mapuche in central Chile remained outside of colonial control.

It was in the colonial period that native peoples became "Indians." The label "Indian" (or *indio* in Spanish) was used in error by Christopher Columbus, who thought that by sailing west he had landed in India. After the Conquest, Spanish as well as other European colonizers described the native peoples of the New World in this way. The term "Indian" became important for its legal implications (many Indians had to pay tribute or provide labor services) and eventually began to be accepted by the native peoples themselves.

Many indigenous peasants, because they could not leave their land to fight against their new overlords, instead found subtle ways of resisting colonial control, such as filing lawsuits. They used their designation of "Indian" to wrest concessions from their dominators and so turned their new status against their conquerors. This method continued well into the twentieth century and, with some modifications, is still practiced today.

The colonial period in Latin America was punctuated by Indian revolts, although almost none of them succeeded in ridding the region of the invaders. After the first decades of colonial rule, ethnic mixture and an acceptance of some European norms, especially by the indigenous elites, made outright rebellion more difficult. Some members of the native elites had intermarried with Spaniards or become members of Spanish society. Only a cycle of violence beginning in the late eighteenth century, of which the Túpac Amaru rebellion in Peru and Bolivia is the most famous, severely strained European-Indian relations. Túpac Amaru and other Indian leaders rose up to fight against colonial exploitation, which had increased during the Spanish reforms of the eighteenth century in which the Crown attempted to wrest ever more revenue from the empire. At first, Túpac Amaru called on the Creoles (people of Spanish descent who were born in the Americas) to join him against the Spaniards, but in the end few non-Indians took part in his movement. Despite the violence and the widespread nature of these revolts, the Spaniards crushed them.[3] Ironically, the repression of these movements just before the end of the colonial period reduced the role of indigenous peoples as independent actors in the independence struggles that followed.

Between the European invasion and independence, most indigenous groups had shrunk both numerically and in terms of their ethnic identification. The colonial experience had been uniformly disastrous. Once-proud confederations had ceased to exist, and some peoples thought of themselves as belonging to a certain village or a certain region rather than to larger ethnic or linguistic units. The late eighteenth century brought some demographic recovery, and so did the first fifty years of independence, when weak states found it difficult to exploit or control indigenous groups to the same extent as in the colonial period. Nevertheless, the nineteenth century also experienced multiple ethnic rebellions, with the most notable one being the Caste War among the Maya on Mexico's Yucatán Peninsula (1848–1902), although most were smaller in scale than in the colonial period. Moreover, by the late nineteenth century Liberal ideology, which did not recognize indigenous communities as viable institutions, made ethnic survival and maintenance of village lands very difficult. The creole urban elites had absorbed Liberalism from Europe and tried to apply it to the very different context of Latin America.

The period from the late nineteenth to the early twentieth century represented the nadir of indigenous peoples. Not only did a racist ideology that placed indigenous peoples at the lowest levels of humanity (and thus open to exploitation) infect Latin American governments' policies toward natives, but a great push to conquer the still-independent indigenous groups also led to the consolidation of territorial control by nation-states. Invasions by national armies wiped out the independent territories in the Pampas, the Chaco, and Patagonia in Argentina, the Mapuche lands in southern Chile, and the Apache and Comanche territories in northern Mexico. The only place where some native peoples were able to hold on during this period was the vast Amazon basin, where the tropical climate, threats of disease, and dense jungle made it difficult for government forces to assert military control. Even there, the rubber boom in the second half of the nineteenth century made life difficult for indigenous peoples.

Most of the twentieth century was a period of neglect. The nationalistic regimes of the midtwentieth century favored the integration of indigenous peoples into the nation-state as "citizens" without recognizing their distinctive ethnic origins. Natives found themselves marginalized, and even progressive regimes thought in terms of class (Indians became peasants) rather than ethnicity. Indigenous peoples could not object to programs by claiming a different ethnic or racial status, for that category was seen as unmodern and did not have legal standing. Although in some cases this neglect appeared to be relatively benign, it led to an implicit policy of ethnocide, for the distinctive cultural characteristics of native peoples were supposed to be subsumed into the greater body politic. At best, the Indians were exoticized, and their distinctive dress and "millenarian characteristics" were seen as a means to attract tourist dollars. Even in countries where the Indian ideal served as an important national symbol, as in Chile, the indigenous peoples themselves were ignored.[4]

In addition, economic development policies brought about widespread destruction of native lands. This loss was especially remarkable in the

Amazon region, where the Brazilian military dictatorship (1964–1985) privileged the economic development of the Amazon basin through free-trade zones, dams, industrial development, and a concerted effort to criss-cross the jungle with the Trans-Amazon Highway. Indigenous land rights were largely ignored. The ensuing invasion of settlers from the coastal regions and the gold rush in the far north of the country brought disease, land conflicts, and death and destruction to many native peoples. Similar processes occurred in Ecuador, where oil companies polluted vital rivers and where white oil workers killed Indians at will. In the Chiapas region of Mexico, loggers and cattle barons likewise usurped native lands with the connivance of local officials.

Over the past five centuries, therefore, indigenous peoples have en-gaged in different types of resistance and accommodation. These tactics ranged from the relatively rare outright rebellion, to using the legal sys-tem, to everyday forms of resistance. Moreover, many indigenous peoples were only incompletely integrated into the body politic, even as subaltern groups. Only in the twentieth century have the state and multinational companies been able to reach into the most difficult terrain and eliminate frontiers. By the late twentieth century, most of the native peoples were interconnected and felt, in one way or another, the presence of the state and the international economy.

Fittingly, it was this process of globalization that made possible the modern movements. The universal nature of economic and social pro-cesses, combined with the triumph of the European nation-state model, made possible a new ethnic resurgence and consciousness that earlier had been absent. It also connected the various ethnic movements on the na-tional level, giving them the clout and the ability to link to progressive urban movements that had some sympathy for indigenous peoples. Until the 1970s, there were few national-level native organizations that brought together the diverse regionally based groups. By the 1990s, not only had effective national-level organizations emerged, but they also gained new international strength through increased ease of travel throughout the hemi-sphere, the breakthrough in telecommunications (including the use of the Internet), and the growth of nongovernmental organizations (NGOs) that supported indigenous rights. The latter phenomenon was due to the pain-ful process of "structural readjustment" of the state, which shrank in size. The NGOs took up some of the slack in social measures that the state had previously funded, both by employing many middle-class Latin Ameri-cans in the city who otherwise would have become bureaucrats and by providing a rudimentary social net for the poor. However, by giving away some of its social functions, the state in Latin America also lost much of its ability to determine the agenda for helping the poor. Indigenous groups were able to garner support for programs that the Latin American govern-ments probably would not have funded on their own.

The return of democracy was vital for the proliferation of indigenous movements and their appearance as serious and constructive actors on the national stage. Previously, some indigenous groups, such as the Kataristas in Bolivia, originated as important opposition forces to military dictatorships. Others had few national political ambitions—instead, mostly local concerns about land usurpations, economic development, and the like—but the military regimes from the 1960s to the 1980s saw these indigenous organizations as subversive. This was the case most notably in Guatemala and Chile, where authoritarian governments used extremely violent tactics to suppress native groups. Also, in many regions the military viewed the Indians as naturally sympathetic to the programs of guerrillas. Both guerrillas (to their regret) and the military often found out that this was not necessarily the case. In Peru, for example, the military, after spending the first years fighting the peasants, in the early 1980s finally began to employ them to help eliminate the Sendero Luminoso insurgency. (See the essay by Orin Starn, Chapter 7.)

Democracy made it possible for indigenous groups to organize openly. Their leaders were no longer automatically feared as subversives. Moreover, politicians saw indigenous movements as the source of votes in elections. Democracy also made possible the creation of national-level networks with less fear of repression. Most native groups usually found greater opposition from local elites, as the Indians' actions were aimed at powerholders in their own region rather than at the national level. Further, democracy made it possible to link up with other social and political actors, such as the Catholic Church and the host of NGOs that were created to alleviate poverty and help preserve cultural or environmental resources.

The year 1992 was an important turning point, ironically, because of the celebrations for the Quincentenary of Columbus's momentous journey to the New World. Although some wanted to celebrate this event as a politically neutral "encounter"—the Spanish government in particular, which in 1992 also hosted the World's Fair in Seville, from where many of the galleons had departed for the Americas—this focus proved impossible. While several governments tried, with Madrid's support, to showcase the benefits that European culture had brought to the Americas, indigenous groups were incensed. They argued that 1492 marked the beginning of a tragedy that did not merit applause. For them, they asserted, that year meant the start of a European invasion that devastated native cultures and peoples. It had led to the destruction of native polities, the death of millions of people due to disease, warfare, and overwork, and the imposition of foreign rule throughout the two continents.

Indigenous leaders had begun to organize themselves before the Quincentenary in a series of meetings beginning in 1987 to counteract the Columbus celebrations. They also allied themselves with a number of international NGOs, such as Cultural Survival, to provide funding and forums. Thus, the event was also marked by the first large-scale flexing of international alliances that remained characteristic of the indigenous movement thereafter. The Earth Summit of 1992 in Rio de Janeiro also was a highly publicized event in which indigenous peoples created new awareness on the international stage. Both the Columbus festivities in each country and the Rio Summit provided the indigenous groups with an opportunity for heavy media coverage both within their own countries and throughout the world. The media-savvy events by native groups heightened awareness of indigenous causes and eventually drew much-needed funding from European and North American sources. As we will see, the international dimension has been very important for native movements at the turn of this century, but first let us turn to the internal dynamics of indigenous organizations.

The Internal Dynamics of Indigenous Movements

The label "Indian" hides the incredible diversity of indigenous peoples in Latin America.[5] They range from small groups of hunters and horticulturalists in the Amazon jungle to the densely populated village societies of peasants in the Andean highlands and Mesoamerica. Today (this role is new in Latin America) many people consider themselves to be of native origin and as "Indians" reside in the large cities of Mexico City, Guatemala City, Lima, or La Paz.[6] In countries such as Colombia and Ecuador, those of African descent who live in the countryside have also pressed to be included as Indians, complicating the situation even further.

Until recently (and still in many cases), "Indian" (or *indio*) has been a derogatory word in many Latin American countries, often most closely associated with the word *sucio* (dirty). Thus, in many heavily indigenous countries where significant land reforms occurred, such as Bolivia after 1952 and Peru after 1968, *indio* was abolished from official discourse and replaced with *campesino*. In the reformist regimes where this change occurred, it meant that government leaders were trying to impose a class analysis, believing that keeping the old colonial terminology placed the country folk in an inferior social position. These reformist regimes assumed that using "modern" terms that referred to class status instead of ethnic origin made a progressive and more accurate analysis of the situation in the countryside. Although well intentioned, the policies led to a type of cultural ethnocide and did nothing to change the denigration of native groups, their languages, and their cultures. These groups have had to fight against this classist position by trying to recoup their ethnic identity and, most important, by creating respect for their languages and cultures. Ethnic pride became a goal of many indigenous groups from the

1980s onward, but it only reached its full flowering in the last decade of the twentieth century.

The insistence on ethnic pride and uniqueness posed many problems for organizing the many different groups on a national or even regional level. Often, some ethnic groups defined themselves as superior to others in an attempt to subsume other groups as part of their own. Given that each group relied on its own ethnic markers as sources of pride, this type of "cultural imperialism" was not welcomed. This has been the case with the strong Aymara movement emanating from northern Bolivia that has attempted to harness Quechua speakers from central and southern Bolivia into its program as subalterns.[7] (See Felipe Quispe's speech in Chapter 13.) In fact, in almost all cases the strength of the indigenous movement has come from the alliance of the separate ethnic groups. Since each one considers itself superior, it has often been difficult for members of a particular indigenous group to attract the votes of others during elections.

The diversity of indigenous peoples has made it difficult for them to organize effectively on a national basis for other reasons. In states where there was a relatively homogeneous Indian mass, such as Guatemala, the Maya groups speak many different dialects and have their own separate histories that claim oppression by other Maya speakers. The struggle to bring together these peasants into a coherent pan-Maya movement was fraught with difficulties. Only the active intervention of public Maya intellectuals, both by those remaining in the country and by those exiled during the brutal civil war, helped to bring about a fragile alliance by the late 1980s. They focused on the Maya language as a way of organizing in a very repressive regime. Enough common—and politically neutral—ground was found for the different linguistic groups to coalesce into a meaningful national structure. (See the selection by Kay Warren, Chapter 8.)

In most countries, such as Ecuador or Mexico, indigenous peoples are extremely diverse and do not see much similarity between themselves and other native groups. For example, in Ecuador the Amazonian peoples are most concerned with colonists who settle their land and with the oil companies that have ruined habitat and polluted streams. The peoples of the Andean highlands in Ecuador, in turn, have been more concerned with land tenure issues and the price of gasoline. After all, rather than hunters and horticulturalists who range over wide territories in the jungle, the highland people are sedentary agriculturalists who have farmed small plots intensively over centuries. However, by the late 1980s, the democratic opening, inspired leadership, resistance to new market forces, and foreign help led to the loose indigenous alliance called CONAIE (Confederation of Indigenous Nationalities of Ecuador).

Another issue that has come to the forefront throughout indigenous movements is the role of women as leaders.[8] The most recognized are Rigoberta Menchú, the Maya from Guatemala who in 1992 won the Nobel

Peace Prize for her work; and Nina Pacari, one of the principals in the Ecuadorian movement and a deputy in Congress for the Pachakutik Party. Female participation and percentage of women leaders at all different levels have been higher in indigenous movements than in Latin American politics as a whole. Although more research needs to be done, it is likely that this pattern of female participation in revolts has been traditionally high among native groups. What is new is the recognition of women as leaders within these movements. This strategy has been deliberate in some cases, such as in Ecuador, where a school exists exclusively for developing leadership skills among indigenous women. Also, many NGOs were interested in developing the potential of indigenous women, and these efforts have been one result.

The participation of women in leadership positions, however, has varied widely, reflecting the diverse mosaic of culture among indigenous peoples and their attitudes about women. In the Aymara area, there have been few women in positions of authority, but instead it has been suggested that wives are indispensable as complements to their husbands and that the leadership role is a dual male/female one. This view is part of the Andean attitude toward gender relations as distinct from the Hispanic heritage imposed by the Spaniards.[9]

With higher levels of female participation, women have often been in the forefront of demonstrations. They are able to use the perception of themselves as fragile and Virgin Mary-like in Iberian culture to confront police and soldiers in ways that men cannot. In many Latin societies, the male forces of repression are less willing to use their truncheons or guns against women. Also, newspaper photos of armed men beating women tends to resonate in the larger society and generates sympathy for the Indian cause. The indigenous movement is willing to use Iberian cultural conventions against its erstwhile oppressors, a pattern that has existed since colonial times.

The tactics employed by the groups to press their case have varied widely, according to the level of organization and to external constraints. Indigenous movements had a difficult time organizing and becoming effective during the dictatorial regimes of the 1960s and 1970s. The Katarista movement in Bolivia was the exception, as the Banzer dictatorship (1971–1978) at first was less worried about an ethnically based movement than about traditional class-based ones from labor organizations or leftist parties. Likewise, the Maya activists in Guatemala first organized as cultural organizations, since the succession of genocidal military regimes interpreted any Maya political activity as subversive. Once democracy returned to the region, the tactics of indigenous movements took on many forms. In Bolivia and Ecuador, the closing of main roads in the countryside to cut off the cities from their lines of supply was a common and very successful tactic. Marches on the capital by large numbers of indigenous peoples were another favored tactic, such as the one from Chiapas to Mexico City in 2001 and numerous times in Bolivia from the 1990s onward. In Chile the Mapuche also used roadblocks as well as land takeovers, before the 1973 military coup. Since then, the authoritarian structure of the Chilean state has not permitted violent activities; instead, the Mapuche protested by organizing marches and trying to get government officials to attend to their demands. Under democracy, many governments created offices that dealt with indigenous affairs. Others, such as Brazil, already had such agencies—in this case the famed FUNAI (National Indigenous Foundation)—but they had been created to "bring civilization to the Indians" rather than deal with native groups as equals. This situation changed in the 1990s, when indigenous peoples demanded their own rights rather than wait for federal bureaucrats to try to integrate them into the nation.

Alliance with international NGOs also helped to put pressure on governments to take into account indigenous demands. NGOs within Latin American countries aided native groups by providing funding and legal expertise for lawsuits. Some even went so far, such as the Huaroani of Ecuador, to bring suits in U.S. courts, in one case against Texaco. Lawsuits worked best for concrete issues such as land claims and stopping the building of a dam but were not always successful in matters of cultural preservation or the fight against guerrilla movements.

In the political arena, the best-organized movements have elected their own representatives to local and national offices. The Ecuadorian natives have been most effective, though the nativist Pachakutik Party has many fewer representatives than the relative numbers of people defined as Indians in the country. In Bolivia, Evo Morales, an Aymara, came in second place in the 2002 presidential elections with 21 percent of the vote (the winner, Gonzalo Sánchez de Lozada, only had 22 percent in a crowded field). However, his appeal was less that he was an Indian than that he ran on the Socialist ticket and opposed the neoliberal policies imposed since 1985 by the state.[10] A better indication of the success of a purely Indian political movement was the failure of presidential candidate Felipe Quispe in 2002, who ran on an indigenist platform. He only won about 2 percent of the vote.

The only indigenous movement that got involved in major rebellions was CONAIE of Ecuador. Violence flared in 1992 and 1994, although in most cases its source was the police and army. However, the threat of violence in the road closings has been implicit. In 2000, CONAIE leaders participated in a coup against the government. As Erin O'Connor shows (Chapter 4), the results were less than favorable for the movement. But Ecuador here is the exception, and it is not likely that indigenous movements will again resort to that level of violence. The most effective methods have been lawsuits, pressure on government officials, and peaceful mobilizations in the countryside and in the cities.

Native Americans and the State

How do the twenty-first-century indigenous movements participate in the state but at the same time maintain their ethnic identity? As we have seen, until very recently the policy of many Latin American states was to wipe out ethnic differences in an effort to create homogeneous citizens. Although some native leaders have advocated a completely independent line that does not recognize the legitimacy of the state (such as Felipe Quispe of Bolivia[11]), most movements have tried to find political power for themselves and their ethnic group within the state. Such is the case in Ecuador with the most important indigenous movement as well as in Chiapas, Mexico, and elsewhere. Many have advocated the creation of a state that recognizes the multiethnic nature of their own society. In the case of Bolivia the 1993 Constitution incorporates this principle into its first article.

In many countries, the issue of the relative independence of indigenous groups and their place in society is hotly contested. Although there are many legal matters involved that revolve around terms such as "ethnic group" versus "peoples" (with the former not having rights beyond the nation-state), the important issue is that many governments see the relative autonomy of native peoples as threatening. This view is nowhere more the case than in Brazil, where most indigenous groups that clamor for autonomy live in difficult-to-reach places and along poorly patrolled borders in the Amazon region. With the continued threat of drug smuggling and coca cultivation spilling over the borders into Brazil, its armed forces have defined the relative autonomy of indigenous groups as a national security issue. As a result, the ability for movement within the Brazilian system has been relatively limited for those groups unfortunate enough to live close to national boundaries. This problem occurs also in Colombia, Venezuela, and Chile.

In other countries, leaders of indigenous movements have become well integrated into the body politic. Other than Nina Pacari in Ecuador (a member of the opposition), the most important figure has been Víctor Hugo Cárdenas, an Aymara who in 1993 became vice president of Bolivia on the ticket of Gonzalo Sánchez de Lozada, a member of the aristocracy, the owner of the largest mining company in Bolivia, and the leader of the Movimiento Nacional Revolucionario (MNR). However, Cárdenas's participation in government caused him to lose political allies because he became associated with the neoliberal policies of the MNR regime that do not favor peasants or Indian communities. Some accused the MNR of buying Cárdenas as a sort of fig leaf to cover up the antipopular measures that the government in the end wanted to impose. However, Cárdenas pledged to bring to the fore indigenous rights, and it was in part due to him that the constitution was changed in 1993 to recognize the multicultural and pluriethnic nature of Bolivian society.

Since then, indigenous politics in Bolivia have veered in the opposite direction, with the rise of former guerrilla leader and hard-line Aymara-rights advocate Felipe Quispe. As the selection of one of his speeches demonstrates, Quispe sees Bolivia (and much of the Andes) as Aymara, in which whites have no place. This new direction moves away from the multiethnicity that most other mainstream Indian movements have advocated. His election loss might push him further along that route.

In Peru, where there has been no significant indigenous rights movement over the past few decades, the issue of native peoples nevertheless is important. After all, indigenous protests had marked the history of Peru during much of the twentieth century. Moreover, the leader of APRA (Alianza Popular Revolucionaria Americana—American Popular Revolutionary Alliance), Víctor Haya de la Torre, had proclaimed in the 1920s that Latin America should be called "Indoamerica" because of the significance of the native population. Mention of his own heritage was an important element of President Alejandro Toledo's 2001 campaign, inducing pride among the large indigenous population in the Andean nation. However, his story as a refugee from the Andean highlands shows integration rather than separatism, as he rose from shoeshine boy and then (in part through a university education in the United States) to the presidency of Peru.

International Dimensions

One of the truly interesting issues in the florescence of native ethnic consciousness—which by definition highlights the local and the unique among people—has been the large role that international organizations have played in the development of indigenous movements. The most important include the International Labor Organization (ILO), the United Nations, the Catholic Church, and a whole host of NGOs, both those concerned with cultural issues and those involved with ecological ones. These rather different institutions have had varied impacts, but nevertheless it is hard to imagine the development of most indigenous movements without them. This is not to say that the international agencies were instrumental in bringing about these movements, but only that they have gained scope and power in large part due to extranational support.

The fact that native movements span international boundaries is not terribly surprising. As is even more egregiously the case in Africa, the postcolonial states that emerged from the Iberian colonies in the nineteenth century rarely respected ethnic territories when they demarcated national boundaries. Many ethnic and linguistic groups were split between different states, such as the Maya, who ended up in Mexico, Guatemala, and Belize; or the Aymara, whose population became Peruvian, Bolivian, and (after the War of the Pacific in 1884) Chilean. Likewise, the Mapuche live in both Chile and Argentina, the Yanomami in Venezuela and Brazil. Other than the Yanomami and other such tribal peoples in the Amazon where the state has only recently begun to make inroads, each government has tried to instill a patriotic fervor that went against the ethnic continuities between countries. In the case of Latin America, the state's attempt to have people define themselves as citizens of Peru, Guatemala, Mexico, and so on has been relatively successful. Only recently have some ethnic organizations tried to create extranational movements. However, in most cases the movement toward recognizing a pan-ethnic identity has generally remained on the rhetorical level. The most effective movements remain regional or national.

Much of the initial impetus for indigenous movements that have redefined the legal status of native peoples has come from international organizations. Most important in this regard was the International Labor Organization (ILO). Its Convention 170 covered indigenous peoples regarding slavery and semi-slavery, but by the 1980s ILO Convention 169 proclaimed the rights of native peoples throughout the world. Many indigenous groups have based their rights to organize and preserve their societies and cultures on the international law embodied in this document, and NGOs in turn have based their rights to aid native peoples on this law. Convention 169 has been largely accepted in most Latin American countries in the 1990s, with Bolivia in the lead in 1992. Likewise, the United Nations has also become involved, but it has only provided draft agreements rather than a coherent body of international law. Both the United Nations and the Organization of American States (OAS)—which has been even less proactive—have done less than might otherwise be expected because some of their nation-state members see a threat in increasing the autonomy of their own native peoples.

In addition to ILO Convention 169, NGOs have made major differences in indigenous movements. International connections, rather than those between countries within Latin America, have come from the industrialized nations of the Northern Hemisphere, mainly from those headquartered in Western Europe. Chief among them is the Catholic Church.[12] The impetus for aiding native groups was inspired by the reforms of Vatican II in the early 1960s, in which the Church pledged to fight for the "preferential option for the poor." Later, the Medellín Conference in 1968 gave rise to the most radical manifestation of the new theological currents through Liberation Theology, which linked class analysis and need for revolutionary changes to the traditional Church concerns of aiding the poor. Jesuits, Maryknoll priests, and Salesians were in the forefront of this effort in Latin America to help the largely powerless indigenous groups organize and to provide them with financial aid. Initially, at least, many touched by Liberation Theology wanted to impose a class analysis on indigenous peoples, but in the end the close contact between priests and missionaries and the natives gave way to the acceptance of ethnicity as a means to understand the severe maldistribution of wealth and power within Latin American society. The 1971 World Council of Churches meeting in Barbados, focusing on the "Liberation of the Indian," provided one of the first outlets for these new concerns.[13]

Since then, many Catholic organizations have aided in the development of indigenous organizations and consciousness. The famous example of the bishop of San Bartolomé de Las Casas as mediator in the Chiapas conflict is indicative. He was heavily involved in indigenous self-help projects and thus had considerable stature among the Chiapas peasants. The example of Bolivia is telling in this regard too. The Asamblea del Pueblo Guaraní (APG) was founded with the help of Jesuit priests and, as Silvia Hirsch's article (Chapter 5) shows, it has been very effective among the Guaraní speakers of southeastern Bolivia. Other Jesuit organizations in Bolivia have aided in the development of the Katarista movement and also have initiated many economic development projects. Equally important, organizations such as the Jesuit-led CIPCA have served as centers for reflection on notions of Aymara ethnicity both in the city and the countryside through their workshops and publications.

Protestant churches, although they have proliferated in Latin America in the past few decades, generally have not been as important in developing or supporting indigenous movements. Many missionary efforts remain profoundly paternalistic, such as the Summer Institute of Linguistics, which purported to translate the Bible into native languages and to set up missions in out-of-the-way places where attempts were made to have natives assimilate into the dominant culture. Only in Guatemala, where a large proportion (and perhaps the majority) of highland Maya have become Protestant, has there been some emphasis on the preservation of indigenous culture. The Anglican Church in the Gran Chaco region of Central South America has begun to focus on cultural preservation and indigenous advocacy. Elsewhere, Protestant natives tend to assimilate into Iberian culture, although the issue of religious conversion is a complex one. In many cases, native people try out various sects and change religions over their life span, depending on what community they belong to. Although this vacillation is most marked among marginal urban populations (of which indigenous migrants often represent a large proportion), it is also becoming more common in the countryside where missionaries from different sects compete in the same villages for converts.

Emigrants of indigenous origin have had some impact on native organizations. In the case of the Maya, government repression in the 1980s created a large exile community. Most exiles were poor peasants who remained in refugee camps, but a few with some university training were able to publicize the plight of their peoples. For example, Víctor Montejo, a professor at a U.S. university, provided much guidance to the pan-Maya movement and was able to denounce the ethnocide occurring in his country. There are many other indigenous men and women who now are studying in the United States or in Western Europe who will be part of the next generation of leadership in their countries.

The most important international connections that led to the creation and strengthening of indigenous movements have been the NGOs. They have generally fallen into three categories; those associated with human rights, those addressing cultural issues, and those preserving the environment. There is also some overlap from other agencies, especially from those who deal with the reduction of poverty and with education and literacy programs. The Inter-American Development Bank, for example, until 2002 provided aid to indigenous groups under its Poverty Reduction Program; from that year onward, native peoples were put into a separate category. Human rights agencies were most important before 1990. Over the past decades they have lost some of their impact on indigenous issues because of the region's democratization. Only in countries such as Colombia, where a bitter civil war is being fought, do human rights NGOs such as Amnesty International and Human Rights Watch, among others, still have close connections to indigenous issues. There, the kidnapping and murder of native leaders and the coercion of Indian peoples into coca growing by both guerrilla forces and paramilitary organizations have remained important issues.

NGOs focusing on cultural issues have had the highest long-range impact. They have provided native leaders and movements with international publicity, advised them on how to organize and make their voices heard both on national and international levels, and created a support network outside of the country of origin, which has greatly strengthened indigenous movements in dealing with national governments. The oldest of this type has been Cultural Survival (CS). Founded in the 1960s by anthropologists concerned with the disappearance of native cultures throughout the world, this Harvard University-sponsored program spearheaded efforts against the assimilationist policies of governments and development projects that threatened indigenous peoples. It worked against an earlier type of organization, such as the Inter-American Indigenous Institute, founded in the 1940s by the OAS, that was, as might be expected from its nation-state perspective, profoundly assimilationist. It also built a network of supporters throughout the world (especially in the United States) that received updates on various international causes through newsletters and its journal, *Cultural Survival*. Much of this organization's efforts have gone into providing advocacy for peoples who do not have much of a voice because of their lack of integration into the modern nation-state. Thus, to cite one example, CS's advocacy focused more on the Kayapó Indians in the Amazon jungle than on Andean peasants who over centuries have been part of the state, although in a subordinate position.[14]

An alliance between groups concerned with the environment and indigenous groups has grown strong since the 1990s. The key event in this alliance was the 1992 Earth Summit in Rio de Janeiro on environmental issues. For environmental groups, the best way to call attention to the loss of wilderness in the Americas was to bring in Indians who represented the pristine way of life that was in congruence with the ecology of the forest. These people could talk eloquently about their loss of way of life in ways that resonated with a loss of habitat, especially in the Amazon forest where deforestation, mining, and invasions by settlers created crisis conditions. NGOs concerned with environmental issues found logical allies among the indigenous peoples, for the preservation of forest environments also provided for the conservation of native cultures. Thus, the World Wildlife Foundation, the Sierra Club, Greenpeace, and other similar organizations supported movements among indigenous peoples to preserve their way of life because protection of the local environment would also be included.

The ecological perspective has become more urgent because of the new industry of biogenetics. Indigenous peoples, especially in tropical areas, fear that they will lose control not only over their land but also over their genes. Companies are beginning to patent genes of plants, animals, and people found in the rainforest, with no compensation for the owners of these resources. At some point, indigenous groups fear that they will have to pay First World prices for goods and services that originated in their territories and even in their own bodies, without having been compensated. Some of the environmental groups have the sophistication to deal with these issues, which involve complex legal and ethical aspects.

Although money-rich environmental NGOs provide support to native peoples, there are a host of problems with this alliance. One is that indigenous peoples are not necessarily environmentally friendly. Many Indians have not altered the environment only because they lack expensive tools such as bulldozers or chainsaws. In the forest regions where the alliance between environmental NGOs and indigenous peoples has been strongest, the native groups are very small and thus do not have a major impact. Still, the environmental groups, merely by their presence, have perhaps changed the agenda of natives who are aware that preserving their environment might be lucrative in its own right.

Another problem is that, at least in terms of image, native forest peoples, by becoming the representatives of environmental groups, are relegated to the level of the local fauna and thus in the popular imagery return to the nineteenth century and earlier. They again become exotic creatures and "savages," although in this case "good savages." Thus, the proud chiefs in their feathered headdresses become a kind of shorthand for the Amazon jungle rather than individuals who have their own aspirations that might be different from those of environmental groups.

Since the late 1990s, the equation of power between indigenous groups and NGOs has changed because of the new communications technology, in particular the Internet. NGO members themselves began to connect indigenous organizations to the Web. Use of the Internet made it possible for native groups to communicate directly with the outside world on their own terms. This development lessened the dependence that indigenous leaders had had on outsiders to get their message out. Often because of their isolation or lack of voters, many ethnic groups have scant representation, and until the last decade of the twentieth century they had few outside links beyond the nonprofits that were interested in indigenous issues. The Internet also broke the virtual monopolies that certain NGOs had on different ethnic groups; in many cases NGOs in a country informally divided up who worked with what ethnicity. Through the Internet, indigenous groups could present themselves to other organizations that could aid them as well as gain access to information previously difficult to get at from remote locations. Access to information has traditionally been one of the most important factors that limit the effectiveness of indigenous peoples in organizing and asserting their legal rights. The computer revolution, where there is an Internet café in even small cities in Latin America, has created new opportunities for ethnic minorities.

The process of gaining independence from the same funding sources is ongoing. In many cases the most literate (and computer-savvy) members of indigenous groups are tied to NGOs. In many cases the NGOs themselves have created not only the Websites but also the networks in which the Websites are found. Also, indigenous peoples tend to be the least literate and the poorest members of society with limited access to computers and their knowledge. "Urban Indians" have been crucial in the appearance of indigenous peoples on the Internet—people who often have interests diverging from the largely illiterate and poor natives in the countryside. Nevertheless, the Internet has helped immensely in putting native issues out front for the world to see in ways that no other medium has done.

Chapter Organization

The book is divided into four sections, each with a central theme. Each selection can be read separately but also cross-referenced with other sections. Thus, for example, Mario Sznajder's essay on the Mapuche political movement (Chapter 2) can be read in conjunction with journalist R. Marhikewun's article (Chapter 14). Also, Marta Silva's testimonial about the conditions of the Guaraní in the Pantanal region of Brazil (Chapter 9) can be contrasted to the situation of the Guaraní speakers in Bolivia and Argentina (Chapter 5). However, given the wide diversity of indigenous movements within Latin America, no effort has been made to cover them all. Instead, I have tried to provide information on geographically dispersed peoples as well as on ones with widely differing cultures, ranging from relatively small groups in the Amazon who rely heavily on small-scale horticulture and hunting to large and even partially urban ethnic groups such as the Aymara or the Quechua in the Andean highlands.

The four great themes of contemporary indigenous movements—territorial integrity, indigenous political participation, ties to guerrilla movements, and cultural survival—are interwoven and at times overlap. In Part I the fight for keeping ethnic territory is represented by the struggles of the Wauja in Brazil and by the Mapuche in Chile, as described by Emilienne Ireland and Sznajder. Ironically, in both cases, dams threaten to displace people from their ancestral lands, but this problem can also be seen as a conflict between economic development at the cost of indigenous rights. Since most native peoples overwhelmingly live off the land, control over their territory is crucial to their survival.

The issue of political participation is dealt with in Part II. How do native peoples organize, and how effective are their organizations? How can they take part in the political process and not lose their identity? The case of the Ecuadorian indigenous peoples looms large. A background piece by León Zamosc provides the long-term context and then is followed by the essay by O'Connor, who analyzes the 2000 coup led in part by CONAIE, arguably the most important political move on a national scale by an indigenous group in a century. Hirsch compares the relative political strength of the Guaraní in Bolivia and Argentina. Chapter 6 deals with a case of cultural preservation that has been little known, that of indigenous peoples in Paraguay. René Harder Horst brings out the contradictory policies of the Asunción government and the real difficulties that exist when native peoples are so oppressed that it is hard for them to find their own voice.

The link between guerrilla movements that have attempted to overthrow the state and indigenous peoples is the theme of Part III. Although certain sectors of the governments under siege have tried to tie native movements to guerrilla activity, this relationship has been tenuous at best. Starn's essay shows how the Peruvian army used the Andean peasants to fight the Senderista guerrillas. In the process he offers reasons why no indigenous movement was possible in Peru during the civil war in the 1980s and 1990s. In Guatemala, Warren's chapter analyzes how the Maya have tried to overcome the great obstacles placed by the war between guerrillas and the government on developing a pan-Maya movement there.

The fragility of such movements shows that guerrilla activity, while it purports to liberate the masses, does not permit the kind of ethnic organization that more democratic countries have made possible.

The book ends with Part IV, a collection of speeches, interviews, and denunciations by six indigenous leaders. What is striking is the wide variety of voices, from a Yanomami and a Guaraní complaining about disease, dislocation, and land usurpation to the thoughts of a congressional deputy in Ecuador, who shows how the indigenous movement has been integrated into the body politic. This view contrasts with the speech by an Aymara nationalist, who tries to refocus the region's history and language into an Aymara perspective.

Conclusion

As the selections in the following pages make clear, the situation of indigenous peoples is complex in Latin America. Each ethnic group has a different dynamic and suffers from different problems. Unfortunately, just as in North America, the native peoples are among the most poverty-stricken and unhealthy in their countries. Nevertheless, it is clear that the indigenous movements in Latin America are in the forefront of the struggles against the global forces that threaten to engulf many cultures. Whether they will be successful (perhaps through cutting-edge technology like the Internet) is not clear at all. However, it is clear that this trend toward greater ethnic identification in a world that is becoming otherwise more homogeneous will continue, and it will affect Latin American politics for some time into the future.

Notes

1. For greater elaboration on this theme and a collection of some of the best essays on the topic, see John E. Kicza, ed., *The Indian in Latin American History: Resistance, Resilience, and Acculturation* (Wilmington, DE: Scholarly Resources, 1993).

2. For excellent essays on rebellions in Mexico and the Andes, respectively, see Friedrich Katz, ed., *Riot, Rebellion, and Revolution: Rural Social Conflict in Mexico* (Princeton: Princeton University Press, 1988); and Steve J. Stern, ed., *Resistance, Rebellion, and Consciousness in the Andean Peasant World, 18th to 20th Centuries* (Madison: University of Wisconsin Press, 1987).

3. For a recent overview of these revolts, see Luis Miguel Glave, "The 'Republic of Indians' in Revolt (c. 1680–1790)," *The Cambridge History of the Native Peoples of the Americas*, Vol. III, *South America, Part 2*, eds. Frank Salomon and Stuart B. Schwartz (Cambridge: Cambridge University Press, 1999), 502–57.

4. There was a brief moment of Mapuche political mobilization in Chile in the 1940s and 1950s where a Mapuche party had some success in getting its candidates elected to Congress and minor offices, but this progress had faded by the 1960s. See Xavier Albó, "Andean People in the Twentieth Century," *The Cambridge History of the Native Peoples of the Americas*, Vol. III, *South America,*

Part 2, eds. Frank Salomon and Stuart B. Schwartz (Cambridge: Cambridge University Press, 1999), 816–23.

5. Of course, the same can be said for North America.

6. Previously, indigenous peoples who moved to the city tried to blend in and pass as mestizos. They wore city clothes, spoke only the dominant European language in public, and kept private their distinctively indigenous practices.

7. By "subaltern," I mean people who are thought of as subordinate to another group.

8. I am grateful to Marc Becker for his insights on this issue, which I have incorporated into these paragraphs.

9. For the most forceful statement of these differences between Andeans and Spaniards, see Irene Silverblatt, *Moon, Suns, and Witches: Ideologies and Class in Inca and Colonial Peru* (Princeton: Princeton University Press, 1987).

10. Also, the U.S. embassy helped inflate Morales's standing when the U.S. ambassador declared that Bolivia would lose its aid dollars if Morales were elected. Many Bolivians believed that the United States was interfering in their internal affairs and voted for Morales in protest.

11. But even he participated in the presidential elections of 2002.

12. It might be argued that the Catholic Church is, in fact, a part of each Latin American country and thus cannot be classified as an "international organization." While this statement is true on one level, most of the impetus to concentrate on indigenous issues has come from foreign-born clergy, and most of the money supporting activities in favor of indigenous peoples has come from outside, mostly European, sources.

13. Donna Lee Van Cott, "Indigenous Peoples and Democracy: Issues for Policymakers," *Indigenous Peoples and Democracy in Latin America*, ed. Donna Lee Van Cott (New York: St. Martin's Press, 1994), 6.

14. It must be said that CS also highlighted the ethnocide of the Maya Indians in Guatemala during the 1980s, although its campaign was not as successful as with other groups such as the Kayapó.

I

In the Defense of Land

1

Neither Warriors nor Victims: The Wauja Peacefully Organize to Defend Their Land

Emilienne Ireland

One of the great regions of controversy over land rights in South America is the Amazon. Relatively small groups of hunters and gatherers and horticulturalists are being threatened by cattle ranchers and other migrants from the Brazilian coastal areas. This process accelerated during the 1980s, when the military government built a vast highway network in the Amazon as a way to develop the region economically and also to alleviate some of the overcrowding in Brazil's teeming cities. The results of this development scheme have been unexpected. It triggered the destruction of vast swaths of jungle, with all the ecological consequences that are now common knowledge. Moreover, it has not lured many people from the urban slums; instead, the opening up of the Amazon has threatened the existence of the Indian groups who remain in the region. The government has attempted to counter the problems by creating indigenous reservations to preserve the largest ethnic groups from injurious contact and usurpation from whites, but this strategy has been at best only partially successful.

In this brief article, Emilienne Ireland describes some of the problems that the Wauja have encountered. One difficulty has been that the reservations themselves were set up without any direct input from the indigenous groups concerned. The resultant legal case has many repercussions for other groups in Brazil as well. It also shows the barriers raised against the input of preliterate peoples in a process that affects them in profound ways and that is set up (at least in theory) to benefit them.

Emilienne Ireland is a Yale-trained anthropologist who works as a consultant in Bethesda, Maryland. For eighteen months in 1980–1982

From Emilienne Ireland, "Neither Warriors nor Victims: The Wauja Peacefully Organize to Defend Their Land," *Latin American Anthropology Review* 2:1 (1990): 3–12. Reprinted by permission of the author.

*and again in 1989 she lived in Brazil among the Wauja in their village of
Piyulaga.*

An idea is spreading in the rainforests of Central Brazil perhaps even
more rapidly than the fires of deforestation. The idea is that Indians
as a group are politically powerful. Indians living in isolated rainforest
villages throughout Amazonia are coming to think of themselves as sharing an identity as Indian people.

In February of 1989, the Kayapó and their allies staged an historic
peaceful demonstration against a proposed hydroelectric project at
Altamira, Brazil (see Chernela 1988a, 1988b; Turner 1989a, 1989b, 1989c,
1989d, 1990, 1991). The project, to be funded by the World Bank, would
have flooded vast areas of Kayapó land and destroyed most of their rivers
for fishing. Outraged that they had not even been consulted, the Kayapó
organized themselves and mounted a spectacular media event in protest.
Their campaign was so creative and well executed that the ensuing international outcry caused the World Bank to withdraw its support for the dam
project. The success of this initiative at Altamira profoundly changed political reality and expectations for Indian people in Brazil and beyond.
The stereotype of Indian as victim was broken.

One example of this legacy is the current effort of the Wauja[1] of the
Upper Xingu to reclaim peacefully, under Brazilian law, traditional fishing grounds and a sacred ceremonial site, *Kamukuaka*. Both are currently
being invaded or occupied by ranchers and poachers.

Background on the Wauja

The Wauja are a community of about 200 relatively traditional Arawak-
speaking Indians who live by fishing and swidden horticulture in the Xingu
National Park in Northern Mato Grosso. Although during the past generation their economy has become dependent on steel tools, fishhooks,
and other manufactured goods, Wauja involvement in the cash economy
is still minimal and sporadic, limited mainly to sale of handcrafts.

Like virtually all Indian people, during the early period of contact
they suffered horrific population losses due to recurrent epidemics of introduced disease (Ireland 1988). Unlike most other Indians, however, much
of their traditional land was reserved for them under law soon after regular contact began in the 1940s.[2] Despite this measure of protection, an
essential part of their traditional territory was left out of the park. This
unprotected area includes fishing grounds, agricultural land, and, most
important, *Kamukuaka*, a sacred cavern and ceremonial ground beside a
waterfall on the Batovi-Tamitatoala River.[3]

When the Wauja first began to understand that only part of their traditional territory fell within park boundaries, they protested to the gov-

ernment Indian agency, FUNAI, that the excluded area was essential to their survival as Indian people. In response to the Wauja's most recent protests on the matter, FUNAI stated that a five-year study is needed before action can be taken.

Invasion of Wauja Lands

The Wauja say that if nothing is done, in five years their ancestral land will be overrun and lost to them forever. Ranchers already occupy *Kamukuaka*, the most sacred Wauja ceremonial site, situated on the upper Batovi River. Atamai, political chief of the Wauja, describes it as an extraordinary place, a great stone house beside a waterfall. At the mouth of the cavern are rock carvings made by ancestors of the Wauja, images of the parts of women that create life. The Wauja say the carvings have power to make living things increase and become abundant.[4]

In addition, the Wauja revere *Kamukuaka* as the dwelling place of spirits. These spirits are respectfully addressed as kin, and referred to in the Wauja language as *inyãkãnãu*, "those who teach." The spirits guide the elders, appearing to them in visions, helping them heal the sick and maintain harmony within the village. To honor these spirits, the Wauja and their neighbors, the Bacairi, have performed ceremonies at *Kamukuaka* for many generations. Wauja elders emphasize that their most sacred ceremony, *kawika*, was performed at that place, and can proudly list deceased relatives who played *kawika* flutes at *Kamukuaka*. Mayaya, brother of Atamai and ceremonial leader of the Wauja, once sought to express his attachment to *Kamukuaka* without reducing it to words. An accomplished musician, he softly sang the melody of the sacred flute ceremony, concluding, "therefore that land means everything to us."

In Wauja oral tradition, *Kamukuaka* has existed since the beginning of the world, before men were created. Chief Atamai says his late father took his children there before he died, and told them the sacred story linked to that place, of how the Sun dwelt in the great stone house when he still walked the earth in human form. Atamai himself has seen the gaping hole in the side of the cavern where, according to the ancestors, the Sun tried to tear the house apart in those ancient times.

Now the ranchers keep the Wauja out. The ancient ceremonies cannot be performed, and young people know *Kamukuaka* only through the stories of their elders. Even worse, the Wauja say, is the desecration the ranchers have brought:

> They have turned *Kamukuaka* into a cattle pasture. There used to be giant trees all around the stone cavern, right up [*sic*] leaving the earth bare and pitiful. They graze cattle there now. Our ceremonial ground is covered with stinking cattle droppings. The whiteman has covered the dust of our ancestors with shit.

The loss of *Kamukuaka* has had economic consequences for the Wauja as well, since the area along the Batovi near *Kamukuaka* is the only source for certain essential raw materials, including ceramic pigments. medicinal plants, and shells used in trade.[5]

But *Kamukuaka* is not the only area where outsiders are invading the Wauja's ancestral land. In 1988 and again in 1989, Atamai complained to government officials that poachers were penetrating deep into Wauja territory to take commercial quantities of fish, destined for sale in Brazilian towns along the upper Batovi river. The poachers enter Wauja waters in boats filled with heavily armed men, and transport the fish to small trucks waiting at designated locations outside Wauja territory (Cruz 1988, 1989).

Wauja attempts to keep poachers out have led to violent confrontations, in which poachers have shot at Wauja fishermen without provocation (Ireland 1989a, 1989b). Because of poachers, ordinary overnight fishing trips have suddenly become dangerous. Parents now discourage their adolescent boys from going on fishing trips unless accompanied by an elder who can be trusted to handle a threatening situation.

In addition to the physical danger of armed invaders, the sheer loss of fish is a serious problem, since the Wauja depend on fish for most of the protein in their diet. The areas currently being invaded by poachers are some of the best traditional fishing grounds. Generations of Wauja have relied on these areas to provide the large numbers of fish needed for ceremonial feasts. As a result of the continuing depredation by poachers, the Wauja say these areas are becoming fished out. Poaching therefore threatens the traditional Wauja economy, based in large part on communal sharing and ceremonial redistribution as opposed to private profit and accumulated wealth.

Wauja Organize to Reclaim Their Land

The incident in early 1989, when the chief and other elders were shot at by poachers, was a turning point for the Wauja. That summer they decided the government would not defend their land and resources, and that they would have to do it themselves. They built a new village, Aldeia Batovi, within the park but near the area where the poachers and ranchers were penetrating. Gardens were cleared and planted, three large traditional houses were built, and several families took up permanent residence there, maintaining contact with the main village at Lake Piyulaga by radio.

In June of 1990, this new village was burned to the ground by an employee of a local rancher. The three houses were lost, along with all they contained: tools, stores of food, and medical supplies. Responding to letters of protest from abroad, the Brazilian government tried to minimize this incident, alleging the ranchers merely torched a makeshift campsite the Wauja had used overnight and abandoned. This is not the case. No temporary Wauja campsite has first-year gardens, and the village was inhabited. Confrontation was avoided only because the occupants were away attending a ceremony at another village during the attack.[6]

The Brazilian government insists these incidents were not violent, even though shots were fired and houses burned. The Wauja do not agree. They consider themselves under attack, and blame the escalating violence on faulty demarcation of their territory years ago, when the Xingu National Park was created. To correct the situation, the Wauja say park boundaries must be moved south by a distance of 30-40 kilometers, to include critical parts of their traditional territory. The area of land is not large, but it is crucial to the Wauja and to peace in the region. Though it forms the outer margin of their territory, it is at the center of their traditions and their identity as Indian people.

The Wauja have already rebuilt their burned village and renamed it Aldeia Ulupuene. To maintain an increased presence in the area, they are adding an airstrip at the site of the attack. Soon after their village was burned, the Wauja asked the government to survey the land officially outside the park, in order to have it included in the park and thereby protected. Officials replied that they lacked funds for such a project. In response, the Wauja, together with members of other indigenous communities, decided to survey the land themselves.

In August, a volunteer force of about fifty men drawn from Kayapó, Kajabi, Suya, Trumai, Yawalapiti, and Wauja communities assembled at the burned village site to survey the land. This in itself is a major achievement by the Wauja, and a credit to the volunteers. In the first half of this century, some of these communities fought pitched battles against each other and, in several well-remembered instances, inflicted heavy casualties and took women and children captive. Thus the men in this volunteer group are working closely beside traditional enemies of their fathers and grandfathers. That they all are united in a common purpose bespeaks their determination to protect their shared future as Indian people.

The volunteers have begun clearing surveying sightlines and building the airstrip. The project is expected to take three to six months, depending on support from outside sources. Since the new village is a six-day journey from the main village by dugout canoe, the Wauja need motorboats to transport men and supplies, as well as food to feed the volunteers.

The Rainforest Foundation, founded in 1988 by Kayapó chief Ropni and rock musician Sting to support Indian-initiated efforts to protect the rainforest, has taken on the Wauja project as a top priority. Olympio Serra, formerly director of the Xingu National Park, now working on the Rainforest Foundation's Brazilian board, Fundação Mata Virgem, reports that 4,000 liters of gasoline and food for the volunteers were shipped to the Wauja the first week of October. These supplies should enable the Wauja to finish the job before the heavy rains arrive in December.

José Carlos Libãnio, at the Nucleus for Indigenous Rights (NDI) in Brasilia, explains that surveying the area is an important step in protecting it for Indian people under Brazilian law. He says the Wauja's legal case, currently under preparation, stands to set a legal precedent on behalf of all Brazilian Indians. To expand the Xingu Park boundaries, the Wauja's lawyers must challenge an administrative decree that currently prohibits alteration to existing boundaries of indigenous reserves. This decree works against Indians, denying them redress against boundary decisions made without their knowledge or consent.[7]

Libãnio says the Wauja case is strong, and he expects them to win it. However, it will take at least a year for the case to proceed through the Brazilian courts. During that time, the Wauja will need support from the international community. A public information and letter-writing campaign is currently being organized to help create a climate of opinion in Brazil favorable to a just resolution of the Wauja's legal case.

Importance of the Wauja Case

Although all Amazonian Indians are facing serious threats to their survival (Hemming 1987; Price 1989; Maybury-Lewis 1989; Taylor 1988), the Wauja's case is crucial in several respects. First, their legal case stands to set a major precedent on behalf of all Brazilian Indians. If the Wauja win the right to reclaim traditional territory under law, all Brazilian Indians benefit.

Second, the Wauja campaign for non-violent, legal reclamation of territory is setting an historical precedent as well. The Wauja have never attacked or killed Brazilian settlers. If they are successful in reclaiming their territory through entirely non-violent means, it will be a landmark victory for both Indian rights and rainforest conservation.

Third, the Wauja's case presents a unique opportunity simply because they stand a good chance of winning. The Yanomami situation (CCPY 1989a) is currently receiving worldwide attention. Survival International rightly calls it one of the great humanitarian campaigns of the late twentieth century. Both in numbers of people affected, and in severity of human rights violations, the Yanomami case outweighs the Wauja case. But the Yanomami campaign faces great odds, and will be very difficult to win. The gold miners are organized and determined, and the political situation is complex and entrenched. The suffering of the Yanomami is so intense and unrelenting that it is a public relations problem to maintain enough optimism to keep the international community actively involved.

The Wauja case, on the other hand, is relatively straightforward and easy to win. A win for the Wauja will help the Yanomami as well, because success attracts optimism and support. The Yanomami situation seems almost hopeless, and this is a great part of the problem. If the Wauja create a well-publicized victory for indigenous rights in Brazil, the cause of the Yanomami and other Brazilian Indians will be advanced, just as the Wauja's own cause was advanced by the Kayapó victory at Altamira.

Wauja Perspectives on Their Situation

It is difficult to convey to members of an international community that is increasingly mobile and secular how the Wauja, and other people in traditional small-scale societies, are connected to their ancestral lands not only by economic necessity, but by far deeper bonds. The Wauja's land provides far more than food, tools, and shelter. It is the dwelling place of the spirits who guide them, the birthplace of their children, and the resting place of their ancestors. It is the sacred landscape of all their poetry, stories, songs, and prayers—it is their one place upon the earth. Everything needed for human life, everything sacred and precious, flows from that land. If this land is ripped away from the Wauja, if they lose it, they lose their future as Indian people, and they keenly appreciate this.

And yet, equally important to their identity as Wauja is their rejection of war and violence as behavior befitting honorable men. The Wauja have seen that the Kayapó's warrior image has served them well in their dealings with the military elite that has so long dominated Brazilian politics. While the Wauja greatly respect the Kayapó's determination to survive on their own terms, the confrontational tactics of the Kayapó are antithetical to Wauja notions of honor and dignity.

As provocations by invaders become increasingly violent, the Wauja say they soon will be forced to respond in kind and even, perhaps, to kill (Ireland 1989a, 1989b). This is their dilemma. If the Wauja renounce violence and refuse to confront the invaders, they may lose their ancestral land, and with it their way of life. But if in order to keep the land they become violent and brutal men, who trade in fear and solve problems by killing, they will no longer be Wauja and will inhabit the land of their ancestors as strangers.

The Wauja's view of warfare and violence as morally degrading is revealed in their story of creation. The passage condensed here describes how the Sun gave defining attributes to each tribe of man:

> The Sun offers a rifle to the ancestor of the Wauja, but the Wauja merely turns it over in his hands, not knowing how to use it. The Sun takes the rifle from the Wauja and offers it to the ancestor of the warlike Indians who live to the north of the Wauja. This Indian is also baffled by the

rifle, and so the Sun takes it away again and this time hands it to the ancestor of the whiteman.

The whiteman immediately lifts the rifle to his shoulder and fires it successfully, thus laying claim to the superior technology that would be his. The Sun then gave hardwood bows to the Indians, with which they were well satisfied.

Next the Sun passed around a gourd dipper from which each man was asked to drink. The ancestor of the Wauja approached, but found to his horror that the dipper was filled to the brim with blood. He refused to touch it, but when the warlike Indian was offered the dipper, he readily drank from it. When the Sun finally offered the dipper of blood to the whiteman, he drank it down greedily in great gulps.

That is why the whiteman and the warlike Indian tribes are so violent today; even in ancient times, they were thirsty for the taste of blood. To the Wauja, however, the Sun gave a dipper of manioc porridge. And that is why the Wauja drink manioc porridge today, and why they are not a brutal and violent people.

Yet while this story expresses some of the Wauja's attitudes toward violence, it no longer can be said to reflect their view of other Indian people, for this has changed dramatically in the last decade.

In 1980, the Wauja divided human beings into three categories: *putaka*, denoting the peaceful tribes of the Upper Xingu; *muteitsi*, glossing roughly as "enemy Indian" or "wild Indian," and referring to warlike tribes, including the Kayapó; and *kajaipa*, referring to non-Indians. There was no cover term for Indian people. Upper Xingu Indians (*putaka*) and warlike enemy Indians (*muteitsi*) could not be subsumed under one linguistic category simply because they were not the same kind of human being. *Muteitsi* and their way of life were viewed with scorn. Wauja parents scolded unruly children by saying that only *muteitsi* would marry them when they grew up. In 1980 the Wauja used the term *muteitsi* exclusively as an epithet, and never in the presence of a member of that class.

By 1989, however, a dramatic conceptual shift had occurred. The Wauja had begun referring to themselves with pride as *muteitsi*, meaning "Indian people." For the first time, the Wauja had a cover term that recognized all Indian people as a group. The warlike tribes were no longer "our enemies" (*apalunaun*), but instead "our brothers" (*apawanaun*). The meaning of *muteitsi* had not been broadened—it had been radically changed. I never again heard the term used as an epithet or a marker that divided Indians from each other. Instead, *muteitsi* had become a unifying term, and a label of pride.

In past generations, Wauja intermarried with *muteitsi* only as the dreaded consequence of being taken captive in warfare. That is no longer so. The first voluntary intermarriage recently occurred when the daughter of the Wauja chief married a Kayapó in a match approved by both families.

Yet despite this willingness to accept culturally distinct groups as fully human and even as brothers with shared Indian identity, the Wauja see no need to imitate them or adopt their cultural values. The Wauja now accept the Kayapó, but they still renounce violence as a way of life. Far from viewing physical aggression with awe and admiration, they see it as pathetic and a mark of failed leadership. The Wauja term for warrior or soldier, *peyeteki yekeho*, can be translated as "a man whose greatest talent is losing his self-control."

The Wauja value their traditions and moral perspective on the world as much as they value the land of their ancestors. And so their statements to the outside world take the form not of boasting or angry threats, but of carefully reasoned moral arguments. In September 1989, Chief Atamai, seated in the central plaza in the company of the assembled elders, tried to convey these concerns in a filmed interview:[8]

When that whiteman shot at us with his rifle it offended me more than I can say. What if his bullet had killed me? My daughters, my little ones, would be left without me. They would grieve as only children can. They would suffer without their father. Why does the whiteman presume to make orphans of my children? Why does the whiteman seek to kill us?

Does he think Indians do not have families? Perhaps he thinks that Indians do not have children. As he is, so are we. We are men! Doesn't he know that? Our thoughts, our desires, our lives, they are as his own! What we carry within our bellies, what is in our hearts, is the same. Can't he see that?

We are not different. That is why we do not wish to kill the whiteman. We know that whitemen have children, just as we do ourselves. If we kill the fathers, we cause the children to suffer. Killing makes misery, and that is why we do not undertake it lightly.

I bear you no ill will, I say. I have no quarrel with you, whiteman. We are Wauja; we are not a brutal and violent people. But—don't grab for yourself the land of our grandfathers. That is OURS.

Look, imagine what would happen if we decided to invade land belonging to some rancher, some whiteman. He would not just let us have it! Of course he would defend it with everything he had. He would fight, he would shoot us, he would kill us. Should we, then, be any different? Should we value our land any less than the whiteman values his? This is our land, and we SHALL defend it. To keep this land, I would kill. These are not empty words.

We'll summon the Kayapó. They have told me I can count on them. "If the ranchers invade your land," they said, "don't hesitate to call on us. Come to us from your village, and we will hear you. We will smash the houses of those bastards! We will wipe them out! They are our enemies." So say the Kayapó. "Don't take pity on those ranchers. They are your mortal enemies."

"All right," I said, "when it comes to that, we'll make war on them together."

But if they leave us in peace, if they don't invade us, there will be no trouble. They too are our brothers, after all.

Notes

1. The Wauja are commonly referred to by outsiders as the Aurá or Waurá. These names are incorrect, resulting from mispronunciation. The Wauja wish to be known by their true name for themselves, which is spelled Wauja and pronounced WOW-sha.

2. That the Wauja and their Upper Xingu neighbors still occupy the land of their fathers and grandfathers is largely thanks to the efforts of Claudio and Orlando Villas Boas, who helped create the Xingu National Park in the 1950s. For a history of the Xingu Park in the context of national Indian policy in Brazil, see Davis 1977:47–61.

3. The term translated here as sacred is *kakayapai*, spoken with great emphasis. It glosses generally as "dear, of utmost value, something not to be lost." In the context of ceremonial performance, *kakayapai* takes on the added meaning of something precious and irreplaceable handed down from the ancestors and deriving its value from religious belief.

The Wauja have no term that translates literally as "sacred" or "holy," but bilingual Wauja say the Portuguese term *sagrado* translates into Wauja as *kakayapai*, in the sense of "something of utmost value."

4. Brazilian anthropologist Marcelo Óppido-Fiorini reports a cave beside a waterfall, also containing images of female generative power, as a site held sacred by the Wasuhsu, a Nambicuara people. Óppido-Fiorini says similar sites are held sacred by the Sararé, the Alãtesu, the Hahãintesu, the Mamaindé, and the Negaroté.

In 1987, Óppido-Fiorini submitted to FUNAI an extensively documented proposal to protect this sacred site as a reserve, but nothing was done. Soon after, in the fall of 1988, the Nambicuara destroyed a still undetermined amount of agricultural machinery (reports vary between $15,000 and $60,000 in damage) that in their view was desecrating their sacred site. FUNAI is now said to be reconsidering Fiorini's proposal.

5. Demarcation of Indian land has typically failed to take into account Indian land-use patterns. While colonists require only enough real estate to carve out a space for houses and fields, Indians use traditional knowledge to exploit a variety of distinct (and sometimes distant) ecozones, each with associated soils, plants, and animals, all thriving and interacting in specific and predictable ways. Posey (1981, 1982, 1990) shows how the Kayapó expertly create and manage ecozones that appear so "natural" that Western scientists often do not recognize they are human artifacts.

Because Indian cultures depend on sophisticated knowledge of specific ecosystems in specific geographic areas, forced relocation of Indian people to unfamiliar terrain destroys traditional culture, if not the people themselves. Although proponents of hydroelectric and other development projects have typically argued that destruction of indigenous culture and lives is an unavoidable cost of development, scientists increasingly view these same conventional energy-supply models as both environmentally and economically unsustainable. They now call for a more rational, end use-technology approach to energy development that does not require destruction of indigenous people and the natural environment (see Reddy and Goldemberg 1990).

6. According to some reports, one Wauja family did not attend the ceremony and discovered the burned village upon returning in late afternoon from a family fishing trip. Exact circumstances of the fire remain to be determined.

7. According to the government, the intent of the decree is to protect Indians by preventing any attempt to reduce Indian lands already demarcated. In practice, however, the decree does not work this way. To cite just one example, in

1989 the government was able to get around this decree and reduce the territory of the Uru-Eu-Wau-Wau of the Guaporé Valley in Rondônia. It did this by simply nullifying the existing demarcation of their territory and subsequently issuing a new demarcation granting them a fraction of what they had before.

The boundaries could not be altered, but it was easy enough simply to nullify them and start over. Only the President of the Republic has the power to do this; Indians cannot. And because of the decree that allegedly protects them, Indians are blocked from seeking redress under law when their territory is taken from them in this way. A victory for the Wauja would end this unjust situation.

8. This passage has been condensed from the recorded transcript.

References

CCPY (Commision for Creation of the Yanomami Park)
>   1989a   "The Threatened Yanomami." *Cultural Survival Quarterly* 13(1):45–46.

Chernela, Janet M.
>   1988a   "Proposed Altamira-Xingú Complex Threatens 27 Indigenous Groups." *Society for Latin American Anthropology Newsletter* IV:7–9.
>   1988b   "Potential Impacts of a Proposed Amazon Hydropower Project." *Cultural Survival Quarterly* 12(2):20–24.

Cruz, Joel dos Santos
>   1988   *Relatório da Viagem dos Waurás ao Rio Batovi-Tamitatualu.* September 1988 report to FUNAI on poaching.
>   1989   *Expedição Waurá no Rio Batovi em 7 de Maio de 1989.* Report to FUNAI on continuing problems with poachers and on construction of Aldeia Batovi.

Davis. Shelton H.
>   1977   *Victims of the Miracle: Development and the Indians of Brazil.* Cambridge: Cambridge University Press.

Hemming, John
>   1987   *Amazon Frontier: The Defeat of the Brazilian Indians.* Cambridge: Harvard University Press.

Ireland, Emilienne
>   1988   "Cerebral Savage: The Whiteman and Symbol of Cleverness and Savagery in Waurá Myth." In *Rethinking History and Myth: Indigenous South American Perspectives on the Past,* Jonathan Hill, editor, pp. 157–173. Urbana: University of Illinois Press.
>   1989a   "Chief Atamai Describes Invasion of Wauja Land by Poachers and Ranchers." Transcript of interview recorded in Wauja village of Piyulaga, August 1989. 17 p.
>   1989b   "Invasion of Wauja Land." Unedited film footage dubbed in English; 19 minutes. John-Paul Davidson, director; E. Ireland, interviewer.

1989c   *The Storyteller.* 46 minute video; in Wauja (Arawak) and English with English subtitles. John-Paul Davidson, director;
E. Ireland, anthropological consultant. BBC Television.

Maybury-Lewis, David
1989   "Indians in Brazil: The Struggle Intensifies." *Cultural Survival Quarterly* 13(1):2–5.

Óppido-Fiorini, Marcelo
n.d.   *Taihãntesu: Preservação de um Santuário Natural.* Proposal
to create reserve at Wasuhsu (Nambiquara) sacred site, 1987.

Pinto, Lúcio Flávio
1989   "Calha Norte: The Special Project for the Occupation of the
Frontiers." *Cultural Survival Quarterly* 13(1):40–41.

Posey, Darrell Addison
1981   "Wasps, Warriors, and Fearless Men: Ethnoentomology of
the Kayapó Indians of Central Brazil." *Journal of Ethnobi-
ology* 1(1):165–174.
1982   "The Keepers of the Forest." *New York Botanical Garden
Magazine* 6(1):18–24.
1990   "The Science of the Mebêngôkre." *Orion Nature Quarterly*
9(3):16–23.

Price, David
1989   *Before the Bulldozer: The Nambiquara Indians and the World
Bank.* Cabin John, Maryland: Seven Locks Press.

Reddy, Amulya K. N., and José Goldemberg
1990   "Energy for the Developing World." *Scientific American*
263(3):110–118.

Taylor, Kenneth I.
1988   "Indian Rights in Amazonia." In *People of the Tropical Rain
Forest*, J. S. Denslow and C. Padoch, editors, pp. 91–92. Berkeley: University of California Press.

Turner, Terence
1989a   "Kayapó Plan Meeting to Discuss Dams." *Cultural Survival
Quarterly* 13(1).
1989b   *The Kayapó: Out of the Forest.* 52 minute video. M. Beckham,
director; T. Turner, anthropological consultant. Granada Television International.
1989c   "Amazonian Indians Lead Fight to Save Their Forest World."
Latin American Anthropology Review 1(1):2–4.
1989d   "Five Days in Altimira: Kayapó Indians Organize Protest
Against Proposed Hydroelectric Dam." *Kayapó Support
Group Newsletter* 1 (Spring):1–3.
1990   "Visual Media, Cultural Politics, and Anthropological Practice: Some Implications of Recent Uses of Film and Video

Among the Kayapó of Brazil." *Commission on Visual Anthropology Review* (Spring):8–13.

1991   "Representing, Resisting, Rethinking: Transformations of Kayapó Culture and Anthropological Consciousness, 1962–1990." In *The History of Anthropology*, George Stocking, editor. Chicago: University of Chicago Press.

Txucarramãe, Megaron

n.d.   *Relatório de Viagem ao Batovi*. Report to FUNAI of fact-finding trip to Wauja village of Aldeia Batovi after it was burned down in June 1990.

2

Ethnodevelopment and Democratic Consolidation in Chile: The Mapuche Question

Mario Sznajder

As Mario Sznajder shows here, the Mapuche have a long history of resistance to absorption by Europeans. Whether or not, as the author points out, they "violently resisted the Spanish invasion of their land to a greater degree than any other Indian people in America" (the Yaqui of Mexico, the Ava-Guaraní of Bolivia, and others come to mind), it is clear that the Mapuche have historically been one of the most successful. After the initial shock of European invasion, the Mapuche organized their society for war and even expanded into new territories—the fertile Pampas on the Argentine side of the Andes—in the eighteenth and nineteenth centuries.

The more recent history of the Mapuche has, in contrast, not been so felicitous. The brutal military dictatorship of Augusto Pinochet (1973–1990) was especially hard on the Mapuche, since they were associated with leftist parties. In addition, the Pinochet government expressed a long-held desire by Chilean elites of integrating the Indians into the nation-state as regular citizens, with no special status. While this goal might sound laudable on paper, the effects of such measures have been disastrous for indigenous groups, for reasons Sznajder makes clear in his essay. As is often the case, the issue of cultural and social continuity boiled down to the ownership of land.

Attempts by the democratic administrations in the aftermath of the Pinochet dictatorship to remedy some of the problems of the Mapuche have run up against the strictures that the military regime was able to impose through the Chilean constitution, in which right-wing parties and the military wield effective veto power over any significant change in the social contract. How might this situation differ from those of the Aymara movements in neighboring Bolivia?

From Mario Sznajder, "Ethnodevelopment and Democratic Consolidation in Chile: The Mapuche Question," *Migration* 28 (1995): 29–54. Reprinted by permission of the Berliner Institut für Vergleichende Sozialforschung and the author.

Mario Sznajder is a professor of political science at the Hebrew University of Jerusalem.

The Mapuche ("People of the Land"; *mapu*–land, *che*–people) constitute the largest indigenous group in modern Chile. The Spaniards called this indigenous group Araucanians, or people from Arauco, a region south of Concepción, the third largest city in contemporary Chile. The name Arauco seems to be onomatopoeic for *rau*—the sound made by the roaring of a river—or related to the Ragco River, which is in the same area (*Gunckel*: 1966). As with other indigenous groups in America, it is hard to establish the numbers of the Mapuches. The Chilean government eliminated the category Mapuche from the national census, regarding this as a democratizing and antiracial measure. Nevertheless, research on the subject estimates that 360,000 to 537,000 Mapuches live on their lands in the center-south of Chile; the number of those who have emigrated to the urban centers of the country is estimated to be from 100,000 to 150,000. To this must be added another 15,000 Mapuches who live in the rural sector but outside of organized communities (*Bengoa*: 1990, pp. 238–239). Thus, the Mapuches constitute 4 to 5 percent of Chile's total estimated contemporary population of around 13.5 million, although Mapuche organizations sometimes declare that this proportion is up to 10 percent. The entire indigenous population of Chile is estimated at 918,000, or 6.8 percent of the total population, a somewhat higher percentage than that of the indigenous populations of all of continental Latin America, which is estimated at 6 percent (*Latin American Special Reports*: 1994d, p. 2).

The Mapuches are territorially concentrated in Chile's IX Region—specifically, in the valley some 800 kilometers south of Santiago, and especially in the province of Cautín. The Mapuches comprise three main groups. In the north of this area of concentration dwell the Picunches ("Men of the North"), in the provinces of Arauco, Bío-Bío, and Malleco. The Pehuenches ("Men of the Pehuen"—the araucaria tree, symbol of the Chilean rain forest) live in the Andean valleys of Cautín. The Huiliches ("Men of the South") are found in the provinces of Valdivia, Osorno, and Llanquihue. Most of the Mapuches long preserved their traditional social organization, and the communities they lived in occupied more than 1,385,000 acres of land. In 1968 there were 3,068 Mapuche communities, 70 percent of which had undivided lands, generally registered in the name of the *cacique*—the leader of the community, usually the head of an extended family—and only 30 percent of the land had been divided according to the criteria established by the 1927 land law. During 1973–1990, however, the period of military government, the situation changed radically. In 1979, the military enacted a new land law that brought about the division of 90 percent of the land. This process was destructive to the Mapuches, not only because of the disharmony it created between their traditional way of life and the new system of land tenure, finally resulting in the disintegration of the communities and emigration, but also because it was the main factor in their pauperization. Field research estimated that in 1966 the yearly income of the average Mapuche family was equivalent to 120 sacks of wheat, and that it decreased to the equivalent of 84 sacks per family in 1981. In 1981, the yearly income of a Mapuche individual was estimated at 209 $U.S., well below the Chilean national average. This figure, indeed, established the Mapuches as the poorest group in the country (*Bengoa*: 1990, pp. 239–240).

A History of Resistance

Historically the Mapuches violently resisted the Spanish invasion of their land, to a greater degree than any other Indian people in America. The Mapuches whom the Spaniards found were gatherers, hunters, and vegetable and fruit growers; the encounter with the Spaniards, however, brought about rapid change among the Mapuches as they adapted themselves to the requirements of war. Before the war with the Spaniards, Mapuche society was organized around the extended family but did not possess any other significant institutions. A system of alliances for war, but also for economic purposes—such as gathering of nuts and araucaria fruit, acquisition of basic foodstuffs, and fishing—did not involve any kind of social stratification or hierarchy beyond that of the family. It was the war with Spain, beginning in 1546, that produced deep changes in Mapuche society.

Together with becoming warlike, the society was greatly affected by illnesses imported from Europe and by the consumption of alcohol. Cattle raising became the main economic activity, but the extended family as the basic social unit still continued to function, precluding larger groupings and preserving the traditional occupations of gathering, hunting, and orchard agriculture (*Bengoa*: 1991, pp. 26–28). The capacity to adapt to the challenges posed by the Spanish conquest enabled the Mapuches to keep fighting with various degrees of success for more than ninety years, until peace was signed with the Spanish monarchy; but the phase thus inaugurated was characterized by ongoing conflict with violations of the recognized border by both sides. Through a combination of war and negotiations, the Mapuches succeeded in surviving independently in their own territory for more than 260 years of Spanish colonization in Chile. It was during this period that Mapuche society evolved into a cattle-raising and agricultural society, developing trade links with the interior, in the Spanish colony, and even beyond the Andes with the indigenous population of what was later to be southwestern Argentina.

If, during the period of Spanish colonial domination, the authorities maintained the territorial status quo through a combination of incursions into Mapuche lands and *parlamentos*—meetings between the Spaniards and the Mapuche leaders to discuss peace, the last of which was held in Negrete in 1803—and if the authorities regarded the indigenous rebels as barbarians, the situation changed when the struggle for Chilean independence began. The rejection of Spanish influence brought about a different attitude toward the Mapuches—now seen as the symbol of anti-Spanish resistance and somewhat idealized as the "untamed Arauco" (*Bengoa*: 1991, pp. 135–141). After 1819, however, political realities caused the Mapuches to cooperate with the Spaniards against the newly born Chilean state in what was called *La guerra a muerte*—"the war to the death." This was a ferocious war in which the Mapuches, tied to the Spaniards by various treaties, were influenced by the royalist clergy and divided between a majority that sided with Spain and those that sided with Chile.

In the republican era, the relationship between the Mapuches and the Chilean state evolved into a new confrontation. For one thing, the economic needs of the new state led to the exploitation of coal in the northern part of the Mapuche territories, driving the Indians southward; they were also driven southward by colonization. But the major factor in the situation was that the Mapuche control of the lands between the Bío-Bío and Tolten rivers created a territorial discontinuity in Chile and was perceived as an obstacle to national integration and an obstruction in the quest for the determination of borders between Chile and Argentina. Both countries simultaneously took control of Indian lands in the south, enforcing their sovereignty over wide stretches of territory and in this way defining their common border. It was in this situation that the image of the Mapuches changed again, becoming extremely negative. On the eve of the final military confrontation between the Mapuches and the Chilean state, the former were portrayed, in the Chilean propaganda campaign favoring conquest of Araucania, as savages—cruel rather than brave, lazy, drunken, slothful, and idle, fostering a stereotype that has survived until today. "We cannot," notes Bengoa, "understand how people with such characteristics could have kept at bay the infantry battalions of Spain and the glorious Chilean army" (*Bengoa*: 1991, pp. 148–149).

During the 19th century, the situation in the Mapuche lands and on the borders deteriorated. In the 1860s, the occupation of Araucania began to be discussed in political and military circles. Finally, plans presented by Cornelio Saavedra, who was the motive force behind the idea of the invasion, were accepted and carried out. The basic idea was to advance into the Indian lands, build a line of military forts, take over the occupied territory on behalf of the state, and subdivide and colonize it by settling Chileans and immigrants in it (*Bengoa*: 1991, pp. 170–174). Two extremely violent waves of military conquest, the first in 1869 and the second transpiring from the Mapuche uprising of 1881 to early 1883, finally achieved de facto Chilean sovereignty and created territorial continuity in the south of Chile. These events put an end to Mapuche control over their ancestral lands.

Integration into Chilean Society

The Mapuches were forced into "indigenous reductions"—i.e., reservations. From 1884 to 1919, the Chilean state granted 3,078 titles of property to Mapuche communities, comprising 77,751 individuals and 475,423 hectares (1,174,770 acres) of land. The total area of Mapuche land allocated to Mapuche and to white settlers amounted to ten million hectares (24,700,000 acres). Whereas the Mapuches received an average of 17 acres per person, the non-Mapuche—*huinca* or white—colonizers each received an average of 1,235 acres (*Mariqueo*: 1979, p. 20). The 1907 census reported a total population of 107,000 Mapuches in the south of Chile. If, up until 1919, land was allocated to 77,751 Mapuches, around 40,000 (nearly 37 percent of the total Mapuche population) were left landless (*Bengoa*: 1991, pp. 356–357). All this was done within the framework of an 1866 law, the *Ley de Radicación de Indígenas*, which regulated Indian land settlement. This law was abrogated in 1929, putting an end to the process of allocating land to the Mapuches.

Since the loss of control over their lands, the Mapuches' main concern has been their integration into Chilean society—and its corollary, the loss of their ethnic identity. The centuries-long war and the final defeat of the Mapuches and loss of their ancestral lands fostered powerful resentment. The defeat was perceived as the cause of the Mapuches' degeneration, pauperization, and self-identification as a marginal and discriminated-against minority. Their agricultural marginalization, resulting from the loss of control over large areas of territory, impaired their capacity to continue raising cattle extensively. The Mapuches, forced into communities in the Andean valleys and peripheral areas, lost the best grazing lands and, together with them, most of their capital: i.e., their herds of cattle and horses. The subdivision of the community's lands, and the fact that these were already marginal and less fertile, resulted in poverty and the disintegration of large families through emigration. Yet, despite all this, the Mapuches still tend to preserve their social connections, and are paradoxically helped in this by the discrimination and racism from which they suffer, especially when settling on the fringes of Chile's large urban concentrations (*Bengoa*: 1990, pp. 242–244).

The processes we have described turned the Mapuches from Indians into *campesinos*—laborers on the land. Mapuche society was dispersed into more than three thousand communities without strong internal links, and the people lost much of its cohesion. Yet, despite this, and in spite of strong external pressures to integrate, Mapuche society experienced a process of involution within the communities, in which social and cultural identity was preserved and adapted to the new conditions of living: namely, poverty, and the pressures to abandon their traditional culture. In the communities, the Mapuches not only preserved their traditions, within smaller but well-defined territorial boundaries, but also resisted violence and usurpations of land, developed weak but stable economic structures, shared resources and elaborated a new ceremonial system, and in general adjusted to the new realities of Chilean domination.

The relationship between Chilean society and the Mapuches again turned violent as a result of the process of land usurpations from 1910 to 1930. The reaction to land usurpations and anti-Indian violence, especially the marking of Mapuches with firebrands like cattle and the severing of their ears, led to a protest movement among the Mapuches that, from 1913 onward, adopted new forms of resistance and engaged in political participation in Chile's public life (*Bengoa*: 1991, pp. 370–382). In 1911, the Sociedad Caupolicán Defensora de la Araucanía was founded in Temuco. This marked the first clear manifestation of the Mapuches' presence in the framework of Chile's civil society. This organization aimed to promote both the ethnic preservation and education of the Mapuches. It was mainly led by Mapuche schoolteachers, who believed that through education a real integration of the Mapuches into Chilean society could be achieved. A member of this organization, Francisco Melivilu Henríquez, was elected a deputy of the Chilean parliament in 1924, as a candidate of the Partido Demócrata, thus becoming the first Mapuche to integrate into the state apparatus in Chile (*Bengoa*: 1990, p. 246). This was one of the sociopolitical options that some groups of Mapuches chose in order to confront the reality of life within the Chilean state.

Another option, its radical alternative, was total opposition to any kind of integration into Chilean society, through a reaffirmation of the Mapuche ethnic identity and an attempt to achieve a maximum of autonomy. A group representing this point of view crystallized as a result of numerous confrontations over problems of land expropriation between Mapuches and the landowners, backed by the authorities and the *carabineros* (the police). The group's leader, Manuel Aburto Panguilef, founded the Sociedad Mapuche de Protección Mutua in 1914. This association asked the government to stop land usurpations and to apply the law according to its letter and spirit for the benefit of the Indians. It also tried to promote Mapuche culture through a political theater group, La Compañía Araucana, that went from village to village performing Mapuche songs and dances and concluding the performances with political lectures. In 1920 Panguilef founded the Federación Araucana, and from 1920 to 1939 he held yearly meetings of the Mapuche leaders in which the old Mapuche rites of the chiefs' councils were reenacted (*Bengoa*: 1991, pp. 391–400). This movement was very active in politics, trying to pressure the Chilean government to accept Mapuche demands. It leaned toward the left, supporting President Arturo Alessandri, later opposing the junta that overthrew him and supporting the short-lived Socialist Republic set up in 1932 (see *Gil*: 1966, pp. 56–62).

For most of the century, the policy of the various governments in Chile was to attempt to integrate the Mapuches into Chilean society, mainly through education and especially the dissemination of literacy and the teaching of the Spanish language. Parallel to this, some governments, like those of Carlos Ibañez (1952–1958) and Eduardo Frei (1964–1970), carried out development plans in the most populated Mapuche areas. Education and development involved a process of modernization in which the Mapuche traditions and identity were gradually lost and replaced by an increasing integration into Chilean society.

A different policy, however, was advocated by the revolutionary left, which called for the solution of the problems of the indigenous peoples within the framework of a socialist revolution. In this approach, the predicament of the indigenous peoples lost its specific character and became an integral part of the plight of the proletariat and the lower classes in general.

Under the government of Salvador Allende (1970–1973), the policies applied to the Mapuches were bound up with the general agrarian reform carried out by the government. The implementation of the Allende government's agrarian reform laws led, in 1971, to the restoration to the Mapuches of 70,000 hectares of usurped land (*Chonchol*: 1978). This government regarded the Mapuches as part of the agrarian proletariat, and it gave them preferential treatment (*Bengoa*: 1990, p. 247). This policy was not without justification; the process of pauperization of the Mapuches ran parallel to their integration into Chilean society. If, at the beginning of the century, the Mapuches held an average of 6.1 hectares (15.07 acres) of land per person, a study conducted in the 1980s in the province of Cautín, where over 200,000 Mapuches live, showed that they now possessed an average of only 1.5 hectares (3.7 acres) per person. From 1966 to 1981, the income per family of the Mapuches dropped 30 percent. Most of this was a result of agricultural marginalization, the subdivision of land into uneconomical miniplots, and the weakening of the Mapuche communities as a result of emigration to urban areas.

Allende's government also tried to alleviate the Mapuches' predicament through its Law No. 17.729 or *Ley Indígena*, enacted in 1972, and by transforming the Dirección de Asuntos Indígenas into a more executive body, the Instituto de Desarrollo Indígena (Institute for Indian Development). The *Ley Indígena* was elaborated with the active participation of the Mapuche community leaders. It aimed at combining agrarian reform with Mapuche ethnodevelopment and at improving the general standard of living of the Mapuche agrarian population. Difficulties arose, however, not only with respect to restoring the rights of the Mapuches to the lands lost during the previous century, but also in devising the right educational policies and providing technical and organizational assistance to the beneficiaries of the law, as well as in enacting judicial and administrative reforms to improve the relations between the Mapuches and Chilean society. Less than a year after the enactment of the law, a violent military coup d'état took place in Chile.

The Mapuches in the Pinochet Period

The tendency toward the impoverishment of the Mapuches and the loss of their lands was reinforced in the period of Pinochet's military government by the repeal of the Agrarian Reform Law and the *Ley Indígena* of 1972 (*Mariqueo*: 1979, pp. 29–31). Other negative steps, from the Mapuche point of view, were the implementation of neoliberal economic policies and the enactment, in 1979, of decree 2.568, which led, by 1987, to a division of lands in most of the 3,048 Mapuche communities that, according to a 1968 study, still existed (*Bengoa*: 1990, pp. 239–240, and also *Uranga*: 1992, p. 32).

The Mapuche leadership, which underwent harsh repression immediately after the military coup because of the connection of its radical sectors with the "red" policies of agrarian reform implemented during Allende's period, had to reorganize. The depoliticization of Chilean society allowed only for the creation of an association of small Mapuche farmers and craftsmen, called AD-MAPU.

In March 1979, without any previous consultation with Mapuche representatives despite the requests for consultation that they had made since 1975, the military government enacted decree 2.568, the aim of which was to "integrate the Mapuche definitely into Chileanity with rights and duties equal to the rest of the country" (*Chile* 1979: p. 57). The AD-MAPU tried to have the new law repealed; when it failed, it tried to ensure that no Mapuche would demand any subdivision of land—an impossible expectation for a large community open to external influences and pressures. This caused a division within the Mapuche leadership. The more radical elements tried to confront the military government and forge ties with other parts of the left-wing Chilean opposition, representing the poorer sectors of the rural, mining, and urban population of the country. Other elements, more concerned with the danger of losing Mapuche identity, distanced themselves from the radicals and tried to recreate the Mapuche cultural centers that existed before the founding of AD-MAPU. This camp believed that socioeconomic radicalism, the links with the political left, and the demands for the restitution of land had provoked the harsh repression of the Mapuche communities by the military in September–October

1973. Their conclusion was that political radicalism risked bringing about the total disappearance of Mapuche identity (*Maybury-Lewis*: 1991).

Meanwhile, the military government applied the new law and thereby changed the situation of the Mapuches for the worse. Pinochet himself referred to the Mapuche problem in his fourth presidential message of September 12, 1978:

> This morning I also wish to announce the promulgation in the near future of a law on indigenous property which, while respecting the cultural values of the Mapuche, will enable those that wish to do so to opt voluntarily and freely for a title to property, replacing the present system of community ownership (*El Mercurio*, September 12, 1993, p. C-11).

This was to be achieved through three measures specified in the law. It would revoke the ceiling of 80 hectares (197 acres) for agricultural farms in the Mapuche-held lands, permit the setting-up of corporations in the Mapuche areas, and provide for the division of Indian land so as to enable the distribution of individual titles of property. This step created the possibility of establishing modern *latifundia* in what was left of the Mapuche reservations.

Since the lands in question were already marginal and were situated in mountainous territory, they attracted the attention of timber companies eager to exploit the age-old forests of araucaria, the sacred tree of the Mapuches. *Decreto ley* 2.568 abolished the protection previously accorded to territories classified as "indigenous lands." Anyone working the land in the Mapuche areas, regardless of his ethnic origins, was considered a settler, thus opening these areas to non-Mapuche settlement on a commercial basis. Provisions favoring Mapuche education, professional training, technical education, the establishment of centers for crafts, and the application of preferential quotas for Mapuche students applying for higher education, characteristic of previous Chilean legislation, and especially of law 17.729, the *Ley Indígena*, were absent from decree 2.568. The special status of the Mapuche reservations was abolished, and the Mapuches were placed in a situation where they had to compete for ownership of their lands with their more powerful Chilean neighbors on terms established by the latter, which reflected the socioeconomic and cultural patterns of Chilean society and were alien and disadvantageous to the Mapuches.

Decree 2.568, together with the general Indian policies of the military government, rapidly resulted in loss of land and impoverishment for the Mapuches. The breakup of communal lands was very rapid, and by 1983 the number of communally organized Indian reservations declined to less than 300. The free-market policies of the military government, which served as the framework for decree 2.568, created a situation in which the individual possession of lands by the Mapuches, even if the plots were minimal, made them eligible for taxation yet denied them access to free social and health services. Free-market policies required the implementation of modern accounting techniques, absolutely alien to the Mapuche farmers and too expensive to be feasible for them. The bureaucratic manipulation of land titles in the process of the subdivision of land resulted in many cases of fraud, false acquisition, and forged contracts, generally to the disadvantage of the Mapuches. The bureaucratic and legal complexities, alien to the Mapuches, worsened the losing position they were already in. All this together with the attitude of the Chilean legal system, never sympathetic to the Mapuche cause and generally disposed to give verdicts against the Indians, made for a very negative picture *(Bengoa*: 1990, pp. 244–245). In this situation, the Mapuches, deprived of government sympathy or support, were left to survive in a free-market society in which they lacked the main ingredients for success: economic power, high levels of education, and a mentality favorable to individual entrepreneurship.

Against the Mapuches was pitted the combination of ideological elements developed by Chilean authoritarianism and institutionalized in the 1980 constitution. The ideological vision of the military government, which underlay its intentions to found a new social, economic, political, and cultural order, was a combination of nationalist political principles, a neoliberal economic outlook, and a modernized version of the concept of a developed civil society in which the social bodies perform the main functions and the state is left to deal with the rest, according to the principle of subsidiarity. This ideological vision was characterized by integral nationalism, in which cultural values and traditions could be preserved so long as they did not contradict the unity of Chile as a nation.

The combination of a definite Mapuche identity, rejecting many of the Christian and Western values that typified Chilean nationalism, with the demand for devolution of usurped lands was utterly unacceptable to the military government. Economic modernization, enforced since the mid-1970s through extreme neoliberal policies, stood in complete opposition to the principles of communal ownership of land and the connection between the land, forest, and culture that characterized the Mapuches. Under the previous Chilean governments, which practiced protectionist economic policies together with various forms of preferential treatment in the fields of health, education, social services, and land ownership, the Mapuches had experienced a slow but continuous process of economic and social decay. Under the military government of the 1970s and 1980s, this process was greatly accelerated by the combination of authoritarian nationalism and neoliberal economics.

Since many Mapuches were perceived by the military as close associates of the Chilean left, and as such were subjected first to persecution and later to close supervision, no basis for a positive approach existed. In

Chilean nationalist doctrine, the Mapuche-Araucanian past constituted part of the national heritage, one factor in the process of racial admixture that had created the Chilean nation. This nation, it was said, had essentially been shaped by Western Christian cultural values. The Mapuches, therefore, were considered to have been at most a traditionally fighting people who, according to one of the main Chilean nationalist intellectuals, Nicolás Palacios, had fused with another fighting race, the Goths, or Northern Spaniards, in order to produce a fighting nation, Chile, which in the 19th century had proved its strength in many victorious wars. This mode of thinking had a profound influence on the formation of the modern military elite that assumed power in Chile in September 1973. Thus, it is not surprising that the attitude and policies of the military government toward the Mapuches resulted in further Mapuche decay.

The Mapuche Problem in the Context of
the Democratization in Chile

The seriousness of the Mapuche problem, together with the changes in the political system resulting from the transition to and consolidation of democracy in Chile, caused it to resurface as a public issue.

One of the factors that brought the Mapuche problem to the fore was the long-standing dispute between the Galletué timber company and the Mapuche (Pehuenche) community of Quinquén. The local Indians resisted the penetration of modern economic activity into their communal lands. After the timber company had done everything possible to evict the 150 Mapuches in the area so as to be able to cut down the age-old araucaria forest, winning court decisions, the representatives of the Quinquén Pehuenches, on October 11, 1990, appealed for help to Patricio Aylwin, the president of Chile (*Bengoa*: 1992, p. 103 ff.).

The government's intervention was carried out within the guidelines established by the Chilean process of democratization, which do not allow for any infringement of the principle of private property or of court decisions. Since the Chilean Supreme Court had already ruled in favor of the timber companies, who were the legal owners of the land. the situation of the Pehuenches was precarious and the scope of government action limited. The government strategy was threefold: through a debate in which all sides participated, the Mapuche problem was given public prominence within a democratic framework; in May 1991, the Quinquén area was declared a National Forest Reserve, thus precluding the possibility of commercially exploiting the araucaria wood in the area without the permission of the Chilean National Forest Corporation; and the government negotiated with the timber companies for the commercial acquisition of the land. Finally, on March 2, 1992, an agreement was reached and 30,000 hectares (74,130 acres) of land were bought by the Chilean state from their legal owners at a price of 6,150,000 dollars, for the purpose of restoring it to the Pehuenche communities (*Bengoa*: 1992, pp. 124–127).

This episode is significant because it represents a reversal of the historical trend of disintegration of the Mapuche communal way of life, and also because it clearly shows that the Chilean model of democratic transition and consolidation requires the addressing of grave social problems, such as that of the Mapuches and particularly in the case of Quinquén, but allows only for certain kinds of negotiated and reformist solutions. It shows that such solutions can be worked out without violating the limits of the neoliberal model of economic development—i.e., without land expropriation, without challenging the rulings of the Chilean courts (known to be traditionally unfavorable to the Mapuches), and, above all, without raising the question of Mapuche territorial autonomy: in other words, without challenging the nationalist conception of Chilean identity.

The redemocratized government of Chile was sensitive to the plight of the Mapuches. Many Mapuches had been executed after the military coup of 1973, and many more were persecuted from the beginning of the military dictatorship. In the late 1970s they became perhaps the first social sector to confront the military government, while trying to defend their communal possession of land. In this they set a precedent for later popular movements of social reform and opposition, and they were seen as an extreme example of the social costs of the politically authoritarian version of economic neoliberalism.

President Aylwin had sometimes vacationed in the Bío-Bío area and was familiar with the plight of the Mapuches. On December 1, 1989, when campaigning as a presidential candidate for the Concertación de Partidos por la Democracia—the democratic opposition to the military government—Aylwin signed the agreement of Nueva Imperial, in which he undertook to include the demands of the Mapuches in the electoral platform of the democratic government. On May 17, 1990, the new government created a special agency to deal with the problem of the indigenous peoples of Chile, the CEPI (Comisión Especial de Pueblos Indígenas), whose chairperson was José Bengoa, a social anthropologist and historian of the Mapuches. This organization included Indian activists as well as experts in matters concerning the indigenous peoples. Thus, the CEPI was able to overcome the inherent tendency of such organizations to co-opt and neutralize the leadership of social protest movements, and it became, on the contrary—especially through the activities of Bengoa—the defender of indigenous interests vis-à-vis the Chilean state.

In 1990, preparation began of a special Indigenous Law or *Ley de Indígenas*. With the cooperation of the CEPI, a draft for this law was formulated and afterward discussed in two thousand indigenous assemblies and meetings. Subsequently, delegates were elected and fifteen provincial congresses were held. In January 1991, three hundred representatives of the indigenous peoples met at the National Congress of Indigenous Peoples and voted on the proposed law article by article (*Uranga*: 1992, p. 33). The year 1991 saw the formation of the Consejo de Todas las Tierras, the Council of All Lands, or in Mapuche, Aukin Wallmapu Ngulam. This organization expressed its views through its spokesperson or *werken* (in Mapuche) Aucan Huilcaman, a law student at the Universidad Autónoma del Sur. Right-wing politicians in Chile pointed at the leftist influences in this organization as well as its links with "foreign" international organizations that dealt with problems of indigenous peoples. The members and supporters of the Council demonstrated repeatedly, demanding autonomy and achieving national and even international recognition. Their demands for autonomy were not restricted to the sphere of language and culture but extended to the possession of a recognized area of territory in the lands to the south of the Bío-Bío River, and control over its resources. In this context, the Consejo de Todas las Tierras demanded constitutional recognition of the rights of the Mapuches as a people (*Maya*: 1991).

Meanwhile, in a conference on the subject of indigenous peoples in Hispanic America held in the Faculty of Law of the University of Chile, a comparative analysis was made of the difference between the former Chilean legislation on indigenous matters and the new projected law and policy. Francisco Huenchumilla, a Christian Democratic member of parliament of Mapuche origin, explained at this conference that the government had relinquished its intention to propose a constitutional reform recognizing the rights of indigenous peoples because the political opposition, tacitly backed by the army, would block such a reform, exploiting the institutional enclaves left over by Pinochet's government. Thus, the government had chosen to postpone the constitutional recognition of the existence of indigenous peoples in Chile to a time when the political balance would allow for constitutional reform. In the meantime, the governmental coalition had enacted a law pragmatically responding to most of the demands of the indigenous organizations (*Boletín Pueblos Indígenas*: 1993a, pp. 2–3).

There is much evidence that the debate accompanying the bill was detailed and thorough, and that the parliamentary commissions that dealt with the bill consulted the chief experts in the field, headed by José Bengoa, and also consulted with the indigenous organizations on a wide range of issues. The law thus proposed was then brought to the Chilean parliament and fully discussed by the appropriate parliamentary commission, revised in accordance with the balance of political forces existing in the country, and again presented to parliament as an approved draft in late August 1993 (see *República de Chile, Senado*: 1993).

Despite the basic pragmatic agreement between the government and the opposition about the law-enactment process and the avoidance of a deep constitutional reform (including the issue of recognizing the indigenous populations as "peoples" and the implications of that step in terms of territorial and economic autonomy), the ideological disagreement between the two sides was clear. Senator Ricardo Navarrete, president of the Commission of Indigenous Affairs of the Chilean Senate and a member of the Radical Party, a part of the government coalition, declared that

> the indigenes in our country have been subjected to systematic human rights violations. . . . This should have produced a greater readiness or political desire to bring about the constitutional reform, which, as we know, was finally abandoned in order to make possible discussion of the bill (*Boletín Pueblos Indígenas*: 1993b, p. 3).

The opposition senator Sergio Diez—a member of the Renovación Nacional, the largest opposition party, and a former supporter of the Pinochet government—expressed the opposite view:

> I am in favor of the integration of all the roots of the Chilean people, into the Chilean people. . . . I believe we all feel we are Chileans and wish to integrate into the national reality, but we do not wish to assimilate to a single pattern in order to become part of that national unity. Therefore it is important to distinguish between "integration" and "assimilation." I am an integrationist (*Boletín Pueblos Indígenas*: 1993c, p. 3).

The difference between the two is clear. The government, at least according to its statements, is willing to contemplate a deep structural change whose formal and symbolic aspect would be a constitutional reform, redefining the Chilean approach toward the indigenous peoples, of which the Mapuches constitute the vast majority. The opposition, on the other hand, wishes to "integrate" the Mapuches and the other indigenous peoples into the Chilean people, while allowing for pragmatic solutions to their immediate problems (lands, water resources, education, health, etc.) and a measure of respect for the cultural identity of each group, as constituting various cultural roots of the same Chilean nationality. In political terms, the issue can be considered within the larger framework of the political and institutional model of limited democracy enshrined in the 1980 constitution. This document speaks clearly of a single Chilean nation within the boundaries of its territorial sovereignty, and of a delicate balance among the different powers and branches of the government, which are as difficult to change as it is to reform the constitution. Therefore, addressing the roots of the problem of the indigenous peoples by reshaping the delicate balance established in the 1980 constitution, and opening up the Chilean nation to redefinition, are issues directly linked to the constitutional nature of Chilean democracy, and to the nature of the transition to democracy and its consolidation according to terms laid down by the former military regime and partially revised in 1989 (on this issue, see *Political Constitution of the Republic of Chile*: 1980, article 5 ff.; *Moya*: 1989). [These were the actions taken during the Aylwin administration.]

Law 19.253, "On the protection, support, and development of the indigenes, and on setting up the National Corporation for Indigenous Development," was approved by the Chilean parliament, enacted, and published in the *Diario Oficial* on October 5, 1994 (*Diario Oficial de la República de Chile*: 1994). President Aylwin had signed the law at a public ceremony on September 28, 1993, in Nueva Imperial, the location where in his presidential campaign in 1989 he had promised the Mapuches to carry out their demands if elected. In response to Aylwin's speech, the representatives of the indigenous peoples expressed their satisfaction with the practical aspects of the new law while pointing out that one of their main demands, namely, constitutional recognition of the indigenous peoples, had not yet been fulfilled (*El Mercurio*, September 29, 1993, p. A1).

Law 19.253, comprising eighty articles and sixteen transitory clauses, may be described as constituting the framework for positive discrimination in favor of the indigenous population of Chile. It mandates prison terms for those found guilty of discriminating against an indigenous person because of his origin or culture. It declares it the duty of the state to respect, promote, and protect the development of the indigenous populations, as well as of their lands and water resources. It announces the creation of a National Corporation of Indigenous Development (CONADI), as an autonomous and decentralized organization, in Temuco, center of the Mapuche heartland (since the majority of the indigenous population in Chile is of Mapuche origin). The purpose of CONADI as a branch of the administration is to promote, implement, and coordinate the actions of the state for the development of indigenous groups and individuals. The new law accepts Indian customary practice as valid in legal confrontations involving indigenous persons of the same ethnic group. It declares the goal of promoting bilingual education and protecting the archeological and cultural heritage of the different indigenous groups. The application of the law together with the activities of CONADI, which received a basic financial allocation of $4.5 million for the first year, could positively affect the lives of 600,000 indigenous persons, nearly 90 percent of whom are Mapuche.

The new law and corporation regularize the already existing policies of the redemocratized government in various areas. Through its former agency, the CEPI, Aylwin's government had already spent more than $3 million on five hundred small development projects as well as on 4,500 educational scholarships for young indigenous persons, nine hundred of which were at university level (*El Mercurio*, September 29, 1993, p. A1). Undoubtedly, the policies of the emerging Chilean democracy constitute a further significant step toward satisfying the demands of the Mapuches and other indigenous peoples of Chile. This has been done in a way that allows the indigenous groups the possibility of finding their place within the evolving civil society in which democracy is being consolidated. The

Chilean parliament and government have enacted a modern law that makes a start at redressing historical tendencies that had led to the attrition of marginal ethnic groups in the country. Still, bound by its own limitations—political, institutional, and budgetary—it has, perhaps, done too little too late.

Conclusions

There are positive signs of ethnodevelopment in contemporary Chile. CONADI and the government are transferring land to Huiliche and Mapuche communities (*Aurora*, August 18, 1994). Funds are being provided for education, the preservation of culture, and small development programs. Yet all these measures seem only a drop in the ocean. Countries such as Brazil, Colombia, and Nicaragua have taken further steps by constitutionally recognizing the rights of their indigenous peoples (*Stavenhagen*: 1992). This recognition changes the terms of the equation, but may be sharply opposed by nationalist sectors and those still preoccupied with notions of "national security." In Chile, the kind of democratic transition and consolidation that has evolved from the military government, and the attempt to create and implement a model of limited democracy, have resulted in a situation in which constitutional recognition of the indigenous peoples is impossible. This is a serious problem, because it may be the case that the only way to fully ensure the human and civil rights of indigenous peoples is to negotiate with them, on an equal footing, the terms of their economic, cultural, political, and even territorial autonomy, concomitant with the constitutional recognition of those rights (*Stavenhagen*: 1993).

References

Allende, S.: 1973, Chile's Road to Socialism. Harmondsworth (Middlesex: Penguin Books).
Arrate, J.: 1991, The Social Debt in the Chilean Development Process, in: Tulchin, J.S./Varas, A., From Dictatorship to Democracy: Rebuilding Political Consensus in Chile. Boulder (Lynne Rienner).
Aurora: 1994, Repartirán 50,000 hectáreas entre indígenas chilenos. Latinoamérica II, August 18.
Bengoa, J.: 1990, La cuestión indígena y la situación de las minorías étnicas, in: Proposiciones, 18.
Bengoa, J.: 1991, Historia del Pueblo Mapuche. Santiago (Ediciones Sur).
Bengoa, J.: 1992, Quinquén. 100 Años de Historia Pehuenche. Santiago (Ediciones Chileamérica CESOC).
Boeninger, E.: 1991, The Chilean Political Transition to Democracy, in: Tulchin, J.S./Varas, A., From Dictatorship to Democracy: Rebuilding Political Consensus in Chile. Boulder (Lynne Rienner).

Boletín Pueblos Indígenas: 1993a, Pasado, presente y futuro de las leyes y los indígenas, July–August.

Boletín Pueblos Indígenas: 1993b, Antes de las Fiestas Patrias podria estar publicada la ley, July–August.

Boletín Pueblos Indígenas: 1993c, Distingo claramente entre asimilación e integración: soy integracionista.

Chile 1979: Chile's New Law on Indian Affairs, p. 57.

Chonchol, J.: 1978, Quatre siècles de résistance. Les mapuches, la terre volée et la persécution, in: Le Monde Diplomatique, June, p. 9.

Cristi, R.: 1992, La síntesis conservadora de los años 70, in: Cristi, R./ Ruiz, C., El pensamiento conservador en Chile. Santiago (Editorial Universitaria), pp. 134–139.

Diario Oficial de la República de Chile: 1994, Ley Num. 19.253. Establece normas sobre protección, fomento y desarrollo de los indígenas, y crea la Corporación de Desarrollo Indígena, pp. 2–8.

El Mercurio: 1978, Mensaje Presidencial a la Nación, September 12.

El Mercurio: 1993, Promulgada ley de trato especial a los indígenas, September 29.

Feinberg, R.L.: 1972, The Triumph of Allende: Chile's Legal Revolution. New York (Mentor Books).

Fuentes, J.: 1984, Lía Cortés, Fernando Castillo Infante y Arturo Valdés Phillips. Diccionario Histórico de Chile. Santiago (Zig-Zag).

Gil, F.G.: 1966, The Political System of Chile. Boston (Houghton Mifflin).

Gunckel, H.: 1966, Variaciones sobre la palabra araucano, in: Boletín de la Universidad de Chile, 2, 69–70, pp. 18 ff.

Latin American Special Reports: 1994a, Indians: New Factor in the Latin American Scene. 94–03 (June).

Latin American Special Reports: 1994b, Recent History of Growing Militancy. 94–03 (June).

Latin American Special Reports: 1994c, The Indians' Decade. 94–03 (June).

Latin American Special Reports: 1994d, The Difficult Task of Counting Heads. 94–03 (June).

Mackenna, B.V.: 1972; La guerra a muerte 1819–1824. Buenos Aires (Editorial Francisco de Aguirre).

Mariqueo, V.: 1979, The Mapuche Tragedy, in: Chile 1979. Copenhagen (IWGIA).

Maya, J.C.: 1991, Consejo de Todas las Tierras. Sus problemas y aspiraciones, in: Ercilla, October 23, n.p.

Maybury-Lewis, D.: 1991, Becoming Indian in the Lowlands of South America, in: Urban, G./Sherzer, J. (eds.), Nation States and Indians in Latin America. Austin (University of Texas Press), pp. 213–214.

Menéndez, E.C. (compilador): 1974, Pensamiento nacionalista. Santiago (Editorial Nacional Gabriela Mistral).

Moya, C.A.G. (compilador): 1989, 54 Reformas a la Constitución Política de Chile. Santiago (Editorial Jurídica Publiley).

Ominami, C.: 1991, Promoting Economic Growth and Stability, in: Tulchin, J.S./Varas, A., From Dictatorship to Democracy: Rebuilding Political Consensus in Chile. Boulder (Lynne Rienner).

Palacios, N.: 1904, La raza chilena. Valparaíso (Imprenta y Litografía Alemana).

Political Constitution of the Republic of Chile: 1980, Santiago.

República de Chile, Senado: 1993, Boletín No. 514-01, Segundo Informe de la Comisión Especial de Pueblos Indígenas, August 31.

Stavenhagen, R.: 1992, Challenging the Nation State in Latin America, in: Journal of International Affairs, 45, 2, pp. 439–440.

Stavenhagen, R.: 1993, Los derechos indígenas: algunos problemas conceptuales, in: Índice, 6, pp. 33–34.

Touraine, A.: 1994, Critica della modernità, in: I viaggi di Erodoto, 8, 22, p. 101.

Tulchin, J.S./Varas, A.: 1991, From Dictatorship to Democracy: Rebuilding Political Consensus in Chile. Boulder (Lynne Rienner).

United Nations Report: 1979, Chile 1979: The Mapuche Tragedy. IWGIA Document 38. Copenhagen.

Uranga, V.: 1992, Pueblos indígenas. La historia de los vencidos, in: Análisis, June 8.

Urzua, H.G.: 1974, El pensamiento nacionalista en Chile a comienzos del siglo XX, in: Menéndez, E.C. (compilador), Pensamiento nacionalista. Santiago (Editorial Nacional Gabriela Mistral), pp. 147–149.

II

Indigenous Political Participation

3

Agrarian Protest and the Indian Movement in the Ecuadorian Highlands

Leon Zamosc

The native peoples of Ecuador have been at the forefront of the ethnic indigenous revival in Latin America. A number of spectacular mobilizations in the 1990s have propelled the indigenous rights movement into the political foreground. In many ways, this might have been a surprising development, given the land reform that Ecuador has undergone since the 1960s. This process broke up many of the large haciendas in the countryside and returned some of the estate lands to the Indian communities that had survived into the late twentieth century.

Professor Leon Zamosc shows why the Indian rights movement began to flourish just as many people expected the indigenous population to meld into the cities and to become indistinguishable from the rest of the Ecuadorians. Instead, the class-based organizations that had attempted to gain the allegiance of the Indians faded as ethnically based popular organizations took over. Zamosc posits that the growing importance of ethnic movements is based on currents of modernization and the kinds of social changes that have occurred as "structural adjustment" measures, which opened up the Ecuadorian economy to the outside, transformed the social and political landscape. One of the great virtues of this essay is not only the acknowledgment of the varieties of Indian groups but also the way in which worldwide changes have affected the ability of the Indians to project themselves onto the national scene.

The author supplies a sophisticated analytical framework within which to examine indigenous movements throughout Latin America. How do the Indians fit into the modern state? Zamosc asserts that they reject the homogenization of modernity, but not their integration of members into the

From Leon Zamosc, "Agrarian Protest and the Indian Movement in the Ecuadorian Highlands," *Latin American Research Review* 29:3 (1994), 37–68. Reprinted by permission of *Latin American Research Review*.

national society with their own legitimate social, political, and cultural demands.

León Zamosc is a professor of sociology at the University of California, San Diego, and has written extensively on peasant movements.

In June of 1990, the mountains of the Ecuadorian Sierra provided the setting for a spectacular display of protest. For an entire week, tens of thousands of Indian peasants stopped delivering farm produce to the towns and blocked the main highways, picketed on the roadsides, and marched en masse in regional capitals. In some places, demonstrators seized the offices of government agencies, and in others, localized skirmishes reportedly broke out where landowners and Indian communities had been embroiled in unresolved land disputes.

The protest was called by CONAIE, the Confederación de Nacionalidades Indígenas del Ecuador. The name given to the event, Levantamiento Nacional Indígena (National Indian Uprising), was chosen to establish continuity with the Indian insurrections of the colonial era and the nineteenth century. It soon became apparent, however, that this *levantamiento* was not actually cast in the mold of the localized, violent upheavals typical of the past. After Indian activists occupied one of the oldest churches in Quito in a symbolic opening move, popular protest swelled into a general civic strike, a massive moratorium suspending all normal activities in favor of an array of contentious acts. Caught by surprise, the Social Democratic government of President Rodrigo Borja deployed the police and the army to restrain the mobilization. But the composed demeanor of the protesters and the prudence displayed by the authorities allowed the episode to wind down with little violence. The turnout was particularly heavy in the central highlands, where the largest concentrations of rural and Indian populations live. In Chimborazo, Cotopaxi, Tungurahua, and Bolívar, Indian delegates submitted lists of grievances, negotiated, and signed agreements with provincial authorities. The protest was called off at the national level when the Borja administration agreed to open a dialogue with the Indians on the economic situation, land conflicts, and other issues raised by CONAIE's sixteen-point memorandum to the nation.[1]

Since the levantamiento, the Catholic Church has been mediating intermittent negotiations between the government and CONAIE. Executive power was transferred to a new Conservative administration, and regional branches of the Indian movement have staged additional protests.[2] While the major political parties have been hostile or noncommittal to the Indian cause, the Ecuadorian generals have denounced the movement as "subversive" and have effectively militarized entire Indian areas under the cover of a vast program of "community support."[3] Although the situation remains fluid and it would be premature to try to gauge the long-term consequences, the levantamiento is undoubtedly the major popular mobilization in recent Ecuadorian history. Two aspects are particularly noteworthy: the sheer magnitude, which revealed a widespread mood of discontent among the rural people of the highlands; and the defining of the event as an Indian mobilization, which opened the eyes of all Ecuadorians to the Indians' return as protagonists who are placing the national question back on the political agenda.

This Indian ethnic resurgence is not a uniquely Ecuadorian phenomenon but part of a broader trend in contemporary Latin America with many forms of expression in everyday practices and public life. Increasingly since the 1970s, the flowering of movements claiming to represent the aspirations of regional and national Indian constituencies has become the clearest political manifestation of this general trend.[4] While the ultimate impact will depend on conditions and processes particular to each case, these movements have major implications for the countries where they arise. From the perspective of social equity and economic growth, they are calling attention to the situation of rural groups among the poorest sectors who are sometimes located in environmentally sensitive areas where natural resources have been targeted for development by the state and multinational corporations. Moreover, the Indian movements seem to be actual or potential bearers of the demand to redefine citizenship in a way that would recognize Indian rights to cultural distinctiveness and political autonomy. Such a demand is at odds with both the model of liberal democracy being enjoined by political elites and the dominant cultural perceptions of national identity in Latin America.

The Ecuadorian levantamiento gave emblematic expression to the relevance of the Indian political comeback. Approaching this event from the social movement perspective, this article seeks to contribute to an emerging literature that is beginning to recast the Indian question in the light of new substantive and theoretical concerns.[5] Before proceeding, two caveats are in order. First, regarding the thematic focus of the discussion, this article has been framed as an inquiry into the origins and the significance of the levantamiento. I approach the 1990 protest as a peak of collective action in an ongoing cycle of mobilization.[6] Rather than dwelling on the details of the event or speculating on possible outcomes of the sequence as a whole, my purpose here is to provide an analytical outline of the factors involved in the ascending phase of the cycle.

The second caveat relates to the regional focus of the analysis. In terms of the Indian question, the most important Ecuadorian regions are the Sierra and Amazonia, the latter home to smaller groups that have always been viewed as more contentious than their Andean counterparts. In this context, the article's focus on the highlands is justified largely by the fact that Amazonian participation in the 1990 levantamiento was marginal. This contrast reemphasized important differences between the circumstances, demands, and patterns of mobilization of the Amazonian and Andean Indians.[7] I will return to the regional contrast in the concluding section. For now, it should be kept in mind that the sources of Indian protest cited herein apply to the highlands, which include the majority of Ecuadorian Indians but not all of them.

Considering the scope and intensity of the levantamiento, it might be tempting to view it as a classic case of collective catharsis. Such a perspective recalls traditional approaches that have viewed mass mobilization as a "release" of accumulated psychological or social tensions.[8] Since the 1970s, however, such mechanistic views have been superseded by theoretical perspectives that envision social movements as active agents and potential catalyzers of social, political, and cultural change. In the United States, two prominent currents converge around the strategic components of collective action: the resource mobilization approach, which emphasizes resource management and the pivotal role of organization; and rational choice theory, which conceives of actors as instrumental agents who behave rationally to maximize their own benefits.[9] In European sociology, the main contributions have tended to focus on two aspects that can also be perceived as convergent or at least complementary: the symbolic content of social movements, and the processes of identity construction and transformation that furnish the bases for collective action.[10]

These approaches have led to greater sophistication in interpreting phenomena like the Indian struggles in Ecuador. But the replacement of paradigms is fraught with problems of its own. Many theorists make a point of completely rejecting the older conceptual perspectives, an approach that tends to underestimate the importance of the structural factors shaping the possibilities for collective action. Furthermore, competition for preeminence seems to be feeding reductionist propensities in that the new approaches tend to overemphasize the centrality of certain factors and try to project their sometimes narrow explanatory logic onto every aspect of the process of social mobilization. Without pretending to resolve these problems completely, I will explore the possibilities of an integrated analysis that respects the different dimensions of collective action and connects them to structural processes. To lay the groundwork for the discussion, I will examine the changes marking the socioeconomic evolution of the Ecuadorian highlands over the last thirty years. Then, based on a conceptualization of the three essential components of collective action, I will examine the instrumental orientation, organizational foundations, and expressive significance of the Indian protest of June 1990. The article will conclude with some general reflections on the levantamiento as a turning point in the trajectory of the Ecuadorian Indian movement, calling attention to conditions that are changing its orientations and prospects.

The Context: Agrarian Transformations in the Highlands

Ecuador entered the second half of the twentieth century as an essentially agrarian country. In the Sierra, an elevated plateau flanked by the highest Andean ranges, almost three-quarters of the population lived in the countryside.[11] The region historically had been the main area of human settlement in the country. In contrast to the export orientation of tropical agriculture in the recently populated mestizo region of the Costa, the agriculture of the highlands remained focused on producing traditional foodstuffs for domestic markets. The first systematic study of the country's rural economy and society, conducted in the early 1960s, showed that much of this production came from the haciendas (the large estates in the highlands), which continued to control most of the land and operate as strategic hubs in the socioeconomic organization of the region.[12]

The reproduction of the hacienda-based agrarian regime hinged on a dual articulation with subordinated peasant sectors. Internally, the hacienda economy incorporated communities of *huasipungueros*, peasant families who labored year after year for landowners in exchange for small subsistence plots and low supplementary wages. Externally, the haciendas maintained various relationships with poor peasants from neighboring Indian communities. Some of these peasants paid in kind for using plots of land, but most were required to contribute labor quotas in return for access to strategic resources such as pasture, water, firewood, and roads. Taking into account the centrality of these servile relations of production (and particularly the predominance of labor rent, the most primitive form of rent), it is not surprising that many viewed the Ecuadorian Sierra as one of the last bastions of feudalism in the Americas.

Agrarian Reform and the New Peasant Sectors

Agrarian reform played a decisive role in transforming this traditional structure. The first phase, during the 1960s, eliminated the servile relations within the haciendas and made the huasipungueros into legal owners of their subsistence plots.[13] The second phase of the reform in the 1970s achieved more visible redistributive effects, as new regulations broadened the criteria for state intervention and permitted effective transfer of some hacienda lands to peasants from neighboring communities.[14] These two stages were implemented by military governments who presented the attempt to modify the old agrarian regime as part of broader projects aimed at modernizing Ecuadorian society. The initiatives were responding to special circumstances: enhanced export-based economic growth, which was induced first by the short-lived boom in the banana sector during the late 1950s and early 1960s and was later renewed by expansion of the oil industry during the 1970s.

The agrarian reform had a considerable impact. Between 1954 and 1982, redistribution involved approximately one-quarter of the total area of haciendas larger than one hundred hectares.[15] An even more important indirect effect derived from the fact that the risk of expropriation convinced many landowners to put land on the market.[16] In the northern Sierra, where proximity to the main urban markets offered excellent prospects for dairy production, most landowners followed the strategy of selling portions of their haciendas in order to capitalize on smaller areas that, once redefined as modern agricultural units, were automatically exempted from the threat of agrarian reform. In the central and southern Sierra, where conditions were less amenable to this alternative, landowners tried to anticipate state intervention by selling the land privately in parcels, seeking always to maximize prices by fostering competition among potential buyers (usually peasants from the Indian communities linked to the hacienda or sometimes mestizos from nearby villages).

It is not possible to examine fully here the interactions between institutional reform, activation of the land market, and the other changes that played roles in the overall agrarian transformation in the Sierra. My purpose here is to highlight one major result of this process: a less concentrated ownership of land. In 1954, large haciendas monopolized more than three-quarters of the total area, but by the mid-1980s, agricultural land was distributed in similar proportions among large, medium, and small farms.[17] The spread reflects a combined pattern of agrarian development in the Ecuadorian Sierra, with different logics of production and reproduction coexisting side by side. This situation is by no means idyllic for the peasants, whose third of the agricultural land is physically insufficient to sustain the majority of the rural population and invariably includes the highest, driest, and least fertile tracts. Even so, as a result of the changes taking place in the highlands, most rural families emerged with some measure of access to land.

At this point, a closer look should be taken at the internal composition of the peasant sector, given that existing studies show great variations in access to land, living standards, and other conditions. These variations reflect processes of differentiation that cut across regions, local communities, and even households within each community. In broad analytical terms, two basic socioeconomic situations can be distinguished.[18] When families have enough land, they tend to concentrate on cultivation for their own consumption and market sale, goals that always entail some degree of specialization in one or more of the traditional crops of the highlands (cereals, leguminous plants, and tubers). Most visible in the northern Sierra, these small producers coexist with medium-sized units and modernized haciendas engaging in entrepreneurial production.

In the second socioeconomic situation, families lacking sufficient land are forced to combine subsistence farming with other activities, which at times include artisanal work and petty commerce. More typically, women and children are left to farm the plots while the men go elsewhere to work. Some of these migrants have adjusted to the seasonal labor demands of capitalist agriculture on the Costa, but the vast majority seek employment in the cities, primarily in the construction industry, returning home to spend weekends with their families. This semi-proletarian sector includes a large proportion of all peasant households in the Sierra and most rural inhabitants in the central provinces.[19]

For both types of peasants, the 1970s brought incorporation into the market and the national economy, along with some improvements in their living conditions. Spurred by the boom in oil exports and industrialization, brisk urban growth increased the demand for foodstuffs produced by market-oriented households while generating many new job opportunities for migrants in construction and other activities requiring unskilled labor.[20] The downside of these changes was that they also created tremendous dependencies. On the one hand, peasant incomes began to hinge on the price of agricultural commodities and also on urban demand for labor. On the other hand, because all these adjustments involved changes in patterns of production and consumption, Ecuadorian peasants found themselves relying more and more on the market for fertilizers, agricultural inputs, transportation, clothing, and even food.[21]

The distinction between small agricultural producers and semi-proletarians is essential for understanding the circumstances of the rural population in Ecuador. Nevertheless, it represents only an initial step in conceptualizing the complex range of situations that can be found today in the Ecuadorian Sierra.[22] For example, those producing for the market have different levels of access to the land and other resources, and their prospects may also vary widely according to regional location and product specialization. Similarly, semi-proletarians display different degrees of involvement in the labor market and varied working and living conditions according to the activities in which they engage. Amid all this variation, however, two constants can be identified. One is the relationship between socioeconomic situation and standard of living, which arises from the fact that market-oriented peasants are almost always much better off than those who depend on migrating and working for wages.[23] The second constant is the relationship between socioeconomic situation and ethnic ascription, defined by the fact that small producers for the market are mostly mestizos, whereas semi-proletarian migrants are mostly Indians. Consider the striking contrast between Carchi and Chimborazo. The northernmost province of the Sierra, Carchi is evenly populated by mestizo potato-growing peasants who are some of the most successful small farmers in Ecuador. The central province of Chimborazo, one of the most solidly Indian areas in the country, has suffered massive labor migration and rural poverty.[24]

Peasant Organizations and the State

Agrarian reform, particularly during the administration of General Guillermo Rodríguez Lara (1972–1976), was part of an ambitious project seeking to modernize Ecuadorian society and the economy through state initiatives. In a country with a history of regional and political fragmentation, it was the military that tried to further this project via a national developmentalist program. Until that time, Ecuador's economy had been an agro-export economy with little industry, low rates of urban growth, and a limited internal market. The real takeoff came during the first half of the 1970s, as the country began to extract and export Amazonian oil amid skyrocketing prices and achieved an average annual growth rate in gross national product of more than 10 percent.[25] With oil resources under state control, the military sought to implement the classic agenda for development via inwardly oriented industrial growth: investments in state enterprises, credits for new private businesses, subsidies and fiscal incentives, overvalued exchange rates, import restrictions, and borrowing from foreign banks when oil prices began to decline.[26] During the second half of the 1970s, the GNP grew at a more modest annual rate of 6.6 percent, but by then the industrial, construction, and service sectors had become the most dynamic in the economy.[27] In this context, the policy of moderate agrarian reform had a dual purpose: to encourage landowners to modernize their haciendas, and to establish a base of small agricultural producers who would contribute to the supply of foodstuffs while helping to enlarge the national market as consumers. These goals were reinforced with sizable public investments in credit programs, technical assistance for agriculture, infrastructural works, and improvement of services in rural areas.[28]

In considering the role of popular organizations in the countryside, two periods can be distinguished. During the period of the reform (the 1960s and 1970s), the key element was the struggle for land. Before that time, only the Communist party had been involved in active political opposition in the rural areas. The Communists failed to play a salient role in the battle over the agrarian reform, however, because they were influential on only a few haciendas and also because their organizational blueprint (which stressed worker demands and favored strikes) was not germane to the special nature of the struggle for land.[29] Moreover, the Communists were repressed by the military, who preferred to deal with FENOC (Federación Nacional de Organizaciones Campesinas), a new organization linked to Christian Democratic political groups.

FENOC played a vital role in organizing land-acquisition committees and regional associations that circulated petitions, negotiated with landowners and IERAC (Instituto Ecuatoriano de la Reforma Agraria), and reinforced general pressure for land redistribution.[30] By 1975, when Socialist militants displaced the Christian Democrats in the FENOC leadership, the organization began to employ more radical methods, resorting more often to land seizures to force transactions. In the highlands, however, peasants were less belligerent than in the Costa, where land invasions proved far more pivotal to implementing agrarian reform.[31] FENOC's turn to the left coincided with the emergence of ECUARUNARI, a new Indian organization taking root in various areas of the Sierra under the influence of radical groups tied to the social programs of the Catholic Church. Like FENOC, ECUARUNARI operated as a federation of regional organizations (its full Indian name means "awakening of the Ecuadorian Indians"). At the local level, however, it sought a foothold in the organizational forms already existing in the Indian communities and their *cabildos* (committees in charge of the affairs of each community).[32] Yet for all the emphasis on ECUARUNARI's distinctiveness as an Indian organization, its discourse scarcely differed from that of FENOC in that it espoused a class-based ideology focused on the struggle for land, linking that struggle to the socialist ideals of the worker-peasant alliance and paying little attention to ethnicity as an issue in itself.

By the second half of the 1970s, it became clear that the military's reformist thrust was foundering rapidly for lack of popular support and due to strong opposition from political, landowning, and business elites. Bracing for an orderly retreat, the triumvirate of conservative generals that had replaced Rodríguez Lara in 1976 recanted on all fronts. One measure redefined the state's agrarian policy, emphasizing greater productivity and narrowing the criteria for further land redistribution.[33] The political space for agrarian reform appeared to be effectively closed, and the situation was not changed by the 1978 transition to democratic rule. Since the first civilian government of President Jaime Roldós, the various successive administrations have consistently followed policies seeking not to transform the agricultural sector but to regulate and stabilize it. Regarding the peasantry, governmental emphasis shifted to integrated rural development and selective assistance programs.[34]

During this second period (the 1980s), peasant organizations underwent significant changes. As the role of FENOC's regional associations as agents in the struggle for land was fulfilled or diminished, these groups began to wane—especially in the Sierra, where they had never attained much organizational consistency. The associations that remained active, particularly in the Costa region, were those that had redefined their role around representing the new demands of the peasants who had gained access to the land.[35] At the national level, FENOC leaders continued to wave the banner of agrarian reform, but they showed little capacity to inspire action on the issue. The organization has languished because the stances taken by its leaders have not heeded changing national circumstances and the needs of FENOC's own grassroots associations. These groups are now largely composed of landed peasants whose chief problems are related to pricing their goods and obtaining support and services in their regions. When asked to account for FENOC's incapacity to respond in a dynamic fashion to the new conditions, most activists and observers point to two factors: the bureaucratic entrenchment of its national leaders, and the ideological crisis that has gripped the Socialist party and the Ecuadorian left in general.[36]

In the Sierra, where FENOC declined most conspicuously, the Indian movement gained ground rapidly due to simultaneous impulses from above and from below. At the grassroots, the key element was revitalizing the traditional organizational framework—the local communities and the cabildos, which began to coalesce into *federaciones de comunidades* and *uniones de cabildos* in parishes and *cantones*. At the regional level, the most important factor was ECUARUNARI's shift in orientation, which balanced standard calls for land reform with new demands arising from the struggle against ethnic discrimination and defense of Indian language and culture.[37] In 1986, ECUARUNARI's increasing cooperation and partnership with CONFENIAE (Confederación de Nacionalidades Indígenas de la Amazonía Ecuatoriana) led to the formation of CONAIE as the national organization representing all Indian groups.[38]

Rather than insisting on traditional themes like the struggle for land and economic improvements, CONAIE concentrated on an ethnic agenda ranging from vindication of cultural rights to more ambitious programmatic demands, such as redefinition of Ecuador as a plurinational country.[39] CONAIE's most notable achievement came in 1988, when it struck an unprecedented deal on bilingual education with the Borja administration.[40] Under this agreement, CONAIE assumed responsibility for helping manage a program of intercultural bilingual education in all Indian areas of the country. This program was to have the same official status as the government-run educational system, with its budget provided entirely by the state. In the leftist political camp and its associated popular organizations, critics of CONAIE denounced the agreement as a sellout to the state that was designed to emasculate the contentious potential of the Indian movement. To these critics and the many observers and government officials who shared such opinions about CONAIE's presumed co-optation, the levantamiento came as a stunning political surprise.

Three Analytical Dimensions of the
Levantamiento Nacional Indígena

A few theoretical and methodological clarifications are in order at this point. In my view, in order to account for an act of social protest, an approach based on the subjectivity of the social actors should provide at least clarification of who mobilized, how they did so, and what goals were being pursued. When considered in reverse order, these questions define the three basic coordinates of collective action: the instrumental dimension, related to the fact that the action is directed toward attaining shared goals; the organizational dimension, or the networking and articulation that make collective action possible; and the expressive dimension, which alludes to the fact that the form and content of collective action have denotative value regarding the social identity of the group in question. Taken together, these three dimensions can help explain a social mobilization from a broad and nonreductionist subjective perspective.

Such an explanation would be incomplete, however, because it would reveal nothing about the connection between agency and structure. The intrinsic handicap of a purely subjectivistic account lies in the fact that it is limited to the conditions and motives of the actors as perceived by the actors themselves. Such an account would overlook basic questions about the ways in which the actors' perceptions and behavior are actually fashioned by their involvement in broader sets of socioeconomic and political relationships. In other words, this kind of account would leave out the contextual structural factors that may condition specification of goals, availability of organizational resources, and definition of the social identity of the actors.

The present analysis of the roots of the Indian levantamiento will attempt to combine these two perspectives. Thematically, the analysis will focus on the three dimensions of collective action as guideposts for tracing the links between the element of agency and the structural processes that shaped the context of the Indian protest. Because the methodological starting point is the subjective perspective of the actors, this analysis will be based on testimonies published in press reports, proclamations and documents circulated during the protest, several hours of unedited video footage (containing scenes of the levantamiento as well as statements by Indian leaders, participants, and observers from different provinces),[41] and a series of interviews that I carried out in the Sierra between October and December of 1990.

In reviewing the published testimonies, I listed the different motives cited to account for the massive Indian participation in the protest. Thus I made an inventory of the factors that, from the subjective perspective of the participants and observers, were considered most pertinent in explaining why individuals and groups participated in the levantamiento. Almost without exception, the items in this inventory can be catalogued within a taxonomy derived from the conceptual scheme of the three dimensions of collective action. Some explanations alluded to instrumentality in emphasizing the demands and rationalizing participation in terms of the declared aims of the protest. Other accounts referred to the logistical factors that made the mobilization possible, highlighting the relevance of what has been defined as the organizational dimension of collective action. Finally, some testimonies, by invoking the logic of social solidarity and belonging, offer clues to the expressive meaning of the levantamiento. The following sections will focus on each of these elements, systematically tracing the discussion back to the structural factors that set the stage for the mobilization.

Economic Recession, Adjustment Policies, and Agrarian Protest

In terms of the instrumental dimension, the most salient aspect of the testimonies were the affirmations that the purpose of the levantamiento was to protest the high cost of living and government indifference. Again and again, peasants repeated that they were getting less for the products they sold and paying more for everything they bought, especially food and fertilizer. They also stressed that the government was doing nothing to ameliorate conditions in the countryside. The question of land did not appear as a generalized theme, although it was a burning issue in places having ongoing conflicts between landowners and peasants. For purposes of this study, the central question revolves around the connection between these perceived grievances and the changes in the socioeconomic situation of the rural population in the Sierra.

The 1980s are now widely regarded as the "lost decade of development" in Latin America. Ecuador exhibited a typical pattern: economic stagnation caused by the exhaustion of import-substitution industrialization, followed by recession resulting from the foreign debt problem, the associated drain on resources, and austerity measures. The Ecuadorian recession was accompanied by aggravating circumstances tied to the collapse of the oil prices, similar to those in Mexico and Venezuela. The adjustment policies begun in 1982 under the Christian Democratic government of Osvaldo Hurtado became draconian during the Conservative administration of León Febres Cordero and were largely maintained by Social Democratic president Rodrigo Borja. Government measures sought to eliminate stimulus programs, abolish protection and subsidies, reduce price controls, promote exports, open up the economy to the international market, reduce public spending, devalue the currency, and foster increases in interest rates.[42] In the 1980s, the average annual growth in GNP fell to 2.4 percent (fluctuating into the negative numbers in 1983 and 1987).[43]

The prospects for the 1990s do not look much brighter: between 1990 and 1993, growth in gross national product averaged 3.3 percent, but a decline has been predicted for the period from 1994 to 1997.[44]

What were the connections between economic recession, adjustment policies, and peasant protest? In the 1980s, the annual growth of the agricultural GNP averaged 4.9 percent, indicating that in aggregate terms the agricultural sector did better than the rest of the economy.[45] When one looks at the performance of various subsectors in agriculture, however, it becomes clear that the success story belonged to the agricultural exporters and the agro-industrial producers of the Costa and the northern Sierra.[46] These subsectors of entrepreneurial production benefited from devaluation and continued to be favored by the general trend among Ecuadorians toward increasing consumption of processed food.[47] One detailed analysis based on this and other evidence concluded that the crisis of the 1980s in the countryside hit the peasant economy, and most brutally in the poorest areas of the highlands.[48] Caught in the crunch of inflationary increases in the price of all basic necessities, reduced opportunity for obtaining credit, exorbitant interest rates, and contraction of state supports and services, the market-oriented peasants found their situation worsening as the real prices paid for their products deteriorated and the cost of the mostly imported agricultural inputs was driven up by the devaluations.

Many of these developments, particularly the rising cost of living, hurt the largest group, the semi-proletarian peasants. Two additional factors affecting them should be mentioned. One was the loss of occupational opportunities due to the slowdown in manufacturing and construction. By the end of the 1980s, employment in manufacturing had sunk 10 percent below the level at the beginning of the decade.[49] In the construction industry, activity declined by half between 1987 and 1990.[50] The second major factor was the drastic decline in real wages, which decreased by almost 30 percent between 1980 and 1985 and even further at an annual rate of 8 percent between 1986 and 1990.[51] The resurgence of land conflicts must be set against this economic backdrop. According to CONAIE data, seventy-two land disputes were pending between peasants and landowners in the Sierra on the eve of the levantamiento.[52] This information and my field observations in Alausí (a canton in Chimborazo where six disputes were taking place) and at a national meeting in Pujili in November 1990 of groups directly involved strongly suggest that these conflicts cannot be viewed as symptoms of a major new peasant offensive to obtain land. In most cases, they began as disagreements that evolved into legal disputes over the terms of ongoing land sales. Their exacerbation reflects the fact that after the recession narrowed the peasants' opportunities for migratory employment, they have become more aggressive in demanding resolution of such disputes.

The connection is unmistakable. In content, the 1990 levantamiento paralleled what appeared in other Latin American countries as "IMF riots," a display of popular protest induced by the profound impact of the economic slump and the adjustment policies of the 1980s.[53] The shock was particularly painful in the Ecuadorian Sierra because the reforms of the 1970s had improved the situation of the peasants somewhat while dramatically increasing their dependence on the country's macroeconomic conditions. This context shaped the instrumental orientation of the levantamiento, defining it as a protest event aimed at ventilating the discontent of the rural population and demanding changes in state policies.

The Organizational Bases of Collective Action

The 1990 levantamiento was notable for its massive turnout of protesters. How were these multitudes assembled? What made individuals leave their homes in droves to picket along the roads and participate in the demonstrations? Most testimonies point to the initiatives taken by the Indian communities and their cabildos, although specifics varied from place to place. In some cases, meetings were held in which the entire community debated CONAIE's proposal, made the decision to join in the protest, and set up special committees to take charge of the preparations. In other places, the cabildos made the decision that the community would participate after consulting informally with the rank and file and took steps to coordinate the turnout. In other places, the decision to participate was made by the regional federations and unions and transmitted from the top down as "an order" to the member communities. The overriding point is that it was primarily the community-based local and regional organizations that took the initiative and coordinated popular participation by mobilizing their influence, resources, and at times capacity for coercion to guarantee contribution of the material resources needed as well as personal involvement in roadblocks, marches, and rallies. To clarify this matter, more needs to be determined about the communities' sources of strength. The following overview will discuss four factors that can be related to the socioeconomic and political changes of the last thirty years.

The first factor was a political power vacuum in the countryside. In the Ecuadorian Sierra, the system based on the hacienda had been more than an agrarian regime. It had also sustained the political and ideological domination that allowed landowners, directly or via the mediation of mestizo priests and village authorities, to monopolize power at the local levels. This local control helped the landowners consolidate as the hegemonic regional class and become involved in national politics as a conservative force.[54] Socioeconomic reorganization during the 1960s and 1970s altered the situation dramatically. Among the peasants who had to organize in order to fight for the land, a sense of collective purpose emerged based on appeals to primordial loyalties. In reactivating the ties of extended kinship and reciprocity, this process reinforced (and in many cases even regenerated) the old Indian community as the natural organizational framework for these relationships. At the same time, the direct and indirect effects of the agrarian reform had undermined the landowners' bases of power. The figure of the landowning *gamonal* (political boss) faded away, and no other political force seriously attempted to enter rural society and fill the void. These circumstances created space for the revitalized Indian community, which in taking up representation of the peasants and raising their new demands began to gain prominence as a relevant actor in local and regional political arenas.[55]

The second factor pertains to the role of external political agents, which is always pivotal to organizing and politicizing the rural population. The subject of peasants' political allies has a complex history in Ecuador. Two trends can be identified over the past twenty years. One was the diminishing influence of the leftist groups (Communists and Socialists). Eager to promote a unitary peasant-based class consciousness, they had always viewed ethnicity as a divisive factor inimical to their projects of social transformation. The other trend was the growing influence of progressive Catholic sectors, inspired by the idea that ethnicity could be useful in promoting a grassroots-based, self-managed model of development founded on the traditional organizational framework of the Indian community.[56] This important shift in external influences can be correlated with the structural changes already outlined here. The ascendancy of the left had been largely due to the fact that the struggle for land generated great receptivity to radical appeals. But the peasants' access to land redefined their situation, and they began to respond to other appeals perceived as more in tune with their new needs and the political realities of the period following the agrarian reform.

The third source of strength of the Indian grassroots organizations was their new role as mediators between the rural population and development agencies. This role was fostered by state policies of the late 1970s and early 1980s that, after shelving the land reform, began to emphasize assistance programs, infrastructure, and provision of services in the rural areas.[57] It is true that subsequent spending cuts and austerity policies resulted in a significant withdrawal by the state. But this change has not diminished the mediating functions of the communities because the state has been partly replaced by an array of national and foreign nongovernmental organizations that have acquired high visibility in the Ecuadorian countryside in bringing aid to foster small-scale projects of self-managed development.[58] The process has generally reinforced the Indian communities because while local members perceive the need for these groups as vehicles for obtaining the external aid, the state and the nongovernmental organizations appreciate their usefulness as organized "partners" who can facilitate realization of programs and the orderly transfer of resources. The interest of the external agencies in boosting the community is evidenced by the fact that many of their projects include special assistance for organizational development and leadership training.

The last favorable factor considered here is the existence of Indian personnel capable of assuming leadership roles. What are the origins of these leaders? A proper answer to this question would require a more detailed analysis of the new social conditions in the countryside, the situation of strategic segments of the Indian population, and the interactions involving development agencies and political allies. Here one can only refer briefly to the most relevant aspects. One of the new social conditions has been greater access to education, which added a basic dimension to incorporating the Indian population into the life of the country, raised the aptitude levels of younger generations, and enabled further qualification for those who managed to go on to institutions of higher learning.[59] A motivating factor within the groups from which many of the Indian leaders come is the "status inconsistency effect": these better-off artisans, petty merchants, and peasants are caught in a contradiction between expectations raised by their economic mobility and the persistence of a negative valuation of their Indian condition by whites and mestizos.[60] Finally, regarding interactions with external agents, formation of an elite of Indian leaders was greatly assisted by the training of educators to carry out state-sponsored literacy campaigns and by countless consciousness-raising drives, community courses, and workshops for activists conducted over the years by leftist groups, the Catholic Church, and development agencies.[61]

Expression of a New Collective Identity

In analyzing the expressive significance of the levantamiento, I began with testimonies asserting that participants joined the mobilization because "we are Indians and this is a protest by all the Indians," or "we come to demand the rights that belong to us as Indians," or "we want to show that we Indians are united, organized, and can make our own demands." Many of such statements included references to the pride of being Indian and to five centuries of discrimination and denial of ancestral rights. These testimonies and other clues like the phenomenon of "participación por contagio" (contagious participation) that developed during the mobilization reveal a strong sense of ethnic solidarity. Expression of this sentiment charged the levantamiento with extraordinary meaning when Indians signaled to fellow Indians and to the rest of Ecuadorian society that a new collective identity was in the making. The key question for my analysis centers on the conditions that have been shaping development of this new identity.

As before, the task must begin with a retrospective look at the recent social history of the Sierra. As discussed, the agrarian regime in the highlands could also be viewed as a regime of political domination. The ethnic dimension of this power system was defined by a basic historical continuity: the use of ethnicity to mark social rank and reinforce relations of economic exploitation. Miscegenation and acculturation occurred extensively in the northern and southern extremes of the Sierra. But in the demographic core (the central axis of the highlands), *mestizaje* and *hispanización* was limited to towns and villages. In the countryside, Inca and Spanish reorganizations had induced a long process of ethnotransformation that blurred the differences among the original ethnic groups and favored what has been aptly described as a "generic" Indian ascription and identity.[62]

In a world where the existence of mestizos softened racial boundaries, the new Indian identity was socially constructed around three basic elements: the Quichua (or Quechua) language, the social and cultural traits characteristic of a traditional peasantry, and subordinate status to white landowners and mestizos in the villages. Thus ethnicity was defined as a sociocultural and political referent that furnished the basis for specifying rank and imparting order and meaning to the collective experience of dominated and dominators. Among the dominated, this referent generated an Indian self-identification profoundly stigmatized by a sense of inferiority. The dominant groups used the ethnic referent to justify their own supremacy, which they rationalized as a necessary consequence of the alleged cultural chasm separating them from *la raza vencida* (the vanquished race).

The breakdown of the hacienda regime and the other changes reviewed here signaled disintegration of the system of "ethnic administration."[63] This outcome created conditions for a new ethnotransformation and for revamping the foundations of Indian collective identity in the Sierra. While this phenomenon can be approached from various perspectives, one can make a case for a sociological interpretation based on two premises: first, that redefining this identity is a process whose content is being gradually constructed through the circumstances of the Indians' encounter with the larger Ecuadorian society; second, that at least for now, the main significance of the process is that the Indians are proving capable of converting the negative connotations of their ethnic ascription into positive self-identification and using it as a strategy for collective action.

The logic of the first premise leads to the following argument. Until the 1950s, Indian identity was "generic" but fragmentary, pertaining to groups that were unrelated among themselves and isolated from the rest of society as a result of their subordination to the haciendas. Changes during the 1960s and 1970s allowed Indians to meet and interact with other groups like themselves and with other Ecuadorians, thus creating opportunities to perceive the specifics of their common situation and look at themselves as a different category within the broader society. This encounter and self-recognition has been taking place at a time when Ecuador is experiencing an accelerated modernization, and thus from the very moment when the Indians look out over the horizon of the country's public life, they are challenged by an existing white-mestizo project of national integration and development. The situation calls for definitions because it poses the imperative of having to respond not only to the specifics of this challenge but also to the perception of new necessities generated by social change.

An excellent example here is the demand for bilingual education. When offered access to education as an integral part of the prevailing project of national integration, the Indians had to take a stand. They had to decide whether they wished to be educated like the rest of the Ecuadorians, or whether their education should incorporate and celebrate their linguistic and cultural differences. Democratizing local politics poses a similar test. What should be the institutional bases of this local democracy—those offered by the white-mestizo project or those existing within the Indian community? Unlike the issue of bilingual education, this is a question that has not yet been addressed systematically by the Indian movement. But at the grassroots level, Indian communities are strengthening their administrative and political functions, reviving and revising their customary laws, and demanding the appointment of Indian prefects in many parishes. Indians must confront other issues like these in their incorporation into national life. In taking stands, they will also be taking further steps toward gaining access to citizenship in a manner that would "acknowledge their difference."[64] Thus the content of the Indian identity, far from being a set of "givens," is something that will continue to be transformed as Indians respond to the challenges of integration according to their perceived needs and aspirations.

An influential thesis on ethnicity proposed by Fredrik Barth maintains that the essential element in inter-ethnic relations is the defining of boundaries between the groups in question.[65] This theory, which emphasizes form over content, is partially relevant to what is happening in Ecuador, where the Indians are gradually demarcating their differences. Unqualified application of the argument could be misleading, however, for the affirmation of cultural difference appears to be inseparable from the quest for integration and access to citizenship.

Clifford Geertz's substantive approach emphasizing the cultural content of ethnicity presents a similar difficulty.[66] For Geertz, one of the most troubling prospects in Asia and Africa is that ethnic conflicts may fragment the nations that emerged after colonialism. Geertz explains these conflicts as a contradiction between an integrative impulse that seeks to create the homogenous identity deemed necessary for modernization and national development and the reactions of segments of the population whose sense of individual self-esteem and collective identity continues to be anchored in the daily realities of consanguinity, language, customs, and traditions. This approach might interpret the Ecuadorian Indian movement as a rejection of the white-mestizo project of integration. But on looking at the problem from this perspective, it is evident that what the Indians are rejecting is not the proposal of integration per se but the plans for cultural homogenization embedded in it. The weak point in Geertz's argument is its failure to question the intrinsic cultural intolerance of the liberal concept of citizenship. If it is accepted that citizenship implies or requires an "ironing out" of all cultural differences, then one cannot appreciate the significance of responses that while oriented toward integration also pose the challenge of forging a new concept of citizenship capable of acknowledging and reconciling cultural diversity. To deal with this complex reality, overarching theories of ethnicity (regardless of their formal or substantive emphasis) would be required to transcend the limits of the modernist attitude and come to terms with the concept of ambivalence.[67]

In the meantime, it might be useful to pay attention to "middle-range" theories that view ethnicity as a basis for collective action. For example, Charles Tilly and Craig Jenkins have argued that the potential for mobilization is greater when groups have a cohesive identity and when their members are connected by dense networks of interpersonal relations.[68] This finding is consistent with research showing that after a history of exploitation of subordinate ethnic groups, these groups tend to reaffirm their ethnicity as a basis for solidarity and resistance.[69]

In this light and following the arguments of Alain Touraine, ethnicity can be perceived as a claim to a capacity for action that enables some social groups to "fight out" their conflicts and try to realize their interests and goals.[70] Recent events in Ecuador clearly fit this conceptualization, given the redefinition of the way a social group perceives itself (from a stigmatized group to a collectivity with rights) and a bid to fulfill a broad array of aspirations based on this new awareness of collective identity. These outcomes were encouraged by the fact that the Ecuadorian state displayed some receptivity to the Indians. During the 1980s, the state approached the Indian communities with development programs, dealt with CONAIE and its member organizations, committed governmental support to bilingual education, and hinted at a willingness to negotiate some degree of territorial autonomy for Amazonian groups. In doing so, the state legitimized the Indian organizations and also reinforced the idea that ethnicity is a viable channel for advancing demands and gaining access to social benefits. . . .

Conclusion

. . . One of the most puzzling Latin American paradoxes of recent times is the fact that despite the regressive impact of the adjustment policies on the conditions of most of the population, popular movements appear to be ebbing. In Ecuador, as in other countries, this retreat can be traced to the ideological effects of the return of liberal democracy and the ongoing crisis within labor and peasant organizations, usually influenced by left-ist political groups that have been unable to redefine their Utopias or of-fer alternatives to neoliberal economics and social policy. In these circumstances, social protest tends to take spontaneous forms of expression that lack direction and organization and therefore have little pros-pect of being effective, as illustrated by the so-called IMF riots in several countries. In the Ecuadorian Sierra, however, the situation differed be-cause as the conditions for rural protest matured, the rising Indian move-ment could channel a broad and orderly expression of grievances. Without planning or foresight, CONAIE found itself the only popular organiza-tion that could represent the distressed rural population of the Sierra. This point is demonstrated by the fact that the idea of undertaking a major mobilization came not from the national leadership (which was initially very reluctant) but was almost imposed by regional delegates. At a meet-ing convened in Pujili in April 1990, they exposed the severity of the crisis and insisted that something had to be done to respond to calls for action that were pouring in from the communities.[71] During the levantamiento, CONAIE's unique position as the "right agent" to articu-late rural protest was evidenced by expressions of support from mestizo peasant sectors and by the fact that several mestizo groups asked CONAIE to represent them in negotiations with the government on land disputes.[72]

Thus abruptly and without warning, CONAIE was forced by pressure from below to take up agrarian demands not central to its agenda and also to change tactics, shifting from pleading and lobbying to a more assertive stand backed by popular mobilization. Given the circumstances, the orga-nization deserves high marks for its ability to respond. The summons to mobilize was conveyed effectively throughout the highlands. The list of demands aptly combined calls for immediate government action on press-ing economic issues (price increases for peasant products, price freezes on inputs and essential consumer goods, and speedy resolution of the land conflicts) with programmatic ethnic demands (such as the constitutional definition of Ecuador as a plurinational country, territorial autonomy for the Amazonian groups, enactment of the bilingual education program, and legalization of Indian medicine).[73] Yet the popular turnout and the actual protest events were not the work of CONAIE but of grassroots-based local and regional organizations. Moreover, CONAIE showed limi-tations in subsequent negotiations with the government. In these dialogues, the Indian delegates appeared ill informed on the issues, lacked a clear mandate to make decisions, and showed little capacity to set priorities, define agendas, and deal with the evasive tactics of government ministers.[74] Although these flaws can be attributed partly to limited time to prepare for the negotiations, they also reflect the rudimentary development of many of CONAIE's organizational abilities. . . .

Finally, in terms of the broader Latin American context, this inquiry into the Ecuadorian Sierra has touched on factors that should be relevant to studying Indian movements in comparable highland regions of the other Andean countries, Mexico, and Central America. Taken as a whole, these factors suggest a general interpretive framework in which contemporary Indian movements can be read as a radical critique of the kind of modernity that has prevailed in Latin America. The "really existing" modernity that befell the Indians and the popular sectors was utterly alien to the ideal modernity that had been touted since the Enlightenment as rationalizing progress in the service of freedom and the enrichment of human life. What Indians experienced instead was a reckless modernity whose growth-centered models of capitalist development disregarded the basic needs of the people and failed to establish safety nets to attenuate the repercussions of its crises. It was a cowardly modernity whose sometimes truncated, often cosmetic, and always insufficient agrarian reforms led to rural transformations that shoved entire populations into the national mainstream without giving them a real chance at dignified economic and social integration. It was a hypocritical modernity whose rhetoric on universal political citizenship was never matched by consolidating democratic institutions that would allow and even encourage popular participation in decision making. It was a bigoted modernity whose imagery of national identity stereotyped Indianness as backward and justified humiliating discriminatory practices and repression or "folklorization" of Indian culture.

In Ecuador as elsewhere in Latin America, the Indian resurgence comes at a time when the modernist-nationalist-developmentalist project in its variants appears to have lost all vitality. A state that proved incapable of fulfilling the project of national integration, which in the warped modernist perspective should have included "turning the Indians into Ecuadorians," is now retreating to a minimalist role. Political and business elites have forsaken developmentalist agendas to embrace the do-nothing recipe of neoliberalism. The leftist avant-gardes that had always played a role in popular mobilization have evaporated as a relevant factor. And the Indians, free at last from the onslaught of modernizers of all stripes, are stepping in to claim their right to a better life, autonomy, and difference. In my view, it would be wrong to read their challenge as a wholesale rejection of modernity. The Indians' explicit demands show that they are interested in the material benefits of development and wish to be citizens of the Ecuadorian state. What they seem to want is a different kind of modernity: one that would provide self-determination, a space of their own to try to be what they are discovering they want to be. The ultimate irony is that if the Indians are allowed to do so, they may end up fulfilling for themselves the original emancipatory project of modernity that liberals, reformers, and socialists failed to accomplish.

Notes

1. The press reports on the levantamiento were compiled in *Kipu, el Mundo Indígena en la Prensa Ecuatoriana*, nos. 14–15 (1990). In English, see Les W. Field, "Ecuador's Pan-Indian Uprising," *NACLA Report on the Americas* 25, no. 3 (1991):38–44. For the perspectives of various social and institutional actors, see *Indios: una reflexión sobre el levantamiento indígena de 1990*, edited by Diego Cornejo Menancho (Quito: Instituto Latinoamericano de Investigaciones Sociales, 1991); and Comisión por la Defensa de los Derechos Humanos, *El levantamiento indígena y la cuestión nacional* (Quito: Abya-Yala, 1990).

2. In October 1991 and October 1992, sizable rallies were held protesting the Columbus Quincentenary. In May 1993, Indians participated substantially in a national strike organized by the trade-union centrals and the main popular organizations. The most important event was the impressive march for territorial autonomy staged in April 1992 by Indians from the Amazonian province of Pastaza. On this march, see the journalistic reports in *Kipu, el Mundo Indígena en la Prensa Ecuatoriana*, no. 18, Special Supplement (1992).

3. On the parties and the Indian question, see the interviews in *Los políticos y los indígenas*, edited by Erwin Frank, Ninfa Patiño, and Marta Rodríguez (Quito: Instituto Latinoamericano de Investigaciones Sociales, 1992). On the activities of the military, see *Punto de Vista*, no. 459 (1991):12–13; and *Kipu, el Mundo Indígena en la Prensa Ecuatoriana*, no. 18 (1992):33–34, 55.

4. For a comprehensive compilation of statements and proclamations made by Indian movements from virtually every Latin American country, see the two volumes of *Documentos indios: declaraciones y pronunciamientos*, edited by José Juncosa (Quito: Abya-Yala, 1992).

5. In English, excellent essays were published in *Resistance, Rebellion, and Consciousness in the Andean Peasant World*, edited by Steve Stern (Madison: University of Wisconsin Press, 1987); *Ethnicities and Nations: Processes of Interethnic Relations in Latin America, Southeast Asia, and the Pacific*, edited by Remo Guidieri, Francesco Pellizzi, and Stanley Tambiah (Austin: University of Texas Press, 1988); and *Nation-States and Indians in Latin America*, edited by Greg Urban and Joel Sherzer (Austin: University of Texas Press, 1991). For engaging comparative reflections, see Florencia Mallon, "Indian Communities, Political Cultures, and the State in Latin America, 1780–1990," *Journal of Latin American Studies* 24, Quincentenary Supplement (1992):35–53.

6. For a conceptual discussion of cycles of protest, see Sidney Tarrow, *Struggle, Politics, and Reform: Collective Action, Social Movements, and Cycles of Protest* (Ithaca, N.Y.: Western Societies Program, Cornell University, 1989).

7. The Ecuadorian Andean-Amazonian counterpoint exemplifies the more general contrast between highland and lowland Indians in many countries of Latin America. See Greg Urban and Joel Sherzer, "Introduction: Indians, Nation-States, and Culture," in Urban and Sherzer, *Nation-States and Indians*, 12–13.

8. The most sophisticated versions of these theories were articulated by Neil Smelser in *Theory of Collective Behavior* (New York: Free Press, 1963); and Ted Gurr in *Why Men Rebel* (Princeton, N.J.: Princeton University Press, 1970).

9. On the first approach, see *The Dynamics of Social Movements: Resource Mobilization, Social Control, and Tactics*, edited by Meyer N. Zald and John D. McCarthy (Cambridge, Mass.: Winthrop, 1979); and J. Craig Jenkins, "Resource Mobilization Theory and the Study of Social Movements," *Annual Review of Sociology* 9 (1983):527–53. On the second approach, see the classic work of Mancur Olson, *The Logic of Collective Action: Public Goods and the Theory of Groups* (Cambridge, Mass.: Harvard University Press, 1971); and *Rational Choice*, edited by Jon Elster (New York: New York University Press, 1986). The most interesting application of rational-choice theory to peasant collective action is found in Samuel L. Popkin, *The Rational Peasant: The Political Economy of Rural Society in Vietnam* (Berkeley and Los Angeles: University of California Press, 1979).

10. See Alberto Melucci, *Nomads of the Present: Social Movements and Individual Needs in Contemporary Society* (Philadelphia, Pa.: Temple University Press, 1989); and Alain Touraine, *Return of the Actor: Social Theory in Postindustrial Society* (Minneapolis: University of Minnesota Press, 1988).

11. In 1950 the rural population amounted to 73.8 percent of the total Sierra population of 1.8 million. The total population of Ecuador was 3.2 million. See the joint publication by the Consejo Nacional de Desarrollo (CONADE) and United Nations Fund for Population Activities (UNFPA), *Población y cambios sociales: diagnóstico sociodemográfico del Ecuador, 1950–1982* (Quito: Corporación Editora Nacional, 1987), 16, 194, 218.

12. The study, coordinated by Rafael Baraona for the Comité Interamericano de Desarrollo Agrícola, was published as CIDA, *Ecuador: tenencia de la tierra y desarrollo socioeconómico del sector agrícola* (Washington, D.C.: CIDA, 1965). For other general works on the characteristics of the traditional agrarian regime, see Andrés Guerrero, *Haciendas, capital y lucha de clases andinas* (Quito: El Conejo, 1983); Fernando Velasco, *Reforma agraria y movimiento campesino indígena en la sierra* (Quito: El Conejo, 1983); and Osvaldo Barsky, *La reforma agraria ecuatoriana* (Quito: Corporación Editora Nacional, 1984). My brief description is based on these sources.

13. See my overview of the first phase of the agrarian reform in Leon Zamosc, *Peasant Struggles and Agrarian Reform: The Ecuadorian Sierra and the Colombian Atlantic Coast in Comparative Perspective*, Latin American Issues Monograph no. 8 (Meadville, Pa.: Allegheny College, 1990), 5–27.

14. On the second phase, see Barsky, *La reforma agraria ecuatoriana*, 199–272; and Manuel Chiriboga, "La reforma agraria ecuatoriana y los cambios en la distribución de la propiedad de la tierra," in *Transformaciones agrarias en el Ecuador*, edited by Pierre Gondard, Juan León, and Paola Sylva (Quito: Centro Ecuatoriano de Investigación Geográfica, 1988), 39–57.

15. My estimate is 24.5 percent, based on data presented in Barsky, *La reforma agraria ecuatoriana*, 43; and Chiriboga, "La reforma agraria ecuatoriana y los cambios," 51.

16. On the activation of the land market, see José V. Zevallos, "Reforma agraria y cambio estructural: Ecuador desde 1964," *Ecuador Debate*, no. 20 (1990): 47–54; and Mark Thurner, "Disolución de la hacienda, luchas campesinas y mercado de tierras en la sierra central del Ecuador," *Ecuador Debate*, no. 20 (1990): 69–145. See also Gustavo Cosse, *Estado y agro en el Ecuador* (Quito: Corporación Editora Nacional, 1984), 44–46.

17. In 1954, 16.4 percent of the area was found in small units (consisting of less than twenty hectares), 19.2 percent in medium-sized units (twenty to one hundred hectares), and 64.4 percent in large units (more than one hundred hectares). By 1985, the land distribution was 33.5 percent in small units, 30.3 percent in medium-sized units, and 36.2 percent in large units. See Barsky, *La reforma agraria ecuatoriana,* 43; and Chiriboga, "La reforma agraria ecuatoriana y los cambios," 51.

18. For a more detailed description of the strategies of both kinds of peasants, see William F. Waters and Frederick H. Buttel, "Diferenciación sin descampesinización: acceso a la tierra y persistencia del campesinado andino ecuatoriano," *Estudios Rurales Latinoamericanos* 10, no. 3 (1987):355–81.

19. On the migratory processes, see *Población, migración y empleo en el Ecuador,* edited by Simón Pachano (Quito: Instituto Latinoamericano de Investigaciones Sociales, 1988); and Gilda Farrel, Simón Pachano, and Hernán Carrasco, *Caminantes y retornos* (Quito: Instituto de Estudios Ecuatoriano, 1988).

20. On these processes, see Rob Vos, "Petróleo, estado y cambio agrario: Ecuador, 1972–1984," in Gondard et al., *Transformaciones,* 15–38.

21. The peasant diet now depends heavily on rice (which comes from the Costa) and cheap industrially processed starches (bread and pasta).

22. For studies illustrating this diversity, see Barsky, *La reforma agraria ecuatoriana,* 358–87; Asociación Latinoamericana de Organizaciones de Promoción, *La situación de los campesinos en ocho zonas del Ecuador* (Quito: ALOP, 1984); and *Los cimientos de una nueva sociedad: campesinos, cantones y desarrollo,* edited by Manuel Chiriboga, Renato Landín, and Jaime Borja (Quito: Instituto Interamericano de Cooperación para la Agricultura, 1989), 13–27.

23. See the income figures in Rob Vos, "El modelo de desarrollo y el sector agrícola en el Ecuador, 1965–1982," *Trimestre Económico* 52, no. 4 (1985):1126; see also the data on poverty quoted by Vos in "Petróleo, estado y cambio agrario," 34.

24. See Emil B. Haney and Wava G. Haney, "La transición agraria en la sierra del Ecuador: del semifeudalismo al capitalismo en Chimborazo," *Ecuador Debate,* no. 20 (1990); Ignacio Llovet, Osvaldo Barsky, and Miguel Murmis, "Caracterización de estructuras de clase en el agro ecuatoriano," in *Clase y región en el agro ecuatoriano,* edited by Miguel Murmis (Quito: Corporación Editora Nacional, 1986):17–78; and David Lehmann, *Sharecropping and the Capitalist Transition in Agriculture: Some Evidence from the Highlands of Ecuador,* Working Paper no. 40 (Cambridge: Centre of Latin American Studies, University of Cambridge, 1985).

25. Alain De Janvry, Elisabeth Sadoulet, and André Fargeix, *Adjustment and Equity in Ecuador* (Paris: Organization for Economic Cooperation and Development, 1991), 22.

26. Ibid.

27. Ibid., 55.

28. Vos, "Petróleo, estado y cambio agrario," 26–29; and Cosse, *Estado y agro,* 46–56.

29. Zamosc, *Peasant Struggles,* 11–12.

30. See FENOC, *La FENOC y la movilización campesina: las luchas campesinas entre 1970 y 1978* (Quito: Centro de Estudios y Difusión Social, 1980).

31. On land invasions in the Costa region, see Michael R. Redclift, *Agrarian Reform and Peasant Organization on the Ecuadorian Coast* (London: Athlone, 1978). In the highlands, land invasions were rare. Rather than engaging in open

confrontations, peasants waged a "war of attrition": on one hand, they vexed the landowners with constant pleas to relinquish or sell the land; on the other, they exerted relentless indirect pressure through pilfering, poaching, and petty sabotage against the haciendas. I categorized these tactics elsewhere according to the "Brechtian" forms of struggle analyzed by James C. Scott in *Weapons of the Weak: Everyday Forms of Peasant Resistance* (New Haven, Conn.: Yale University Press, 1985). See Zamosc, *Peasant Struggles*, 17–18.

32. See Roberto Santana, "El caso de ECUARUNARI," *Nariz del Diablo*, no. 7 (1981); and Jorge León, "Las organizaciones indígenas: igualdad y diferencia," in Cornejo Menacho, *Indios*, 392–96.

33. Barsky, *La reforma agraria ecuatoriana*, 237–52.

34. Manuel Chiriboga, "El estado y las políticas hacia el sector rural (1979–1982)," in *Ecuador agrario: ensayos de interpretación*, edited by Manuel Chiriboga et al. (Quito: El Conejo, 1984), 128–39. See also Cosse, *Estado y agro*, 57–68.

35. Based on interviews with national and regional peasant leaders. See also Manuel Chiriboga, "Crisis económica y movimiento campesino e indígena en Ecuador," *Revista Andina* 4, no. 1 (1986):7–30.

36. Interviews with political cadres, trade union activists, and leaders of peasant and Indian organizations, obtained in July–Aug. 1989 and Oct.–Dec. 1990 in Quito, Guayaquil, and Cuenca.

37. Interviews with leaders of ECUARUNARI, July–Aug. 1989 and Oct.–Dec. 1990 in Quito, Riobamba, Cuenca, and Pujilí. See also CONAIE, *Las nacionalidades indígenas en el Ecuador: nuestro proceso organizativo* (Quito: Tinkui, 1988), 245–66; and Santana, "El caso de ECUARUNARI."

38. See CONAIE, *Las nacionalidades indígenas*, 293–306; and León, "Las organizaciones indígenas," 406–14.

39. For an official report, see CONAIE, *Memorias del Segundo Congreso* (Quito: Tinkui, 1988).

40. See Ruth Moya, "A Decade of Bilingual Education and Indigenous Participation in Ecuador," *Prospects* 20, no. 3 (1990):337–42.

41. Edited parts of this footage are included in the thirty-eight-minute video entitled "El levantamiento indígena de junio de 1990," coproduced by Centro de Estudios y Difusión Social (CEDIS) and CONAIE in 1990.

42. De Janvry et al., *Adjustment and Equity*, 46, 49.

43. Based on data quoted in ibid., 55; and in *Economist Intelligence Unit*, "Ecuador: Country Profile, 1992–1993" (1992):9.

44. Figures quoted from *Economist Intelligence Unit*, "Ecuador: Country Forecast," no. 1 (1994):12–13. The average GNP growth predicted for the 1994–1997 period is 2–3 percent.

45. Carlos Arcos and Gustavo Guerra, "Producción de alimentos y economía campesina en los ochenta," in *La crisis y el desarrollo social en el Ecuador, 1980–1990*, edited by César Montúfar (Quito: El Conejo, 1990), 127.

46. Ibid., 126–33, 138–40. See also De Janvry et al., *Adjustment and Equity*, 53; and Morris D. Whitaker and Jaime Alzamora, "The Performance of Agriculture," in *Agriculture and Economic Survival: The Role of Agriculture in Ecuador's Development*, edited by Whitaker and Dale Colyer (Boulder, Colo.: Westview, 1990), 47–51.

47. On the changing patterns of food consumption, see Arcos and Guerra, "Producción de alimentos," 140–46; and Whitaker and Alzamora, "Performance of Agriculture," 58–68.

48. Arcos and Guerra, "Producción de alimentos," 133–38. See also Fernando Rosero, "Política agraria: crítica y propuestas," paper presented at the Séptimo Foro Nacional por los Derechos Humanos, Riobamba, 16–17 Nov. 1990.

49. The number of workers employed in manufacturing fell from 113,000 in 1980 to 102,000 in 1986. See De Janvry et al., *Adjustment and Equity*, 71.

50. Construction plummeted from three million square meters in 1987 to half of that in 1990. See *Economist Intelligence Unit*, "Ecuador: Country Profile," 26.

51. *Economist Intelligence Unit*, "Ecuador: Country Profile," 13; and Juan Falconi, Patricio León, and Salvador Marconi, "Ecuador de los años ochenta: entre el ajuste y la crisis," in Montúfar, *Crisis y desarrollo*, 71.

52. CONA1E, "Trámites y conflictos de tierras presentados por la CONA1E ante la Comisión de Diálogo," unpublished 1990 document. See also Fernando Rosero, "Defensa y recuperación de la tierra: campesinado, identidad etnocultural y nación," in Cornejo Menacho, *Indios*, 419–48.

53. On the "IMF riots," see John Walton, "Debt, Protest, and the State in Latin America," in *Power and Popular Protest: Latin American Social Movements*, edited by Susan Eckstein (Berkeley and Los Angeles: University of California Press, 1989), 299–328.

54. On the hacienda-based system of domination, see Cosse, *Estado y agro*, 20–25; Osvaldo Hurtado, "El proceso político," in *Ecuador hoy*, edited by Gerhard Drekonja et al. (Bogotá: Siglo Veintiuno, 1978), 166–69; and Andrés Guerrero, *La desintegración de la administración éthnica en el Ecuador: de sujetos-indios a ciudadanos-étnicos*, CEDIME working paper (Quito: Centro de Investigación de los Movimientos Sociales del Ecuador, 1990), 10–20.

55. No systematic study has been published on the revitalization of the Indian communities. For partial references, see Galo Ramón, "La comunidad indígena ecuatoriana: planteos políticos," in *Comunidad andina: alternativas políticas de desarrollo*, edited by the Centro Andino de Acción Popular (Quito: CAAP, 1981), 69–70; León, "Las organizaciones indígenas," 384–89; and Guerrero, *La desintegración de la administración étnica*, 24–26. It would be interesting to analyze the process according to some of the insights offered by Victor V. Magagna in *Communities of Grain: Rural Rebellion in Comparative Perspective* (Ithaca, N.Y.: Cornell University Press, 1991).

56. These remarks are based on interviews with national leaders, regional activists, and external observers of peasant and Indian organizations. Despite the importance of the relationships among these organizations, the leftist groups, and the Catholic Church, they have not been systematically researched.

57. See Alicia Ibarra, *Los indígenas y el estado en el Ecuador* (Quito: Abya-Yala, 1987), 171–88; Jorge Almeida, "Vigencia de lo indígena en el Ecuador," in *Etnia en el Ecuador: situaciones y análisis*, edited by the Centro Andino de Acción Popular (Quito: CAAP, 1984), 21–23; and Mary Crain, "The Social Construction of National Identity in Highland Ecuador," *Anthropological Quarterly* 63, no. 1 (1990):48–49.

58. In the mid-1980s, fifty-six nongovernmental organizations (forty-one domestic and fifteen foreign) were running programs in Ecuador along with thirty-six international institutions (twelve bilateral and twenty-four multilateral). For a complete listing, see Food and Agriculture Organization-Ecuador, *Directorio de organizaciones no gubernamentales ecuatorianas para el desarrollo rural* (Quito: FAO-Ecuador, 1985).

59. For an interesting essay on the role of education, see Galo Ramón, "Ese secreto poder de la escritura," in Cornejo Menacho, *Indios*, 362–70.

60. See Erwin H. Frank, "Movimiento indígena, identidad étnica y el levantamiento: un proyecto político alternativo en el Ecuador," in Cornejo Menacho, *Indios*, 520–27.

61. In one way or another, participation in these activities and programs had been a key element in the formation of virtually every Indian activist I interviewed in Ecuador.

62. Blanca Muratorio, "Protestantism, Ethnicity, and Class in Chimborazo," in *Cultural Transformations and Ethnicity in Modern Ecuador*, edited by Norman Whitten (Urbana: University of Illinois Press, 1981), 520.

63. Guerrero, *La desintegración de la administración étnica*, 9–15.

64. I am borrowing the phrase "que se reconozca la diferencia," from León, "Las organizaciones indígenas," 416.

65. Fredrik Barth, " Introduction," *Ethnic Groups and Boundaries: The Social Organization of Culture Difference*, edited by Barth (Boston, Mass.: Little, Brown, 1969).

66. Clifford Geertz, "The Integrative Revolution: Primordial Sentiments and Civil Politics in the New States," in Geertz, *The Interpretation of Cultures: Selected Essays* (New York: Basic Books, 1973), 255–310.

67. On the modern mentality's abhorrence of "the scandal of ambivalence," see Zygmunt Bauman, *Modernity and Ambivalence* (Cambridge, Mass.: Polity, 1991).

68. Charles Tilly, *From Mobilization to Revolution* (New York: Random House, 1978), 52–97; and Jenkins, "Resource Mobilization Theory," 538.

69. David Mason, "Introduction: Controversies and Continuities in Race and Ethnic Relations Theory," in *Theories of Race and Ethnic Relations*, edited by John Rex and David Mason (Cambridge: Cambridge University Press, 1986), 8–9.

70. Touraine, *Return of the Actor*, 81–82.

71. Based on interviews with national and regional leaders. See also Luis Macas, "El levantamiento indígena visto por sus protagonistas," in Cornejo Menacho, *Indios*, 30.

72. Interviews with CONAIE's legal advisor and delegates to the negotiations with the national government, Nov. 1990, Quito.

73. See the demands enumerated in Field, "Ecuador's Pan-Indian Uprising," 41.

74. Interviews with CONAIE delegates who negotiated with the national government, Nov. 1990, in Quito and Pujilí.

4

Indians and National Salvation: Placing Ecuador's Indigenous Coup of January 2000 in Historical Perspective

Erin O'Connor

In January 2000 indigenous groups allied with the Ecuadorian military took over government offices in the capital city of Quito, precipitating a coup against the president and bringing about his resignation. Although soon thereafter, under heavy pressure from the United States and other countries, the vice president took office, this was the first time that Indians in Latin America had brought down a government. How did this happen? Does this mean that indigenous rights groups in heavily Indian nations such as Ecuador, Bolivia, Peru, and Guatemala have finally taken the initiative and hold the balance of power? Erin O'Connor addresses some of these issues as well as the historical reasons for this until-then unprecedented event.

The answers to these questions, she argues, lie in the past and the way in which the indigenous movement developed in Ecuador. Although these events are in many respects unique to Ecuador, their underlying issues are common to many other countries. In particular, the ways in which themes such as democracy and political participation are defined are important in understanding this movement. In other words, the Indians have begun to create their own notions of democracy that go beyond the formal (and often inadequate) mechanisms of electoral politics, where little ever seems to change.

Erin O'Connor is an assistant professor of history at West Chester University.

> Most of the time, [the Indian] lacks confidence, is as timid as an eternal child, and has a profound and unveiled aversion to those whom he justly considers his executioners; such is the nature of his character.
>
> —Agustín Cueva, 1912[1]

> Ecuador's Indian Federation has emerged as the
> most organized and influential indigenous move-
> ment in a region where native peoples in sev-
> eral countries are engaged in struggles over land,
> language, and civil and political rights.
> —Monte Hayes, 2000[2]

The two opening quotations highlight the enormity of change that Ecuador's Indian-state relations have undergone in less than a century. Cueva suggested in 1912 that the Ecuadorian Indian was inherently passive, and while he thought that Indians' lives should be improved, he emphasized that salvation would come through the Liberal Party, which would help Indians and use public education to teach them how to be good citizens.[3] Cueva would have been shocked, however, to learn that the descendants of these "passive victims" he wanted to save would become world-renowned activists. By the 1990s, the national indigenous organization, CONAIE, had become a key player in politics even though Indians continued to suffer greatly from the nation's economic problems.

The latest development in Ecuadorian Indian-state relations took place in January 2000, when indigenous activists joined together with members of the military to overtake the legislative palace and demand President Jamil Mahuad's resignation. Within a matter of hours, the president did resign. This event, which took place on January 21–22, marked the first time that an indigenous movement participated in a coup d'état and achieved a change in administration. Antonio Vargas, president of CONAIE, proclaimed the coup "a bloodless revolution" that would lead to deeper changes in national politics.[4] To fulfill this promise, Vargas joined together with General Carlos Mendoza and former president of the Supreme Court Carlos Solórzano in a triumvirate whose purpose was to create a new government of "national salvation." Within hours of its formation, however, the triumvirate fell apart and Mahuad's vice president, Gustavo Noboa, took over the presidency. Noboa planned to continue many of the policies and programs that had led to the coup in the first place.

How did Ecuador's Indians go from being subjects that needed saving to self-proclaimed saviors of the nation? Did the rise of indigenous movements mark a dramatic, even revolutionary change in Ecuadorian Indian-state relations, or was there a longer evolutionary history of indigenous politicization in the country? And what of the 2000 coup itself: was the coup a success because Mahuad stepped down, or was it a failure because his vice president took over and continued the same policies? These questions are the focus of this essay. Rather than treat success/ failure or continuity/change as incompatible opposites, I argue that it is the relationship between these extremes, perhaps even the complementary nature of seeming opposites, that shapes the face of indigenous activism in this small north Andean nation. The coup was both a success and a failure; the movement itself offers an entirely new form of social protest while also building upon a long history of indigenous struggles with the state. There are two notions that pull these paradoxes together into a meaningful, if complex, history: the concepts of democracy and salvation. To explore these intertwined categories and histories, I will move backward through time, beginning with the January 2000 coup, broadening to consider a decade of protests under CONAIE, and ending with an overview of how and why Ecuador became one of the "hot spots" of Indian-state negotiations at the beginning of the twenty-first century.

Ecuador, 1999: Escalation to the Coup of January 2000

The immediate roots of the January 2000 coup can be found in the snow-balling economic crises that Ecuador faced since the 1980s. While the country's economy had been in a gradual state of decline since oil prices fell in the 1980s, the situation went rapidly from bad to worse for a variety of interrelated reasons. In 1995–96, Peru and Ecuador went to war over territory in the resource-rich Amazon basin; Ecuador's defeat meant the loss of lucrative oil exports. Nature also played a role in the escalating economic crises: the El Niño weather pattern hit the country hard in the mid- to late 1990s, bringing floods that destroyed crops and caused severe infrastructural damage. The predicament of the already-strained economy sank into even deeper crisis in 1999. Trade disputes with the European Union over the price of bananas threatened to undermine the value of yet another of Ecuador's critical exports; at the same time, banks were collapsing due to a combination of destruction from flooding and corruption from within the banking system itself.

President Mahuad responded to the economic crisis with austerity programs that generated political confrontations even before the January 2000 coup. In July 1999 taxi and bus drivers went on strike to protest the 300 percent increase in gasoline prices that resulted from the elimination of government subsidies for petroleum products; the strike lasted over two weeks. Indigenous peoples, marching on Quito and other cities in the highlands, joined in the protests. CONAIE's involvement in the July events was based on a desire to show solidarity with the taxi and bus drivers and on the Indians' own mounting complaints over Mahuad's plans to privatize key sectors of the economy. During the same month, hospital workers who had not been paid for weeks also walked out. Although the strikers and the government eventually negotiated compromises, the events of July had a strong impact on the nation. For weeks, the country had been at a virtual standstill: residents of the major cities had to find alternate transportation to get to their jobs, they lived through protests and tire-burning demonstrations that disrupted their lives, and they worried that decreasing supplies from the countryside would result in skyrocketing food prices.[5]

By the fall of 1999, bank collapses, soaring inflation, and natural disasters led the national government to default on U.S.$98 million in foreign debts.[6] Mahuad, searching for a solution to these multilayered problems and still committed to economic austerity, proposed the dollarization of the Ecuadorian economy. Trading in the sucre for the U.S. dollar then became the central focus for pent-up animosities between activist organizations and the state, with indigenous peoples at the center of the disputes. Protests against dollarization were based in part on a patriotic desire to maintain national economic sovereignty; adopting the U.S. dollar would mean that Ecuador "would have to cede political control of its money to the United States Federal Reserve, which only has the well-being of the United States in mind." Indigenous peasants also argued that the change in national specie would deepen rather than solve their economic problems.[7] The president of CONAIE called dollarization "a sinister proposal to protect a corrupt banking bureaucracy and transform Ecuador into an enclave of financial speculation and money-laundering for narco-dollars." He claimed that dollarization of the economy, like privatization programs, was aimed at the destruction of the nation's producers, particularly indigenous peasants.[8] In the month preceding the coup, Indian organizations called for Mahuad's resignation, and Indian "parliaments" met in the countryside to elect delegates to CONAIE's sixth national congress in January and to consider what demands should be made of the national government.[9]

During the week of January 16, indigenous peoples took action. Antonio Vargas was reelected president of CONAIE, thus indicating the organization's ongoing commitment to radical action. The indigenous congress put together various accords and demands to protect the environment, call for legislation to safeguard indigenous interests, and "promote the equitable participation of women in [indigenous] nationalities, villages, and society in general."[10] As CONAIE delegates met, approximately 10,000 protesters (mainly Indians, but also non-Indian workers and students) entered Quito to stage a symbolic takeover of the capital on January 19. Bus drivers, following government orders, denied Indians passage to the city; Indian activists complained that this action was ethnic discrimination. Carmen Yamberla emphasized that bus drivers in the province of Imbabura were mistreating Indians "without taking into account that they were peaceful citizens who were traveling to carry out normal commercial activities for their subsistence."[11] Days later, indigenous activists took over the legislative palace and the coup began.

Success or Failure?: Contradictory Analyses of the Coup's Impact

In heated debates since the coup, both its opponents and defenders focused their arguments around the need to uphold democracy. Ecuadorian as well as international critics emphasized that coup participants struck a "blow to democracy" with their actions in late January. Jaime Mantilla, publisher of Quito's *Diario Hoy*, claimed that the coup undermined the overall good of the nation when he stated: "The real tragedy . . . is that the deposed president, Jamil Mahuad, who was constitutionally elected, fell prey to the political groups *that put their own interests above those of the nation. . . .* They want to form a popular government. In doing so, they ignored a simple rule: You can't achieve a democracy through undemocratic means."[12] Ecuadorians carefully balanced their criticisms with sympathy for the plight of Indians. Mantilla, for example, referred to Indian organizers in the countryside as "a small but respectable group of citizens [who] created their own organizations seeking to influence the decisions that would soon affect their lives." Even Francisco Huerta, the new minister of the interior, followed up his suggestion that Indians were dupes to shamanism and alcohol by carefully stating that "this [Indian] ethnicity is just as important as mine."[13] International reporters and analysts warned of even greater dangers in which Ecuador's democratic failure could have a domino effect throughout South America. Stephen Johnson of the *Miami Herald* wrote: "If the early 1990s marked the spread of democracy in Latin America, then it must seem like the turn of the century is the time of its unraveling."[14] In these analyses, Mahuad was presented as "decent but weak," and indigenous activists were referred to as "special-interest groups."[15]

Not surprisingly, CONAIE and its supporters maintained a very different stance, yet their interpretation of events also centered on questions of democracy. On the eve of the coup, one group claimed that "if [the government] were truly democratic, they would obey the voice of the people . . . [instead] they defend their businesses and their friends who financed their campaigns with thousands of dollars."[16] Antonio Vargas expressed similar ideas to justify activists' actions after the coup had taken place. He asserted that anyone who sought to understand the causes of the coup "should look for them in the corridors of the oligarchies, the parliament, the corrupt courts, and the bankers who with their policies and holdups have deepened the misery, the hunger, the unemployment" of the poor in Ecuador.[17] The call for "true democracy" continued to dominate activists' and sympathizers' demands in the aftermath of the coup. They stressed that the only acceptable result of Noboa's rise to the presidency would have been to rest in "acts of social justice," and "a deepening of democracy" that would "safeguard citizens from oligarchs of any kind."[18]

These contrasting interpretations of democracy and Indians' motives also affected the perception of the coup as a success or failure. In a sympathetic editorial in the Ecuadorian newspaper *Hoy*, the author asserted that "our indigenous brothers . . . have retired, but they will return . . . it was necessary for the Indians to make us feel, in six days of fear, what they have lived in five hundred years of inhumanity."[19] Indigenist activists Salvador Quishpi and Julio Gualan also deemed the coup a successful step in the fight for Indians' rights and committed themselves to "continue the nonviolent battle, and at some moment we will come into power."[20] Some of Ecuador's indigenous peoples were even more optimistic in their evaluation of the event: Indian saleswoman Estela Santillana emphatically maintained that "we did the ultimate. We changed the presidency. That's what we wanted."[21] Conversely, critics identified Noboa's ascension to the presidency as both a sign of the coup's failure and as a hopeful indication that democracy would prevail in Ecuador.

The reality that both Noboa's government and indigenous organizations faced in the aftermath of January 21, 2000, was less clear-cut. Noboa claimed to sympathize with the Indians and entered into a dialogue with their organizations and representatives in Congress; indigenous peoples were simply too well organized and popular to allow the new president to ignore their demands altogether. But Noboa staunchly refused to alter any of his proposed solutions to Ecuador's economic crisis. Likewise, leaders from many of the country's dominant political parties refused to accept demands made by CONAIE to bring an end to privatization or to put a stop to the process of dollarization.

Perhaps more time will allow us all to better understand the significance of the January 2000 coup and its place in the rising power of indigenous organizations in Latin American politics. Certainly, the activism of the 1990s developed in unprecedented and unexpected ways. In 1990, when CONAIE first mounted a nationwide strike and paralyzed Ecuador for over a week, scholars rightly recognized the event as the beginning of a new era in the politics of ethnicity, and it gave CONAIE newfound legitimacy as a voice for Ecuador's indigenous peoples.[22] Since then the indigenous organizations have entered the forefront of national politics: they made demands to protect their economic interests and cultural heritage, staged protests by marching en masse on the capital or blocking roadways to bring the country to a halt, and made alliances across "traditional" boundaries with the Church or the military. For Ecuador's Indians, theory and identity have developed in conjunction with practice as the economic and political crises developed over the past ten years. As Leon Zamosc rightly noted in the early 1990s, "the content of the Indian identity, far from being a set of 'givens,' is something that will continue to be transformed as Indians respond to the challenges of integration according to their perceived needs and aspirations."[23]

The January coup and its aftermath indicated both the great achievements and deepening problems that CONAIE experienced as its power and influence increased on national and international levels. One significant shift in the past decade had to do with support for CONAIE and related movements. Zamosc observed in the early 1990s that "while the major political parties have been hostile or noncommittal to the Indian cause, the Ecuadorian generals have denounced the movement as 'subversive' and have effectively militarized entire Indian areas under the cover of a vast program of 'community support.' "[24] Not only did 71 percent of the Ecuadorian population support the indigenous movement (as shown in a 1999 Gallup poll), but both the military and political parties began to take CONAIE much more seriously than they once did. The military remained divided: although many officers were opponents of indigenous activism, some (especially younger) officers sympathized enough with Indian activists to ally with them. This support for the indigenous cause stemmed in part from Indians' shared concerns with poor non-Indians, since many military men were also relatively poor. As General Carlos Moncayo, the official charged with the security of Congress, stated, "We let them pass [into the legislative palace] because we don't want confrontation with the people."[25] Although the relationship between Indians and the military improved, it was still fraught with tension: not only did indigenous leaders feel betrayed by military allies in the coup, but the military also repressed Indian protests in the mid-1990s as well as in the early 1990s.[26]

Other problems and questions from the early 1990s also began to be addressed. Again, turning to Zamosc's evaluation provides a useful backdrop. He noted that while CONAIE had a strong commitment to "democratize local politics" in the wake of the 1990 strike, it was not yet clear whether the institutional bases for this democratization would come from indigenous communities themselves or would follow white-mestizo political projects.[27] Since 1990, Indians took the initiative in defining and institutionalizing their own political agendas. The process occurred on an even wider scale than most observers anticipated. Indigenous peoples established a voice and presence of their own in the political system through the creation of Pachakutik, a new political party. Pachakutik did not refuse non-Indian members or leaders, and it claimed to speak for the needs of the poor and often "voiceless" members of society in a broad sense. Yet there has been a strong relationship between indigenous identity and Pachakutik membership and leadership: for example, four of the six members of the party who held congressional seats in 2000 were Indians themselves.[28]

Indians also established institutions outside of the political system; they formed their own provincial and district parliaments through which activists organized for the march on the legislative palace in January. Through these regional parliaments, Indians and allied non-Indian activists formed the "People's National Parliament," which demanded Mahuad's resignation and committed itself to establishing a new and truly plurinational government.[29] Although a new government was not created, the People's Parliaments remained in place, and they were one reason that Ecuadorian political analyst Fernando García emphasized that the fall of the triumvirate did not "impede the movement from continuing to gain force . . . their strength is that they have a good organizational structure which has not changed and is very much intact."[30]

Luis Macas, former president of CONAIE, Pachakutik Party member, and congressional representative, summed up the past decade of indigenous activism well. Of the 1990 uprising he said that it was "a historical event that showed the country and the world that we indigenous peoples had not disappeared, that we had not died, to say to the world WE ARE HERE." Of the coup in January 2000, it "indicates that we have overcome adversities to say to the world that we have a proposal . . . for the changes that our country needs. It indicates that between 1990 and 2000, there has been profound reflection not only about the lives of indigenous peoples but also about the global reality of our society, but this has [also] obligated us to make decisions and confront problems."[31]

Indian identity and the politics of ethnicity were constantly redefined and renewed in the last decade of the twentieth century, and it appeared that this process had only just begun. But how far back does this process go? To what extent does this activism of the 1990s offer a completely new form of social protest, and to what extent has it been based on a long history of struggle? This question is my focus in the final section of this essay.

Continuity and Change: The 2000 Coup in Historical Perspective

References to history are frequently used to indicate that Indians have just and deep-seated reasons for their present protests. Even Gustavo Noboa suggested that "the indigenous theme is long-standing and hereditary, the result of a lack of confidence. The fact is they have been deceived for centuries and their demands are right in part."[32] Indigenous activists and their supporters were even more adamant. Raúl López, the bishop from the central highland province of Cotopaxi, justified Indians' activism in the present by contrasting it with their past oppression when he stated that newspaper advertisements once "offered haciendas for sale with Indians included, as if they were cattle or horses."[33] The Indians' history of oppression at the hands of whites and mestizos in Ecuador was also taken to indicate that indigenous activism was both new and exceptional. Steven Buckley stated in the *Washington Post* that "most unusual, however, was the group at the center [of the January coup]—thousands of indigenous people, historically the country's poorest and most politically marginalized group . . . for much of Ecuador's history, Indians generally shunned politics."[34]

It is true that Indians have been one of the most deeply and consistently oppressed groups in Ecuador since the colonial period, and that long history of hardship has helped to shape and give meaning to indigenous identity and politicization into the twenty-first century. It is also true, however, that Indians have an equally long history of resisting oppression by adapting to changing circumstances and by utilizing the political contexts in which they lived. That history has also led to the rise and growth of Indian movements. Some of the best discussions of the history behind the rise of CONAIE focused on Indian-state relations from 1964 to 1990, from the Agrarian Reform Law that broke up large estates in the highlands (affecting many Indians there) to the first nationwide strike that CONAIE orchestrated. Leon Zamosc's essay in this volume (Chapter 3) is an excellent example of such analyses. Since he has done a superb job of explaining the immediate political and economic roots to the rise of CONAIE, I will address other, earlier periods here.[35]

In some ways, the history behind CONAIE's rise is the story of five hundred years of indigenous resistance to European domination.[36] Indian peasant rebellions were the most striking and violent form of resistance from the Conquest through the late nineteenth century. Like peasant rebellions elsewhere, Indian rebellions in Ecuador arose spontaneously in response to specific grievances, were contained within a limited area, and typically lasted only a few days. [37] Resistance could also be nonviolent: Indians actively utilized their oppressors' ideas and political language to their own advantage. Indians called upon Spanish paternalism during the colonial period by emphasizing their "miserable status" as a way to remind court and other officials of their duties to protect the colonized.[38] And while it is true that Indian debt peons (*conciertos*) were sold or rented along with the large estates on which they worked from the colonial period well into the twentieth century, it is also true that *conciertos* expected estate owners and administrators to treat them fairly and to protect them; if these estate authorities did not, *conciertos* were willing to bring them to court.[39] Therefore, although Indian men and women were actively defending their own interests, their strategies when interacting with state and private officials were primarily reactionary and did not involve long-term, widespread, or alternative demands or solutions to oppression.

Although Indians' tactics in dealing with authorities did not change dramatically when Ecuador became an independent nation, their poverty and political marginalization were problems of unprecedented proportions in the nineteenth century. To justify independence, it was important for statesmen to show ways that breaking away from Spanish colonial rule had alleviated racial inequalities. Indians' status, however, changed little until the 1850s, and the changes that came under Conservative president

García Moreno in the 1860s and 1870s were mostly negative. To justify this lack of change, politicians and scholars identified Indians (particularly men) as barbaric and undeserving of equal rights with whites and mestizos.[40]

An important turning point that lay the foundations for modern Indian-state relations in Ecuador came with Liberal rule from 1895 to 1925. The discussion of the history of indigenous relations brings us full circle, back to Agustín Cueva's observation at the beginning of this essay, as he was one of the Liberals deeply involved in redefining "the Indian" during this period. Liberals emphasized supremacy of the law and equality before the law, and they claimed that they would "save" Indians from their traditional oppressors. Conveniently, these oppressors were identified as the Liberals' own greatest competitors for political power, social control within the nation, and access to labor—the Catholic Church and highland hacienda owners. (Most of the Liberals were coastal elites.[41]) Although the actual reforms that Liberals proposed were limited, Indians were able to address grievances and interact with the state in new ways by calling upon Liberal ideology and insisting upon their rights as citizens of the nation.[42] They also continued to use their old strategy of calling upon the state for protection; they frequently declared that local authority-figures were not upholding the Indians' rights as citizens and demanded that the state intervene on their behalf.[43] Thus a critical, albeit incomplete, shift had taken place: Indians would now commit themselves to gaining more rights as citizens throughout the twentieth century, but they still acted deferentially to the state and utilized—rather than shaped—political agendas and ideologies.

Interactions with the state remained, by and large, reactionary and local in nature until the 1940s. At that point, the Federation of Ecuadorian Indians (FEI) was founded as a branch of the Communist Party, and in Cayambe—in the north-central highlands—Ecuador's first bilingual school was formed to teach the children of indigenous hacienda workers. At the center of both of these considerable achievements was an Indian woman named Dolores Cacuango, probably the best-known Indian woman in Ecuadorian history.[44] It was Cacuango who began the process of demanding, and later establishing, bilingual schools, and she was also recognized as a co-founder of the FEI.[45] Thus from within this one woman came indications of two central aspects of what indigenous movements would embrace by the end of the twentieth century: nationwide coalitions among indigenous peoples, and an emphasis on cultural maintenance and dignity. She also forecast the rise of powerful women in these movements as well as the limits and problems that they would face.

Cacuango's life indicates both the strengths and weaknesses that Indian women experienced as indigenous movements arose in Ecuador. As mothers, these women were identified as key figures in keeping indigenous culture alive, particularly since Indian men had to migrate to the cities and assimilate into white-mestizo culture with increasing frequency over the course of the twentieth century. This centrality to indigenous identity, however, was also a burden for many indigenous women who wished to become more active in political organizations: women involved in CONAIE in the 1980s noted that they were often too busy with responsibilities at home to attend meetings on a regular basis, or that they were accused of abandoning the home and indigenous culture if they became too involved in politics.[46] So, while Indian women such as Nina Pacari (now a congressional representative for Pachakutik) and Carmen Yamberla (president of FICI, Federación Indigena y Campesina de Imbabura) are prominent in indigenous politics today, and CONAIE has committed itself to working toward gender equality, the complications and difficulties in achieving this goal can be found in the long history of Indian-state relations that preceded it.[47]

One can also, however, see positive changes that have occurred since the time when Cacuango was trying to establish Ecuador's first bilingual schools, and when the Communist Party first organized Indians into a (seemingly) nationwide group.[48] Whereas Indians in Ecuador were once dependent either on leftist parties or on governmental social institutions such as IERAC (Instituto Ecuatoriano de la Reforma Agraria), they have since 1990 emerged as a dominant political force themselves. Where once Indians had to join class-based organizations or seek paternalistic "protectors" within the government, CONAIE itself became an organization that other groups turned to for support and strength in Ecuador. Since the mid-1990s, class-based organizations and actions sometimes went unnoticed or were largely ineffective unless CONAIE supported them.[49]

Whereas once politicians claimed that they would save and civilize the Indians, in 2000 indigenous activists claimed that they could save and redefine the nation. Although the implications of the coup for the future of Indian-state relations are not clear, the event does offer important examples of how far Indian activism has come in Ecuador, and how many obstacles and challenges still remain. It reminds us that deep and longstanding problems still plague Ecuador's Indians. Like the local rebellions of centuries past, the indigenous coup only maintained power for a brief moment before collapsing; Indian women continued to face obstacles based on their gender as well as on their class and race, and poverty and prejudice still marked the lives of the vast majority of indigenous peoples in Ecuador.[50] Yet the coup also indicated great achievements. Indian strategies for dealing with the state went from being local to national and even global.[51] Historian Hernán Ibarra referred to this process as "cultural globalization" in which not only are old stereotypes rejected but also "autonomous cultural production" is generated on a global as well as a local scale. Zamosc also noted that developments in Ecuador simultaneously redefined the Indian culture and allowed Indians to critique modernity.[52] Indian peoples therefore went from utilizing preexisting political ideas and platforms to actively shaping political ideologies and agendas themselves. Thus, despite the many challenges and questions that Indian organizations in Ecuador still faced, the coup of 2000 showed that indigenous peoples remained at the forefront of debates and struggles to consider more closely the purpose of democracy and the definition of the term "nation."

Notes

1. Agustín Cueva, *El Concertaje de Indios* (Quito: Instituto de Investigaciones Económicas, 1912), 13.

2. Monte Hayes, "Indians Warn of Move against Quito," www.dailynews.com, January 29, 2000.

3. The man who presided over the first half of the Liberal regime (1895–1912), Eloy Alfaro, set the agenda by indicating that it was the Liberal government's obligation to save Indians from their oppressors, as he noted in many speeches. See, for example, Alejandro Noboa, *Recopilación de Mensajes Dirigidos por los Presidentes de la República, Jefes Supremos y Gobiernos Provisorios a las Convenciones Nacionales desde el año 1819 hasta nuestros días* (Guayaquil: Imp. de El Tiempo, 1907), 4:226, 291–92. Also see Agustín Cueva's own emphasis on Indians' ability to be made into good citizens through education, particularly in an article where he claimed that "all races are educable, every race can be transformed," in "Nuestra organización social y la servidumbre," *Revista de la Sociedad Jurídico-Literaria* 16, nos. 25, 26, 27 (Enero, Feb., Marzo, 1912), 48. In spite of these grand claims, however, few schools were built in areas where most Indians lived, and other social reforms fell short as well.

4. Vargas was quoted in the Quito newspaper *El Comercio* as displayed on www.elcomercio.com, Resumen Semanal, January 29, 2000.

5. Information on the events of July 1999 are based on my own experiences living and doing research in Quito at the time. The taxi and bus drivers' strike dominated the newspapers, television news programs, and the majority of conversations that I had with friends and acquaintances that month. Reactions to the strikes and protests were mixed: most people I talked with were sympathetic with the reasons for these strikes, but their support waned as the protests and demonstrations dragged on for weeks. Although I did no systematic research or interviews, people's opinion of indigenous involvements in the July demonstrations seemed most diverse, as they did not necessarily equate the focus of the demonstrations with "Indian" issues or problems. Some Quiteños voiced concern (and dismay) that Indian organizations merely found it "convenient" to ally themselves with the taxi and bus drivers.

6. Stephen Johnson, "Ecuador's Problems Not Just 'Bum Luck,' " www.miamiherald.com, January 29, 2000. Inflation had surpassed 60 percent by the fall of 1999, and the sucre was devaluing quickly. In July 1999, for example, there were about 11,400 sucres to the U.S. dollar; by December 1999 and January 2000, there were over 25,000 sucres to the U.S. dollar.

7. For the quote on the Federal Reserve, see "Indígenas ocupan el Congreso en Ecuador y desconocen el gobierno," www.cnnenespanol.com, January 21, 2000.

Regarding Indian peasants' evaluations of dollarization, see "Bitter Indians Let Ecuador Know Fight Isn't Over," conaie.nativeweb.org; this site lists a series of quotes that CONAIE put together from English newspapers; also see www.elcomercio.com, Resumen Mensual, December 1999.

8. Antonio Vargas, "Boletín para la prensa internacional de la Confederación de Nacionalidades Indígenas del Ecuador, CONAIE," conaie.nativeweb.org, January 16, 2000.

9. For a brief overview of these events, see www.elcomercio.com, Resumen Mensual, December 1999. For indigenous demands in relation to the crisis, see Mns. Alberto Luna Tobar S., Antonio Vargas, and Napoleón Santos, "Resolutions of the People's National Parliament of Ecuador," abyayala.nativeweb.org, January 11, 2000; and Carmen Yamberla, "Uprising for a New Government and State," fici.nativeweb.org, January 13, 2000.

10. Marlon Carrión C., "Ecuador: La CONAIE plantea autonomía de las nacionalidades indígenas," conaie.nativeweb.org, January 19, 2000.

11. Willy Coronel Campos, "Nueva Modalidad de Represión," conaie.nativeweb.org, January 18, 2000. Also see an Internet plea by CONAIE titled "Urgent Action," conaie.nativeweb.org, dated January 2000. Although most protesters were from the north and central highland provinces, there were demonstrations throughout the highlands. In the southern highland city of Cuenca, 35,000 people from different social sectors marched through the urban center. Archbishop Alberto Luna Tobar emphasized that the military's involvement in keeping Indians off buses was "an act of violence and racism rarely seen." For further information on Cuenca, see Kintto Lucas, "Ecuador: Indígenas plantean a FFAA gobierno de salvación nacional y radicalizan sus protestas," icci.nativeweb.org, January 20, 2000.

12. Jaime Mantilla, "Cheating the People to Save Democracy," www.latimes.com, January 28, 2000; emphasis mine.

13. Ibid. The Huerta quote comes from Kintto Lucas, "Ecuador: Indígenas se muestran desengañados de mandos militares," icci.nativeweb.org, January 24, 2000.

14. Stephen Johnson, "Ecuador's Problems Not Just 'Bum Luck,'" www.miamiherald.com, January 29, 2000.

15. The reference to Mahuad is from "A Warning from Ecuador," www.economist.com, January 29, 2000, and the "special-interest groups" reference was made by Stephen Johnson, cited above. The *Economist* article was unusual in that it played down Indian involvement and leadership of the coup; the vast majority of reporters, both Ecuadorian and international, have discussed the centrality of CONAIE to Mahuad's overthrow.

16. Cooperación Técnica Sueca, "Ecuador: Un Volcán Lleno de Cráteres," abyayala.nativeweb.org, January 20, 2000.

17. Antonio Vargas, "Searching for the Coup Participants among the Oligarchy," conaie.nativeweb.org, January 25, 2000. Vargas did, however, initially deny that Indians wanted to overtake the government and suggested that he was pressured to do so by the military members of the coup. He was quoted as saying that "we never had any desire to take power . . . we knew that if we tried to do that there would be a lot of bloodshed." This quote is from Stephen Buckley, "Upheaval in Ecuador Shows Clout of Indians," www.washingtonpost.com, January 27, 2000.

18. The emphasis on social justice is from Antonio Vargas, cited above; the quotation on deepening democracy is from Raúl Vallejo, "Cantinfladas y fariseísmos," www.elcomercio.com, January 29, 2000.

19. Luis Alberto Luna Tobar, "Indios . . . ," www.hoy.com.ec, January 29, 2000.

20. The quote by Julio Gualan appears in Catherine Elton, "Coup Is Over, but Ecuador's Indians Aren't Going Away," www.csmonitor.com, January 26, 2000. Salvador Quishpi, president of ECUARUNARI, made similar statements that appeared in www.hoy.com.ec, January 29, 2000. There were also a few references, however, that if there were no meaningful changes within about five years' time, these struggles could potentially end in violence.

21. Buckley, "Upheaval in Ecuador."

22. See Leon Zamosc, Chapter 3, this volume; also see Melina Selverston, "The Politics of Culture: Indigenous People and the State in Ecuador," in Donna Lee Van Cott, ed., *Indigenous Peoples and Democracy in Latin America* (New York: St. Martin's Press, 1994), 140. There have also been excellent and varied evaluations within Ecuador itself by both scholars and activists. For examples of essay collections focused on the events in 1990, see Diego Cornejo Menacho, ed., *Indios: Una reflexión sobre el levantamiento indígena de 1990* (Quito: ILDIS/Abya-Yala, 1992); José Almeida et al., *Sismo étnico en el Ecuador: Varias perspectivas* (Quito: CEDIME/Abya-Yala, 1993); and Juan Carlos Ribadeneira, ed., *Derecho, pueblos indígenas y reforma del estado* (Quito: Abya-Yala, 1993).

23. Zamosc, 54, this volume.

24. Zamosc, 38, this volume. Also see Tanya Korovkin, "Indigenous Peasant Struggles and the Capitalist Modernization of Agriculture: Chimborazo, 1964–1991," *Latin American Perspectives* 94:1, no. 3 (May 1997): 44.

25. Quoted in the article "Indígenas ocupan el Congreso en Ecuador y desconocen el gobierno," www.cnnenespanol.com, January 21, 2000.

26. Selverston, "The Politics of Culture," 141, 147–48.

27. Zamosc, 54, this volume.

28. Buckley, "Upheaval in Ecuador." Two of the Indian congressional representatives through Pachakutik, Luis Macas and Nina Pacari, first emerged on the national scene as important leaders within CONAIE. Eight city mayors were also from this party, and Pachakutik anticipated winning more local government offices with the municipal elections of May 2000.

29. "Resolutions of the People's National Parliament of Ecuador," abyayala.nativeweb.org, January 11, 2000. Reactions to the parliaments have been mixed. In January 29, 2000, a supportive editorial in Ecuador's periodical *Hoy* noted: "Many think it is scandalous that the 'Indians' have a 'parliament.' None of the critics have tried to understand the significance of both [parliaments] in terms of the traditional expressions of our indigenous people." The editor went on to emphasize that it would be necessary to let go of "creole pride" and closely and fairly examine the parliament in order to truly understand it.

30. García was quoted in Elton, "Coup Is Over."

31. "Entrevista a Luis Macas," icci.nativeweb.org, January 29, 2000.

32. Noboa's statement was included in quotes from the *New York Post* on the CONAIE Website, January 27, 2000.

33. Ibid.

34. Buckley, "Upheaval in Ecuador."

35. Also see Korovkin, "Indigenous Peasant Struggles"; Carola Lentz, "De regidores y alcaldes a cabildos: Cambios en la estructura socio-política de una comunidad indígena de Cajabamba/Chimborazo," *Ecuador Debate* (Quito) 12 (1986): 189–212.

36. CONAIE offers its own summary of the past five hundred years of history. See, for example, CONAIE, *Las nacionalidades indígenas: Nuestro proceso organizativo* (Quito: Tuncui/Abya-Yala, 1989). This book particularly emphasizes rebellion and other overt indigenous protests to oppression over the centuries.

37. The literature on Indian peasant rebellions in Latin America is rich and varied. For Ecuador, known as the Audiencia of Quito in the colonial period, see Segundo Moreno Yáñez, *Sublevaciones indígenas en la Audiencia de Quito: Desde comienzos del siglo XVII hasta fines de la colonia* (Quito: Ediciones de la Pontíficia Universidad Católica, 1976).

38. For groundbreaking work on Indians' use of courts in early colonial Peru, see Steve J. Stern, *Peru's Indian Peoples and the Challenge of Spanish Conquest* (Madison: University of Wisconsin Press, 1982).

39. There is a rich literature on the history of large estates and *concertaje* (the system of debt peonage) in Ecuador. To note a few outstanding works: Andrés Guerrero, *La semántica de la dominación: El concertaje de indios* (Quito: Libri Mundi, 1991); Patricia de la Torre, *Patrones y conciertos: Una hacienda serrana, 1905–1929* (Quito: Abya-Yala/Corporación Editora Nacional, 1989); Roque Espinosa, "Hacienda, concertaje y comunidad en el Ecuador," *Cultura* (Quito) 7:19 (1984): 135–209; and Carlos Marchan Romero, "El sistema hacendario serrano, movilidad y cambio agrario," in the same issue of *Cultura*. For a discussion of gender and labor relations in the late nineteenth century, see Erin E. O'Connor, "Dueling Patriarchies: Gender, Indians, and State Formation in the Ecuadorian Sierra, 1860–1925," Ph.D. dissertation, Boston College, 1997, chapter 6.

40. For a discussion of the dilemmas of Indian-state relations in nineteenth-century Ecuador, see Mark Van Aken, "The Lingering Death of Tribute in Ecuador," *Hispanic American Historical Review* 6:3 (1981): 429–59; and Andrés Guerrero, "Curagas y tenientes políticos: La ley de la costumbre y la ley del estado (Otavalo, 1830–1875)," *Revista Andina* 7:2 (September 1989): 321–65; also O'Connor, "Dueling Patriarchies."

41. These ulterior motives in the quest to save Indians help to explain why the social reforms of the Liberal period were so limited and contradictory. For some excellent discussions of this period, see Enrique Ayala Mora, *Historia de la Revolución Liberal Ecuatoriana* (Quito: Corporación Editora Nacional, 1994); A. Kim Clark, *The Redemptive Work: Railway and Nation in Ecuador, 1895–1930* (Wilmington: Scholarly Resources, 1998); and Andrés Guerrero, "The Construction of a Ventriloquist's Image: Liberal Discourse and the 'Miserable Indian Race' in Late Nineteenth-Century Ecuador," *Journal of Latin American Studies* 29 (1997): 555–90.

42. See O'Connor, "Dueling Patriarchies"; also see A. Kim Clark, "Indians, the State, and Law: Public Works and the Struggle to Control Labor in Liberal Ecuador," *Journal of Historical Sociology* 7:1 (March 1994): 49–72.

43. See Clark, "Indians, the State, and Law;" also see O'Connor, "Dueling Patriarchies," particularly chapter 7. I have noted that this adaptation to Liberal ideology gave Indian men a new, relative advantage over Indian women and was part of a broader process of the masculinization of Indian-state relations during Ecuador's periods of state formation in the late nineteenth and early twentieth centuries.

44. Unfortunately, little has been written about Cacuango in English. There are, however, two books about her life in Spanish, both by Raquel Rodas Morales: *Crónica de un sueño: Las escuelas indígenas de Dolores Cacuango* (Quito: Proyecto de Educación Bilingue Intercultural, 1998), which is also written in Quichua; and *Dolores Cacuango* (Quito: Proyecto de Educación Bilingue Intercultural, 1998).

45. Cacuango founded a bilingual school by collaborating with Luisa Gómez de la Torre—fostering an alliance across class/race lines to educate Indian children

in a way that would not degrade them or their culture. Her co-founder with the FEI was Jesús Gualavisi, an example of Cacuango's alliances and solidarity with men of her own class/race.

46. Mujeres Indígenas de la CONAIE, *De las jornadas del foro de la mujer indígena del Ecuador* (Quito: CONAIE/UNFPA, 1994), 2–4, 94–95, 103.

47. In fact, I argue in "Dueling Patriarchies" that gender ideas and relations were at the heart of the social struggles that founded modern Indian-state relations as the central state took shape in Ecuador. Also see Lynn Phillips's superb article, "Women, Development, and the State in Rural Ecuador," in Carmen Diana Deere and Magdalena León, eds., *Rural Women and State Policy: Feminist Perspectives on Latin American Agricultural Development* (Boulder: Westview Press, 1987), 105–23.

48. I say "seemingly" here because while the FEI was technically a nationwide organization, it only had real strength in the north-central highlands, in the area where Cacuango was born and lived.

49. Selverston, "The Politics of Culture," 132.

50. Monte Hayes offered statistics in January 2000: 83 percent of Ecuador's highland Indians live in poverty, compared to 46 percent of the population as a whole; only 41 percent have potable water, and 44 percent do not have electricity. Indians also have the highest illiteracy rate (16 percent) in the nation.

51. The Internet has greatly facilitated this process of globalization. CONAIE regularly uses its Website to call for international supporters and sympathizers to petition the Ecuadorian government.

52. Hernán Ibarra, "Negación, exaltación y descanto de las culturas populares en América Latina," *Ecuador Debate* (Quito) 41 (1997): 78–92; the phrase is from 91. See Zamosc, 57, this volume; also see Selverston, "The Politics of Culture," particularly 141.

5

The Emergence of Political Organizations among the Guaraní Indians of Bolivia and Argentina: A Comparative Perspective

Silvia María Hirsch

How is it possible for the same indigenous ethnic group to have very different experiences in political organization and effectiveness? This is the question that Dr. Silvia Hirsch asks here. The answer rests largely in the nation-state's recognition of ethnic minorities within its boundaries. In the case of Bolivia, a heavily indigenous country, Indians have gained increasing access to political power, especially since the 1952 revolution, which overthrew a semi-manorial order where large landowners, almost exclusively of European descent, and large mine owners were the rulers. However, the peoples in the subtropical and tropical lowlands continued to be oppressed until very recently. Only since the 1980s have the lowland Indians been able to organize and integrate themselves into the political system.

In the case of Argentina, where there is a lack of recognition of the country's ethnic diversity, the process of political integration for indigenous groups has been much slower. Argentines view Indians mainly as the semi-nomadic southern ethnic groups of the Pampas and Patagonia, whom the national state defeated decisively in 1880. The Guaraní were relatively recent migrants to northern Argentina (since the 1850s) as seasonal laborers for the sugar plantations in Jujuy and Salta provinces. As a result, the land issue was less important than in Bolivia. Also, clientelistic politics in Argentina were more common since the first Peronist regime (1946–1955), incorporating especially marginal groups such as Indians but leaving them with little actual power.

In many ways, Argentina is one of the most advanced countries in South America. For indigenous issues, however, the Argentine Guaraní are looking toward their Bolivian counterparts as mentors and models to follow in organizing along ethnic lines. Ironically, Argentines otherwise look down upon Bolivians and think that they are less advanced. Is this the case here? What is in the Guaraní's best interest—to follow the Bolivian model or to continue to work within established political parties in northern Argentina?

Silvia Hirsch is an Argentine-born anthropologist who received her Ph.D. from the University of California, Los Angeles. She has worked extensively with the Guaraní in both the Izozog region of eastern Bolivia and in the communities of northern Argentina. She presently teaches at Trenton State College in New Jersey.

During the last two decades, Indian political organizations at the regional and national levels have flourished across Latin America. Political mobilization and democratization have led to greater participation by these most impoverished and marginalized sectors of the population. This participation in local and national politics as well as the need for advocates to channel their claims led to the formation of Indian organizations and movements, which struggle for the state's recognition of Indian ethnicity. According to Donna Lee Van Cott, some of the factors that led to the emergence of social movements in Latin America are "a reevaluation of leftist strategies of previous decades; the creation of new networks linking rural and urban citizens across diverse social sectors; and the support of domestic and international development organizations for particularly marginalized sectors, such as women and indigenous groups" (1994:8). Guillermo Bonfil Batalla (1979) considers that the emergence of indigenous political organizations is partly due to endogenous factors that include the persistence of precapitalistic forms of subsistence and ethnic loyalties that are very much entrenched among indigenous peoples.

In certain cases the development of Indian political organizations is closely linked to the influence of nongovernmental organizations (NGOs), which have been implementing development projects among the indigenous groups; in other cases, the state has been the instrument. This article compares the development of indigenous organizations among the Guaraní of Bolivia and Argentina, who not only belong to the same linguistic family and share a common culture but also have conterminous boundaries. In the Bolivian case, the emergence of native organizations is linked to the presence of NGOs, while among the Argentine Guaraní, the state fostered these organizations.

In the 1980s the indigenous peoples of eastern Bolivia organized themselves into new political movements. These movements have led, for the first time in the history of eastern Bolivia, to the development of pan-Indian and intra-ethnic organizations. These groups have now a large constituency and receive funding to implement their own projects. For the Bolivian Guaraní the struggle for their rights has led to a process of empowerment, and the political vindications of native peoples have led to major transformations of the state. Bolivia has redefined its relations with native peoples by sanctioning new laws (for example, the Ley de Participación Popular and Ley de Reforma Educativa) that recognize the ethnic pluralism of the country and give greater autonomy to native peoples. Within the Bolivian case I address two types of political organizations: CIDOB, a pan-Indian confederation that groups the indigenous peoples of eastern Bolivia; and Asamblea del Pueblo Guaraní, an intra-ethnic organization composed only of Guaraní Indians.

In Argentina the emergence of indigenous movements has been slower, and their development is linked to the influence of the state at the local and regional levels. Until recently, NGOs have not operated in the region, and the indigenous populations have looked for alliances and support among political parties and state institutions. In Argentina the state excludes those groups whose culture and practices are not mainstream and whose origin is not European. In spite of the fact that adherence to ethnic loyalties has maintained their situation as disenfranchised persons, native people continue to persist and new forms of organization emerge. In the case of Argentina, I examine community forms of leadership (caciques and Centro Vecinal), and two organizations: one of them the Consejo de Caciques directly linked to state institutions; and the other, the newly formed Asamblea del Pueblo Guaraní Argentina, a pan-Guaraní organization based on its Bolivian counterpart.

The focus of this study is on the process that leads to the formation of indigenous movements, their characteristics and strategies, and the development of political relations with nongovernmental organizations and the state. Up to what extent do these indigenous organizations control and centralize political power of the constituent communities? Are these organizations dependent on the decision making and funding of NGOs and the state? Do they reproduce patterns of bureaucracy and decision making adopted from state and other institutions? Indian movements are immersed in unequal relations of power, but it is important to assess their capacity to resist and transform these relations. According to Janet Hendricks (1991), "the articulation between nation-state and indigenous societies forms an interface in which indigenous responses are not merely reactions to external events, but rather [are] shaped by the internal dynamics of the indigenous culture as well as by the political and economic realities of the contact situation."

In practice an indigenous group living in two different states provides a case in which to observe the influence of two different historical and political contexts. This comparative perspective reveals strategies developed by a disenfranchised group to achieve greater political participation. This study is part of a trend toward analyzing indigenous peoples within a global context, thus countering the notion that native peoples, living in the periphery, are isolated and untouched by modernity.

The Guaraní of Bolivia are proud of their distinct ethnicity. They are not ashamed of speaking their native language in public, wearing the traditional poncho, and declaring that they are Izoceños or Ava. In Argentina the Guaraní try to mask their ethnic identity; in public they speak Spanish among themselves and adopt the customs of the neighboring criollos. Their personal experience with discrimination, their situation as a minority, and their history of oppression hinder their identification with their own culture. In both cases, whatever "traditional" practices are retained, these are being transformed, but the process of transformation becomes a defiance of the homogenizing project of the state and an empowering mechanism for their definition as a distinct ethnic group. If ethnicity is understood as a political strategy, not devoid of symbolic and historical components, then culture becomes a form of empowerment, and indigenous movements the vehicle for empowerment.

The Emergence of Indian Organizations in Eastern Bolivia

The Bolivian Oriente, one of the richest and least known regions of the country, is unparalleled in its rapid development of such important natural resources as oil, gas, and timber. In this region the minority Indian population has received neither the benefits of nor access to their own resources. The state, politicians, and scholars have ignored the existence and importance of the Oriente's native population. Not until the late 1970s were studies conducted among the native peoples and development projects implemented. The Indian population did not participate in the decision-making process that affects their lives, nor did they take part in public political life.

However, in eastern Bolivia, nongovernmental organizations have been allowed to implement projects with somewhat little interference from the state, thus leaving an arena for fostering political and social awareness, for training native leaders, and for the emergence of alternative political groups. It is in this context that the development of pan-Indian organizations such as CIDOB and the Asamblea del Pueblo Guaraní constitutes a breakthrough in the relations between the Indian population and the state. NGOs have been working among the Guaraní for the past eighteen years. These NGOs range from church organizations (both Catholic and Protestant) to agencies directed by anthropologists or humanitarians. Their developmental approaches are diverse, and so has been their impact on native peoples. Many projects implemented by these agencies have gone beyond economic development and have aimed at stimulating ethnic revival and developing both new and traditional political organizations for self-determination. Native leaders have found in these NGOs a vehicle to counter the neglect of the state as well as an opportunity to train and enable themselves to deal with state institutions. Leaders could now present specific demands for land titles, protection from outside encroachment, and improvement of their socioeconomic situation in a more articulate fashion.

At the international level, the link between NGOs and indigenous peoples began in the 1970s and had a great impact on international law, human rights, and on calling attention to the plight of native populations. Between 1971 and 1974 meetings between Indian groups and NGOs led to the formation of the World Council of Indigenous Peoples in 1975 (Wilmer 1993:18). From then on, numerous international meetings have focused on the cultural, territorial, and human rights of native populations and have also advanced their interests at the local level.

While in some Latin American countries Indian organizations began to emerge in the 1960s and early 1970s (Federación de Centros Shuar in Ecuador 1964, ECUARUNARI in Ecuador in 1972, CRIVA in Colombia in 1974), in eastern Bolivia their development has been slower. Not until the 1980s have the indigenous people achieved political unity and institutionalized their claims. Why did these organizations that were predated by similar movements in other Latin American countries fail to arise earlier? Although the reasons are not explored here, some answers are found in the following factors: a high level of out-migration from the communities, which led to decreased participation in communal affairs and disorganized social dynamics; the influence and control exerted by the Catholic Church and Fundamentalist sects, which did not allow any organization to emerge; political repression; and, finally, a historic enmity between different indigenous groups.

Some native groups maintained traditional forms of political organization that enabled them to resist state impositions and obtain land titles and resources for their communities. Such is the case of the Guaraní (Izoceños), who are the main promoters of CIDOB. The largest indigenous group in the Bolivian Oriente, the Guaraní are known for their struggle to uphold their freedom and defend their ethnic frontiers. They engaged in warfare against the white colonizers and destroyed several times the missions established to convert them during colonial times. Finally, after systematic warfare they were subdued and controlled, and an intense missionary process and incorporation into wage labor began. The Guaraní are divided into three distinct groups who occupy the departments of Santa Cruz, Tarija, and Chuquisaca: the Ava, who live at the foothills of the Andes; the Izoceño, who are found in the Izozo region; and the Simba, who live in small enclaves in the departments of Chuquisaca and Tarija. Although known in the literature as Chiriguanos, these groups refer to themselves as Guaraní.

CIDOB's emergence is directly linked to the influence of a great Izoceño-Guaraní leader and to the close relations established with an NGO. The Guaraní maintain a political organization known as the Capitanía, which is based on a hereditary and elected leadership; decisions are made on a consensual basis at communal assemblies. The highest authority is the assembly, a meeting of community leaders. Following the assembly is the Capitán Grande (*mburuvicha guasu*), usually an inherited position. The late Capitán Grande Bonifacio Barrientos Iyambae, who held his position for almost fifty years, struggled to obtain land titles, improve the socioeconomic condition of his people, and maintain the Capitanía system. Barrientos established friendly relations with white neighbors and government authorities, which allowed him to negotiate and obtain resources for his communities. This leader saw the need for unity among the various indigenous groups of eastern Bolivia, and he talked to the generation of younger leaders to develop this project.

The second origin was the practical support given to this idea by Jurgen Riester and Berndt Fischermann. These two anthropologists conducted extensive fieldwork among the Izoceño-Guaraní and Ayoreo Indians, respectively. In 1978, Riester and Fischermann arranged a meeting between the Ayoreo and the Izoceños, who had been enemies. In this meeting the Ayoreo and Izoceño began to exchange ideas and discuss their common problems. Each group thought about forming an independent organization. This idea was discouraged by the anthropologists, who believed it was strategically more important to achieve stronger pan-Indian political unity. This meeting and subsequent Izoceño-Ayoreo visits and exchanges paved the way for the emergence of a pan-Indian organization.

In 1980, Riester and other anthropologists established the APCOB (Ayuda para el Campesino Indígena del Oriente Boliviano) in the city of Santa Cruz de la Sierra. The objective of this NGO agency was to implement grassroots development projects that would improve the socioeconomic situation of the native people and lead to their self-determination. Their first projects were conducted among the Izoceño and Ayoreo Indians.

In 1982, APCOB organized the Primer Encuentro de Pueblos Indígenas del Oriente in Santa Cruz de la Sierra. Seventy delegates from thirty-five different Indian communities—Guaraní (Izoceño and Ava), Ayoreo, Guarayo, and Chiquitano—attended this meeting. For the first time in eastern Bolivia, Indian groups met with each other to discuss their problems and needs. They realized the importance of struggling in a unified way to achieve their goals. To do so, they decided to form a pan-Indian organization, CIDOB (Central de Pueblos Indígenas del Oriente Boliviano). Its initial name was later changed to Confederación de Pueblos y Comunidades Indígenas de la Amazonía, Chaco y Oriente Boliviano, and its first president was an Izoceño-Guaraní Indian.

One of the most outstanding qualities of CIDOB has been its ability to gather culturally diverse native groups. According to Miguel García, a former president of CIDOB, its main goals are to achieve the unification of all the Indian people of eastern Bolivia, coordinate activities with the base groups and popular organizations of the country, and defend and guarantee the rights of the Indian population. García stresses the importance of the right to autonomy and self-determination as well as respect for the traditional political organizations.

CIDOB is not affiliated with any political party or religious group; it establishes and coordinates activities with popular organizations such as CSUTCB (Confederación Sindical Única de Trabajadores Campesinos de Bolivia) and COB (Central Obrera Boliviana). According to Jose Urañavi, another former president of CIDOB, the CSUTCB allies peasants without contemplating ethnic differences. In fact, most indigenous groups in eastern Bolivia have not identified or participated in peasant unions (with the exception of the Ava Guaraní). Most indigenous groups felt stronger loyalties to their traditional leaders than to a union. The Bolivian state's policy toward the Indians has been to classify them as "peasant" without regard to cultural differences and the distinct historical situation of each group.

A prerequisite for becoming a leader of CIDOB is having held a prominent position in the community of origin. Some of CIDOB's leaders have had years of training on the national and international scene. As advocates for indigenous rights, they have attended international meetings and negotiated with funding agencies and government authorities. They are skilled political strategists. CIDOB's leadership is by far more "indigenist and militant" regarding Indians' rights and political participation than is its constituency. As in many other cases, some of CIDOB's leaders who spend a great deal of time in the city are becoming alienated from their communities of origin. These persons become "bureaucratized"; they are criticized by other Indians for becoming wealthy, for traveling abroad, and for spending too much time with white people. In spite of the fact that these accusations may be true, these leaders are skillful at dealing with a variety of officials ranging from anthropologists to World Bank representatives—even the president of Bolivia. These leaders understand the intricacies of bureaucracy and politics in their country.

In Bolivia the Indians constitute 60 percent of the population; however, the national government until recently has ignored the demands of the indigenous population and only reaches them during political campaigns, when the parties go to the communities to seek votes. CIDOB's greatest achievement has been in redefining the paternalistic/clientelistic relationship of Indians with the national society; its image management at the national level has been quite successful. Richard Chase Smith (1985) has developed a typology for the study of Indian political organizations. Within this typology CIDOB is characterized as an ethnic federation. As such, CIDOB's main premise is the recognition of the ethnic dimension of the indigenous population with respect for their cultural practices.

The NGO and the Pan-Indian
Organization: From Mediation to Separation

During its first years, CIDOB's leadership was inseparable from the support, advice, and guidance of APCOB's personnel. The NGO played a
fundamental role in CIDOB's development and in establishing the guidelines for this organization's political strategies. The NGO's mediating role
was especially important; it created a bridge between the indigenous population, state institutions, and funding agencies. NGO personnel trained
native leaders and also fostered the notion of economic and political self-
determination and self-management.

CIDOB relied heavily on funding and counseling provided by APCOB,
which gave the pan-Indian organization greater autonomy from the state
but greater dependency on the NGO. This dependency was criticized by
many indigenous leaders who considered it harmful to the organization's
political autonomy. According to Thomas Carrol (1992:113), NGOs "are
often criticized for hanging on to their beneficiaries for too long and per-
petuating a dependency relationship." In the later years there have been
modifications in APCOB's relations with CIDOB, which has grown, gained
more support from the communities, and begun to train its own people.
APCOB, in turn, began a process of transferring its resources to CIDOB.
For example, the grants that had been allocated to development projects
by international funding agencies were transferred to CIDOB; in turn,
CIDOB would receive direct funding from such agencies without the
mediation of an NGO. CIDOB does not control the projects but acts as a
representative to guarantee and supervise the resources. By 1995, APCOB
had conceded its offices and facilities and moved to a new building. This
concession was not only of a practical nature but it was also highly political: it implied the concrete separation of these two institutions and the
growing autonomy of the indigenous organization. Carrol (1992:114) indicates that the ability of NGOs "to wean base groups also depends on how
well organized the base groups are at the time a project is initiated." In
CIDOB's case the organization had grown and consolidated.

CIDOB was aware that initially APCOB was providing important assistance and that even the most qualified leaders did not have sufficient
skills to carry out accounting tasks and write grant proposals. The NGO's
personnel have been instrumental in planning the organization's strategies at the political and economic levels and in making contacts with funding agencies and support groups at the international level. Without the
support (both economic and political) of an NGO it would have been a
very difficult and lengthy process for a pan-Indian movement to develop.

One of CIDOB's greatest strengths is that its Guaraní constituency
has a long history of struggling for cultural and territorial rights. These
struggles antedate new political organizations and are based on the strength

of the Capitanía and its leadership. As previously mentioned, Guaraní leaders strove to obtain land titles and support from the government, but progress has been slow. Although some of its constituency believes that CIDOB's leaders are alienated from the communities and are benefiting by living in the city and receiving a salary, they are also aware that a leader at the national and international levels requires training and the ability to move easily in two cultures.

Even though CIDOB's economic achievements have been modest, and many projects have failed, their political accomplishments have been concrete and long lasting. The struggle for a territory has become one of the main targets of CIDOB's political strategies, together with the emphasis on ethnic pluralism. Development agencies have strengthened the indigenous organization's capacity and convinced the Indians that there is a solution to their socioeconomic problems. Presently, CIDOB has lost the close link to the bases it initially had, but it has become a national organization that has moved from local communal interests to broader political ones. CIDOB is now the representative of the lowland indigenous peoples at the national and international levels. Moreover, CIDOB has achieved many important objectives, such as the elaboration of a Ley Indigena. It has supported the Ley de Reforma Educativa and the Ley de Participación Popular and has negotiated consistently for indigenous territorial rights. CIDOB's last president, Marcial Fabricano, was a candidate for vice president in the 1997 national presidential elections. All of these achievements constitute major steps in the incorporation of the native population into the civic and political spheres.

Asamblea del Pueblo Guaraní: An Intra-Ethnic Organization

Both CIDOB and Asamblea del Pueblo Guaraní were founded by Guaraní Indians. Both organizations began with a close link to NGOs, and both see themselves as part of a national project of redefining the state as well as the native peoples' relation to the state. What, then, are the differences between each of these organizations? Is the main difference the composition of its constituency, or are there variations in strategies and political practices?

In 1987, under the auspices of CIPCA (Centro de Investigación y Promoción del Campesinado, a Jesuit development agency) and the parish of the town of Charagua (Department of Santa Cruz), a meeting was held to organize and unite the numerous Guaraní communities that were separated historically but shared language and culture. Attended by delegates from forty-three communities, representatives of CIDOB, members of NGOs, and priests from the parish, this meeting resulted in the formation of a pan-Guaraní organization, Asamblea del Pueblo Guaraní (APG). "Guaraní" is used in its title instead of Chiriguano, a term considered pejorative, and "Asamblea" reinforces the traditional form of communal organization. APG incorporates Ava, Izoceño, and Simba communities of eastern Bolivia, with the goal of reproducing native forms of organization based on consensual decision making, achieving group unity among the Guaraní, and struggling to improve their socioeconomic situation. Historically, the Guaraní have been critical of the Bolivian state's cultural and political hegemony; APG has formulated this criticism in terms of political action. Xavier Albó (1996:331) considers APG to be the indispensable spokesperson for the development programs among the Guaraní and also the developer of one of the most challenging programs of ethnic and cultural revitalization, both in education and among adults. Furthermore, one of the leaders of the APG became a member of the Bolivian Congress.

In its initial phase, APG did not receive funding from agencies. Each representative or leader attending APG meetings had to pay his own travel expenses (to which the communities also contribute). The structure of APG differs from that of CIDOB: the leadership of APG is formed by an executive committee composed of representatives from each of the zones and by three executive secretaries. One of these secretaries has a permanent position that lasts two years, while the other two rotate from one zone to the other. Thus, each zone is represented at some time by the executive secretary. This system discourages the accumulation of power. The leadership was insistent about the need to be autonomous from NGOs and the state and thus created a system of self-financing to guarantee that the leaders would work for the community as well as for their salary. According to Guido Chumirai (1989), one of APG's most important leaders, this structure enables APG to have greater basic constituent participation. In the long term, APG required funding in order to operate and pay salaries or stipends to its executive committee and personnel. Thus, it began to receive outside funding in order to continue with its projects. APG meetings are very well attended; the delegates are not necessarily chiefs, but they hold some position of importance in their communities.

One of APG's first objectives was to establish ties with regional and national political organizations. For example, it now has a representative in the CSUTCB, and, in fact, many of APG's most active members have had previous experience with peasant unions and political parties. Both CIDOB and APG have formed networks with unions as a strategy to gain more representation at the regional and national levels and as a means of defining themselves as not an exclusively "Indianist" organization.

Asamblea del Pueblo Guaraní and CIPCA's Projects

CIPCA was the first NGO agency to engage in development projects among the Guaraní. Priests linked to CIPCA have spent years among the people; many of them speak Guaraní fluently and have written numerous books about the history and culture of the society. They have implemented agricultural development projects based on a form of organization termed *comunidades de trabajo* (communal work groups), defined by CIPCA as follows: "This refers to an agricultural cooperative enterprise in which the members work in a collective *chaco* (agricultural field). Their tasks are assigned by *tareas* (agricultural unit) and these are equally distributed among the members. A part of the profit is used to capitalize the *comunidad de trabajo*. The funding derives from the Fondo Rotativo de Crédito of CIPCA-Charagua" (CIPCA-ACLO 1980:114).

The *comunidades de trabajo* have attempted to end dependence on exploitative kinds of wage labor by stimulating agricultural production in the communities. These projects were more successful among the Ava than among the Izoceño Indians; they reinforced the notion of communal work and stimulated the emergence of communal organizations. CIPCA also introduced the Guaraní to peasant unions that in some communities were much more successful than in others. However, political repression during the government of García Meza undermined these new forms of political participation.

In 1986, prior to the meeting that led to the formation of the Asamblea del Pueblo Guaraní, CIPCA together with CORDECRUZ (Corporación de Desarrollo de Santa Cruz), a government development agency, conducted an in-depth survey of the situation of Guaraní communities (CORDECRUZ-CIPCA 1986). This survey resulted in a "Program for Peasant Development" (Programa de Desarrollo Campesino para Provincia Cordillera) that focused on five areas: production, infrastructure, health, education, and land/territory. These five categories were to create new projects leading to socioeconomic improvement. This program constituted the backbone of APG's strategies regarding development and organization. During the first meetings of APG the presence of CIPCA was visible and influential. CIPCA's personnel were instrumental in providing the organization with guidelines, establishing contacts with government institutions and officials, and supporting development projects.

One of APG's most important objectives—greater participation in public life—is achieved by coordinating projects and activities with national and private institutions and by having Guaraní professionals working in these institutions. APG has signed agreements with the National Health Department, the Ministry of Peasant Affairs, and TEKO Guaraní (an NGO dedicated to bilingual and intercultural education). Many Guaraní professionals, working as translators, agricultural technicians, nurses, and educators, are important participants in the NGOs. Although Guaraní Indians have worked in the NGOs since the establishment of these agencies, their role has been secondary in the decision-making process. In the last few years the Guaraní presence has been stronger and more influential;

it has led not only to greater participation in decisions but also in the design and implementation of projects. According to Chumirai (1989), participation and representation of the Guaraní as well as other native groups in public and political life and the acceptance of traditional authorities by national legislation constitute a step to a real democratization of Bolivia.

It must be asserted that CIPCA, the parish of Charagua, and APCOB have stimulated relations between the Izoceño and Ava Indians not only as a means of creating greater unity but also as a means of developing a "pan-Guaraní identity." APG does not need to reconcile the extreme cultural and political differences of its constituency because its members share a common culture. In contrast, CIDOB must negotiate and mediate between groups that have completely different languages, cultures, and relations with the national society.

APG has had a very important role in the development of a bilingual intercultural program (D'Emilio 1991), which was financed by UNICEF and was implemented by TEKO Guaraní. This NGO includes a large staff of Guaraní Indians who work on the elaboration of textbooks and didactic material for the education projects. Moreover, this staff also forms part of the APG "intelligentsia." The emergence of APG in conjunction with the bilingual education project and the greater political presence of the Capitanía of the Izoceño-Guaraní have led to a process of ethnic revitalization. Two important events are critical elements in this process. One of these can be called "the reinvention of Capitanías." In 1987 the Capitanía of Gran Caipependi and Carovaicho (among the Ava Guaraní) was reorganized, after years of a lack of political centralization, when the son of one of the great *capitanes* was named Capitán Grande in a very symbolic and highly attended event. The Capitán Grande of the Izoceño Guaraní invested his counterpart of Caipependi in his new post. This event marked the reorganization of sixteen communities under traditional leadership. Moreover, it was a way of empowering the group and manifesting to the white society that the community was alive and well and willing to adhere to its traditional forms of organization and practices. In the following years three more Capitanías were organized to unify, in this way, dispersed communities and to strengthen their civic and political presence. These new chiefdoms emerged not only through the influence of the Capitanía of Gran Caipependi and Izozo but also through the political work of Asamblea del Pueblo Guaraní (Mendoza 1993).

The second event of great relevance, which transcended the border into the Guaraní communities of Argentina, was the commemoration in February 1992 of the 100th anniversary of the last Guaraní upheaval. This event was attended by representatives of Guaraní communities, members of CIDOB, NGOs, and government agencies, and Siles Suazo, the president of Bolivia. It included a march of more than 100 km to Kuruyuki, the site of the last battle of the Guaraní against the Bolivian army. These events, together with the emergence and consolidation of the indigenous organizations, put the Guaraní on the national political agenda. Since its formation, however, APG has distanced itself from CIPCA. It now receives funding from national and international donors and is dedicated to advocacy issues, human rights, bilingual education projects, and territorial rights.

The Guaraní are proud of having fostered the development of two organizations and having established more egalitarian relations with the state. They are grateful to the NGOs for their help but are also critical of the overdependence on these agencies, and they have taken steps to limit their involvement. APG now faces a great challenge with the sanctioning of the Ley de Participación Popular. This law grants political power and autonomy to what are known as OTB (Organizaciones Territoriales de Base), organizations with a specific territory. APG works at a regional level without a specific territory but incorporates communities that fall into different jurisdictions. It remains to be seen whether the Ley de Participación Popular will diminish the representativity and scope of APG. However, on the other side of the geographical border the situation is quite different and the Bolivian Indian organizations are having a great impact.

The State and the Indians in Argentina: Old and New Forms of Dependency

In Argentina, a country formed by a large influx of European immigrants, the indigenous peoples constitute only 1 percent of the population. National policy regarding the native peoples has been one of exclusion, ethnocide, incorporation as labor force, and evangelization. The Indians in Argentina are the most marginalized and discriminated-against sector of the population. The state has regarded them as obstacles to the modernization of the country, as occupants of territories with important natural resources, and as bearers of a culture different from the majority. Its goal has been the homogenization of its population by erasing cultural differences. Thus, the Argentine state has not left the Indians alone. It has intervened in internal matters, organized and disorganized communities, forced relocation and appropriation of native territories, and imposed change and assimilation on the regional culture through education, evangelization, and wage labor. It is in this context that the development of Indian movements becomes a struggle for the recognition of ethnic and cultural specificity amid a hegemonic practice of exclusion. Up to what degree can an organization emerge and develop a counterhegemonic discourse in this environment? Can an indigenous organization have political autonomy in a country with a strong state intervention?

In Argentina the state never developed a policy of indigenism and protectionism as was the case in, say, Mexico. The Indians were not exactly "a problem" in Argentina because their existence was not recognized. The presence of the indigenous peoples did not constitute a great national concern; and when it did become a concern, major military campaigns were waged against the native population (for example, General Roca's Campaña del Desierto in 1879, General Victorica's Campaña del Chaco in 1884).

At present the state is slowly starting to change its relation with the Indians, and the native peoples themselves are becoming active social actors. In 1990 a new law of indigenous communities was passed by Congress (Ley 23.302, Sobre Política Indígena y Apoyo a las Comunidades Aborígenes), which created a National Institute for Indian Affairs (Instituto Nacional de Asuntos Indígenas). Article 67 of the constitution was amended and Article 75 was issued, guaranteeing respect for Indian identity, bilingual education, and legal rights. In 1991 a Guaraní became the first Indian representative to the congress of the province of Salta, and the second Indian (the first was a Toba of Chaco province) in a provincial congress. National and regional Indian organizations are being heard and are having a greater presence in the media and in regional and national politics.

The Guaraní Presence in Argentina

In the late nineteenth century and during the first decades of the twentieth century there was a large influx of Guaraní migrants from Bolivia to northwestern Argentina. This massive migration was the result of an economic boom in the northwest that required labor for sugarcane plantations, timber mills, and agricultural harvests. Hundreds of Guaraní stayed in Argentina and formed new communities. These migrants did not have land titles; they either settled on land owned by the state with usufruct rights or on land that was privately owned or under the custody of the Franciscan Order. They maintained the political leadership of chiefs (*mburuvicha*), who in Argentina were called caciques, as well as their language and cultural practices. Most of the caciques were the founders of the community or descendants of great chiefs from the past. However, the process of modernization in Argentina engulfed them at a more rapid pace than it did among the Guaraní of Bolivia.

Until the 1960s the Guaraní communities were led by their traditional chiefs, who were their representatives to the outside world. In the 1960s the provincial government created and imposed a new form of organization for the native communities, the Centros Vecinales. These neighborhood centers were to "modernize" the Indian communities, create closer links to the municipality, decrease the role of the traditional chief, and have closer control over community matters. The president of the Centro Vecinal is chosen by the people and serves as an intermediary between the community and the local government. Health and education committees were created with the objective of resolving matters at the local level.

At this point, the posts of the president and the chief conflicted with each other and created factions within the community. Some supported the Centro Vecinal and some backed the chief. The role of the council of elders and communal assemblies lost power and importance, and the communities became dependent on government subsidies, paternalistic practices of local landowners, co-optation by political parties, and domination by the Catholic Church. There are still several communities in which the Franciscan Order has taken control of the internal affairs of the population.

During the same period the province of Salta created the Dirección de Asuntos Aborígenes, a government agency under the jurisdiction of the Ministry of Social Welfare (Ministerio de Bienestar Social). This agency was in charge of the development of Indian communities of the province (Carrasco 1991:96). Several Indians worked in this agency to promote communal development, but the budget was extremely low and the agency became entrapped in the web of bureaucracy.

In 1986 the provincial government of Salta enacted Ley 6373/86, "Promoción y Desarrollo del Aborígen" (Promotion and Development of the Indians), and through this law a new government agency, Instituto Provincial del Aborigen (IPA), was created to represent the indigenous groups, help solve their problems, and further socioeconomic development (Carrasco 1994). IPA was organized in the following way: president, vice president, secretary, council of chiefs from the seven different ethnic groups of the region (Toba, Chorote, Pilaga, Tapiete, Chane, Chiriguano, Wichi). Its first president was a Guaraní, who in 1990 became the first Indian representative in the congress of the province of Salta. However, the creation of IPA can be seen as an attempt at marginalizing Indian autonomy and political participation by engaging in leadership those individuals who have closer links to the outside society and who are able to negotiate and accept the impositions of the local government. Even though IPA is a state agency, it never accrued sufficient political capital to exert pressure at the regional or national level. Although its first president was an Indian, his term was shortlived; he left his post to become a representative to the provincial congress. However, he was able to train other Indians in the "bureaucratic" maneuvering of a state institution.

The next president was a former military officer. The agency then entered into a period of financial crisis and lack of representation. The leaders who did participate in IPA were either the most "acculturated" ones or those who did not have the support of their communities. However, a controversial aspect of IPA's work is that it indirectly fostered, in some communities, the revival of the traditional chief. Many communities who had lost their caciques and adopted the Centro Vecinal wanted to become barrios and more like their criollo neighbors. IPA required traditional chiefs to be representatives of the communities not only as a way of keeping these communities from losing their "Indian and traditional" character but also as a means of gaining political consensus and support. This political maneuver did not necessarily foster ethnic revival and a unified sense of struggle because it was not followed by a cohesive cultural and political project, nor did the communities find themselves represented by IPA. Nevertheless, it did generate discussion about the advantages of identifying as Indians and redefining the relations with the state.

Within the city of Tartagal, another organization was formed. The Consejo de Caciques (council of chiefs) began within a government institution, in this case a municipality restricted in functions, space, and representativity. It is important to add that the municipality hired a large number of Indians for its labor force, some of whom established close contacts with the *intendente*, or mayor. To these individuals contact with the mayor or other functionaries was the first step toward a political career and toward tapping into resources. Political parties have had a long tradition of co-opting indigenous peoples to obtain votes or further their own interests. To many indigenous leaders it is only through involvement, affiliation, and direct militancy in political parties that a political space can be won. In the province of Salta, as in other parts of the country, Indians have formed their own political subgroups within the traditional political parties (Hirsch 1995). These subgroups, called *sublemas*, have their own candidates who compete within the same political party for the same seats. By forming *sublemas* the Indians try to obtain posts at the municipal and provincial levels. The way of doing politics at the local level is characterized by clientelism and paternalism (Carrasco 1994). These deeply rooted political practices are very hard to dismantle. I asked a Guaraní why he had formed a group called Integración Aborígen and why he was a member of the official political party, and he replied: "to gain political space." In this case, the Indians do not see themselves as being co-opted by the political parties or the local caudillos. On the contrary, they see this situation as a strategy to win space in the political arena and to be able to struggle for their own cultural, economic, and political vindications. But in a country in which indigenous peoples have been denied any political participation and representation for such a long time, the line between winning political space and co-optation is too thin.

While these processes of forming subgroups within political parties were taking place, Bolivian Guaraní were visiting their Argentine relatives and friends, and members of APG were establishing contact with the communities in Argentina. This exchange was generating new ideas and the need to establish an organization with autonomy from the state. In

February 1992 a group of Guaraní were invited to Bolivia to attend the 100th anniversary of the last Guaraní upheaval in 1892, and a group of twelve youths were invited to take part in a training course for bilingual teachers. This trip, together with the encounter with the Bolivian APG leaders, who were making contact with communities that maintain their language and political organization and adopting bilingual education, made a deep impression on the Argentine group. Within eleven months an APG was formed among the Guaraní of northern Argentina, and the Bolivian leadership was invited to attend the first meeting.

This organization was started initially without the support of state agencies or NGOs. It began by inviting representatives from rural and urban Guaraní communities of two provinces (Salta and Jujuy). Its first phase was very slow, and it met many obstacles such as lack of financial support and of community backing. Many Guaraní thought that they did not identify anymore as Indians and that this would be another case of a political organization imposed by the government. However, APG in Argentina continued to organize meetings. Now, the meetings were sponsored by ENDEPA (Equipo Nacional de Pastoral Aborigen), a church agency dedicated to education and training, and by GTZ, a German cooperation group working in the region on projects of forestry and agriculture. At this point, APG began to have closer links with nonstate organizations and was able to finance meetings with the help of these organizations. At some of the meetings, the agencies invited lawyers to inform the Indian leaders about their legal and territorial rights, or asked their own agricultural engineers to discuss development projects, or motivated the participants to become more involved in the organization. Initially there was not a clear sense of how APG was to be structured.

One of the founders of APG says: "Many of the caciques said, 'put me as the highest authority,' but we say that this was not a participatory model; we saw that it had to be in another form, and in 1996 we changed. So it was organized by elections, in which a national representative would be chosen, followed by an interprovincial, a departmental, a regional, and then the communal representatives, and then there would be a group of five *arakua iya* (elderly advisors)." The meetings try to motivate the participants to return to their communities with information about APG. In this initial phase of consolidation much of the discourse is centered on the importance of forming an organization, of being united for a common cause. One of the leaders present at a meeting organized in 1996 stated: "If we don't organize, the *ñande reko* (our culture, way of living) won't exist; the *karai* (whites) will treat us as workers."

A project of bilingual education was established in the province of Salta, although in its preliminary phase, it lacks adequate didactic material and qualified personnel. Teachers are assisted by bilingual aides who are young members of the communities studying to become teachers or finishing high school. Both the teachers and the aides were trained by Bolivian Guaraní who were involved in the bilingual education program in their country. These Bolivians have been instrumental in fostering APG and have provided much advice on organizational matters. Furthermore, the Argentine bilingual assistants act as intermediaries between APG and the communities. By attending the meetings of APG and working in the schools and with the communities, they become active social actors engaged in the consolidation of their organization.

In Argentina, APG is still in the process of growth, but it needs to establish a firm base at the community level. However, it is a good example of an organization that has achieved a certain level of autonomy from the state and a moderate level of intervention from NGOs. The challenge is whether this organization will be able to avoid co-optation by the state or political parties and will be able to gain strength and representativity.

According to Adams (1991:181), "Most states are 'ethnocratic,' that is, they are controlled by a particular ethnicity. In ethnocracies the interests of all other ethnicities tend to be subordinated, thus creating conflicts that cannot always be readily distinguished from the structural conflicts inherent in the operation of the state." In the case of Argentina a white "European" minority has always concentrated power and ruled the country. Even though in the provinces the leaders may not be of strict European origin, they have never fully represented the native population.

Even though IPA and other indigenous organizations have drawn criticism that ranges from accusations of corruption to "selling out" to the whites, these organizations contribute new cultural meanings. The construction of new ideologies, which slowly sift into the dominant institutions, lead to a gradual increase in participation by the indigenous population in their decision-making process. As a result, a growing process of ethnic revitalization is taking place together with a greater recognition on the part of the national society of the pluricultural component of the country.

Conclusion

Throughout this article I have presented a comparative case of the emergence of political organizations among the Guaraní of Bolivia and Argentina. In the case of Bolivia, emergence is linked to the presence of NGOs and to a history of struggle and maintenance of traditional forms of leadership. In the case of Argentina, organizations are more dependent on the state, and the appearance of APG is the result of interaction with Bolivian Guaraní and, to a lesser extent, to support provided by NGOs. The Argentine APG is a local organization. The "Indian question" is perceived there as a local matter, not as a national issue as in the case of Bolivia. The Guaraní are subject to many external threats: loss of their territory, economic exploitation, and co-optation by political parties and the state. Their organizations also face internal conflicts: leaders who are too ambitious, distancing from the communities that originally supported them, and problems of mismanagement of funds.

Guaraní leaders and community workers travel back and forth—from Argentina to Bolivia to attend courses and meetings, from Bolivia to Argentina to teach courses and support the political organization. A constant flow of people with a transnational migration of ideas, symbols, and identities is part of the landscape. The transnational character of APG bridges the differences between various Guaraní groups and reinforces a pan-Guaraní identity. At present, the Argentine Guaraní are experiencing a degree of ethnic revitalization due, in part, to changes in the local setting as well as to the transnational ties that they have forged with their Bolivian counterparts. As a result, Argentine Guaraní are using ethnic categories as a political strategy designed to improve their own communities and to enable them to negotiate more effectively with the government and with local authorities. Ethnicity is now not simply a cultural marker but also a political strategy for empowerment.

According to Stefano Varese (1992:16), "this new sociology of the native peoples of Latin America—transnationalized, urban, proletarian, bordercrossing, bilingual and trilingual, professional—poses a direct challenge to established anthropological tradition." The transnational flow of communication, people, and organizations has unforeseeable consequences. Will the Bolivian Guaraní become immersed in political and economic networks with NGOs that will hinder their autonomy? Will the Argentine Guaraní persist in their quest to distance themselves from the state and seek greater self-determination? The Guaraní people are crafting new narratives about themselves; they are searching for alternative routes to a long history of disenfranchisement. The new political organizations appear as viable means for achieving their ethnic projects. The Guaraní have made few economic gains but many political ones. They are subject to political changes in their countries and to the unequal power structure of Bolivian and Argentine society, but their political and discursive skills and the empowering institutions of their society have enabled them to win a position of greater respect and participation.

References

Adams, Richard
  1991   "Strategies of Ethnic Survival in Central America." In *Nation-States and Indians in Latin America*, Greg Urban and Joel Sherzer, eds. Austin: University of Texas Press.

Albó, Xavier
1991   "El retorno del indio." *Revista Andina*, Año 9, Numéro 2. Diciembre.
1996   "Nación de muchas naciones: Nuevas corrientes políticas en Bolivia." In *Democracia y estado multiétnico en América Latina*, Pablo González Casanova and Marcos Roitman Rosenmann, eds. México: Centro de Investigaciones Interdisciplinarias en Ciencias y Humanidades y la Jornada Ediciones.

Bonfil Batalla, Guillermo
1979   "Las nuevas organizaciones indígenas (Hipótesis para la formulación de un modelo analítico)." In *Indianidad y descolonización en América Latina*. México: Nueva Imagen.

Carrasco, Morita
1991   "Hegemonía y políticas indigenistas argentinas en el Chaco Centro Occidental." *América Indígena*, Vol. 51, Número 1. Enero-Marzo.
1994   "Indigenismo y democracia: Clientes, políticos, punteros, caciques gente." *Cuadernos del Instituto Nacional de Antropología y Pensamiento Latinoamericano* 15.

Carrol, Thomas
1992   *Intermediary NGOs: The Supporting Link in Grassroots Development*. West Hartford, CT: Kumarian Press.

Chase Smith, Richard
1985   "A Search for Unity within Diversity: Peasant Unions, Ethnic Federations, and Indianista Movements in the Andean Republics." In *Native Peoples and Economic Development: Six Case Studies from Latin America*, Theodore Macdonald, ed. Cultural Survival. January, N16.

Chumiray, Guido
1989   "Asamblea del Pueblo Guaraní." Ponencia presentada al Seminario Realidad Pluricultural en el Oriente y Chaco Bolivianos (Santa Cruz, diciembre de 1989).

CIPCA-ACLO
1980   *Métodos de evaluación para proyectos de producción agrícola: Bolivia*.

CORDECRUZ-CIPCA
1986   *Plan de desarrollo rural de cordillera: Diagnóstico-estrategia*. Santa Cruz. 7 vols.

D'Emilio, Anna Lucía
1991   "Bolivia: la conquista de la escuela. El proyecto educativo de los guaraní-chiriguanos." In *Etnias, educación y cultura: Defendamos lo nuestro*. Venezuela: Editorial Nueva Sociedad.

Gaceta Oficial de Bolivia
  1994   *Ley de Participación Popular*. 21 de Abril. La Paz.
Hendricks, Janet
  1991   "Symbolic Counterhegemony among the Ecuadorian Shuar."
          In *Nation-States and Indians in Latin America*, Greg Urban
          and Joel Sherzer, eds. Austin: University of Texas Press.
Hirsch, Silvia
  1995   "Organización política y relaciones con el estado entre los
          indígenas chiriguanos de la Argentina." Paper presented at
          the Latin American Studies Association Meeting, Washing-
          ton, DC.
Marinissen, Judith
  1995   *Legislación boliviana y pueblos indígenas: Inventario y
          análisis en la perspectiva de las demandas indígenas*. Santa
          Cruz: Editora El País.
Mendoza, Eduardo
  1993   "Organizaciones indígenas: El caso de los guaraní-chiriguano."
          XII Congreso Internacional de Ciencias Antropológicas y
          Etnológicas. México.
Van Cott, Donna Lee
  1994   *Indigenous Peoples and Democracy in Latin America*. New
          York: St. Martin's Press.
Varese, Stefano
  1992   "Think Locally, Act Globally." *Report on the Americas* 23,
          no. 3. December.
Wilmer, Frank
  1993   *The Indigenous Voice in World Politics*. Newbury Park, CA:
          Sage Publications.

•

6

Consciousness and Contradiction: Indigenous Peoples and Paraguay's Transition to Democracy

René Harder Horst

The events in Ecuador in 2000 have shown that indigenous peoples, if properly organized, can bring down whole governments. What is less well known is that the Indians in Paraguay, who by official count only constitute 3 percent of the total population, played a role in the overthrow of the dictatorial regime of General Alfredo Stroessner (1954–1989). In Paraguay, Indians are defined mostly as those peoples who are still not completely sedentary, unlike those in other Latin American countries. The rural folk in Paraguay who live as peasants and speak Guaraní are generally not considered Indians but rather are integrated into society, in which Guaraní, along with Spanish, is the official language.

Although the role the Indians played was at times direct (such as in the political mobilization of the 1980s), perhaps their most important role was one as victims of the regime, which served to undermine the legitimacy of the Paraguayan dictatorship as it had presented itself to the outside world. In the process, a German anthropologist as well as Pope John Paul II, the U.S. government, and many nongovernmental organizations (NGOs) also played important parts. In fact, in the era of increasing globalization, it is important to keep in mind that NGOs have become ever more significant in world and national politics. Indeed, indigenous organizations themselves are becoming more adept at using international forums to make their case, often supported by groups originating in industrialized countries whose purpose is to aid Indians in Latin America.

Another notable issue that emerges from the discussion of indigenous policy in Paraguay is that of the terms of integration. The Stroessner regime clearly intended to "integrate" the indigenous population into society by placing them as rural laborers on the ranches and in the many Mennonite colonies that are found in the northern part of the country, in the Gran Chaco region. To a large extent, that is what had already happened by the 1970s. Integration on Stroessner's terms, however, also meant the destruction of native culture. Is it possible to incorporate Indians, especially only partially sedentary ones, into society as full and equal members without some form of state tutelage? What kinds of rules must exist for them to become part of a majority mestizo or creole state? What do they gain and what do they lose once they organize themselves politically to fight against abuses? And what role should the government and NGOs play in this process?

René Harder Horst is an assistant professor of history at Appalachian State University in North Carolina.

In the recent "Paraguayan March" of 1999, students, workers, and citizens risked their lives and futures to combat the forces of absolutism and dictatorship when they refused to allow General Lino Oviedo to seize control of their nation. Ten years of democracy had clearly sown among the younger generations a new national pride and the desire to enjoy broad political participation. While some scholars have analyzed the political events that overthrew the Stroessner dictatorship in 1989, no one has showed that Paraguay's indigenous people helped to weaken the dictator's rule and contributed to his collapse.[1] Several reasons account for the oversight of the native role in these important political changes. First, indigenous people are at most only 3 percent of Paraguay's population, proportionally far fewer than natives in Brazil, Bolivia, or Mexico. Moreover, national society has for centuries held a deep-seated prejudice against the native groups that have maintained cultural and ideological boundaries from the majority of persons of mixed racial heritage. Finally, the dictatorship worked arduously to integrate the indigenous minorities, alter their cultural identities, and make independent production within their semi-autonomous communities nearly impossible. This essay will argue, to the contrary, that indigenous groups nevertheless played an important role in eroding General Alfredo Stroessner's power and bringing his dictatorship to an end.

Many scholars have examined the reasons why Latin America moved from military regimes to freer administrations in the 1980s.[2] Few analysts, however, have shown that indigenous resistance and growing native participation in national society weakened authoritarian states and ultimately contributed to their downfall.[3] Despite this oversight, native activism in Paraguay helped to topple the brutal Stroessner regime in 1989. During the late 1980s, in dozens of protests throughout the countryside, native communities demanded the right to continue practicing semi-autonomous subsistence while living on ancestral territories. Some of these struggles were continuing conflicts with *paraguayos* and immigrants over land. Other crises resulted from the extension of cash crops, campesino settlements, and regime development projects into what had previously been native lands. By resisting regime goals, native groups rejected state plans for economic expansion that drastically altered indigenous environ-

ments. Native opposition made the success of such programs more difficult and undermined Stroessner's control over the rural areas. Indigenous
people also called widespread attention to human rights abuses when the
regime tried to push them out of the way; native accounts thus provided
ample fuel for the dictator's critics. The media especially employed indigenous reports to criticize corruption in the regime. By adding their
voices to the Church, labor unions, and opposition political parties, indigenous people therefore helped to cause Stroessner's downfall.

One way to explain why natives were so important, given their small
number, is their historical significance. Paraguay has been famous for its
seventeenth- and eighteenth-century Jesuit missions that figured prominently in its history. When Jesuits first gathered native groups into nearly
thirty missions in eastern Paraguay and the Guairá of Brazil, they came
into conflict with the colonial authorities who desired access to indigenous labor. The Jesuits legitimated their prosperous pueblos by claiming
to defend natives from encomenderos in Paraguay and roving bands of
bandeirantes from Brazil. Following the Jesuit demise, mission natives
who had adopted Catholicism gradually evolved into the Paraguayan peasant class and firmly cemented *mestizaje*, the racial mixture begun early in
the Colonial Period, as well as the national use of the Guaraní language.

When Commander in Chief of the Armed Forces Alfredo Stroessner
overthrew President Federico Chávez and took power in May 1954 with
support from the Colorado Party, he capitalized on this native legacy.[4]
The young military officer, son of a Paraguayan woman and a German
immigrant, was unlike the personalist caudillos elsewhere in Latin America
who flaunted their charisma.[5] Stroessner seemed so dull, plodding, and
uninspiring that no one really expected him to stay in power long and
rivals completely underestimated him.[6] Stroessner used the Colorado Party
to consolidate his control through a system of patronage and surveillance.
With methodical attention he maintained the illusion of a large popular
base of support. In return, the party consistently nominated Stroessner as
its only candidate.

Besides hegemonic political control, the new president also relied on
popular myths of common *mestizaje* origin to further his control. The leader
soon realized that to unite the country behind his rule and minimize opposition to his ambitious economic plans, he would need to build on the
nation's bilingual legacy. Only two years after becoming president,
Stroessner instituted Guaraní as a subject for high schools in Asunción.
To train instructors of Guaraní, in 1961 his Ministry of Education organized the Guaraní Linguistic Institute of Paraguay. Another reason why
the use of Guaraní increased at this time was state-sponsored immigra-
tion from Brazil, Canada, Europe, and East Asia. As competition for jobs
and resources grew, Paraguayans spoke Guaraní to assert their nationality.
Finally, the regime encouraged the legendary explanation that Paraguayan

society was the glorious product of the alliance between Europeans and the Guaraní people to foster national pride. Stroessner's measures united the country's diverse population around the use of an indigenous language. Paraguay was the only nation in Latin America to have a bilingual policy.

The new president's use of the indigenous heritage as a political technique is curious, given the small native population that still resided in isolated rural communities. While natives did contribute labor and products to the economy, at only 3 percent of the population they certainly do not appear to have merited enormous expenditures of time and energy on the part of the president. It was only their historical legacy and different ways of life that made indigenous people important enough for the new regime to even consider them. To this effect the young leader encouraged many of what Benedict Anderson has termed the components of imagined modern nationality: horizontal comradeship, solidarity among whites, and especially a historical background based on a common heritage of racial mixture.[7]

While popular myths of mixed native and European ascendancy helped to rally the elite behind him, the political technique ultimately fell short of ensuring passive popular compliance with the regime.[8] Instead, Stroessner turned to patronage, and his principal goal became the development of the nation's economic potential. He hoped that a growing economy would reward his base of support in the upper classes and lengthen his rule. While the president's plans dramatically increased the nation's agricultural production, they achieved growth at a high cost to the lower classes. Already in 1956, Stroessner imposed an International Monetary Fund (IMF) austerity program that drove down real wages and led to the arrest of 300 trade union leaders after a general strike. When popular discontent prevailed and Congress complained of police brutality, the president dissolved it and exiled all remaining dissidents from inside the Colorado Party. Hundreds of people left Paraguay for neighboring countries. From the outset, Stroessner relied on repression and any other means to ensure a submissive population, a subject labor force, and a political climate stable enough for investment. Steady economic expansion followed throughout much of Stroessner's rule.

Economic growth may have benefited the elite, but development of rural areas proved devastating for the native population. By the midtwentieth century, there were only between 60,000 and 70,000 indigenous people who considered themselves ethnically distinct from the *paraguayo* majority. The Paraguay River geographically divided the seventeen different ethnic groups from five basic linguistic families. East of the river, native peoples belonged to the Tupí-Guaraní language family and spoke some form of Guaraní. In the northern Amambay region the Paï Tavyterã still practiced subsistence horticulture, although they no longer lived in large traditional communities. The Ava Guaraní, culturally the closest to campesinos, lived in the eastern region. Both of these groups had contact with *paraguayos*, and some even worked as peons on ranches. In the central east lived the Mbyá, who still isolated themselves and fled from contact with the national society. Likewise, the nomadic Ache spoke a form of Guaraní, hunted and gathered in small bands, and lived in a few forested outposts in the central eastern regions.

In pre-Columbian times some Tupí-Guaraní had migrated west of the Paraguay River. The Western Guaraní and the Guaraní-Ñandeva still resided close to the border with Bolivia. In the Chaco region lived a variety of non-Guaraní indigenous groups from four different linguistic families. The Ayoreode and the Öshöro belonged to the Zamuco language group and traditionally had inhabited the northern Chaco. The Enxet, Angaité, Sanapaná, Guan'a, and Enenlhit belonged to the Lengua Maskoy linguistic group. These larger groups lived in the central and eastern Chaco, between the Mennonite colonies and the Paraguay River. The Yofuaxa, Nivaclé, and Mak'a shared Mataco-Mataguayo languages and traditionally were found in central and southern Chaco. Finally, the Toba-Qom, of Guaicurú linguistic ancestry, had resided in the southeastern area of the Chaco. Except for the two Guaraní groups, the tribes west of the river shared linguistic ties with natives in the rest of the Gran Chaco, a geographic area including western Paraguay, northern Argentina, southeastern Bolivia, and southwestern Brazil.

By the time Stroessner came to power, every indigenous group had distinct histories of interaction with national society and other Indian peoples, but all shared the legacy of discrimination and inadequate access to legal protection. Some tribes actively avoided interaction with the national population, but in eastern Paraguay especially only religion and place of residence distinguished natives from the campesinos. By 1954, settlers and ranchers had extended crops, cattle raising, and lumber extraction near indigenous communities, and every group had increased contacts with the national population. Every tribe had also lost most of its traditional territory. Stroessner's emphasis on economic development promised conflicts for native groups as they maneuvered for still further interaction with outsiders.

Early Regime *Indigenista* Policy

To clear the native peoples off fertile rural lands, President Stroessner borrowed *indigenista* policies from other Latin American nations. First developed in Mexico following the 1910 Revolution, these strategies promised to both improve indigenous conditions and concurrently oversee their inclusion into national society. In November 1958 the dictator established a guardianship over the indigenous peoples and made them wards of the Defense Department. Stroessner created the Department of Indigenous

Affairs (DAI) to resolve what he called the "indigenous problem" and ordered the new agency to oversee the integration of the Indians. According to the charter,

> Given the need to adopt measures to nucleate the indigenous people scattered throughout the eastern and western regions of the republic into organized colonies, in order to avoid their extinction and adapt them to a sedentary way of life, and considering that Paraguay has assumed commitments to this effect, in its character as a member state of the Inter-American Indigenista Institute; That investigations conducted by the Ministry of National Defense . . . prove the existence of an important autochthonous population in a defenseless and helpless state; it is impossible to postpone the need to adopt measures to direct their reinstatement to national civilized life, we create the Department of Indigenous Affairs . . . with the purpose of centralizing the *indigenista* activities in the national territory.[9]

The president's orders provide insight into his plans. Stroessner and his generals believed the indigenous peoples led an unorganized, uncivilized, and miserable existence because some did not reside in permanent settlements as did the *paraguayo* majority. In reality, however, only the Ache in the east and Ayoreode in the Chaco lived nomadically in the forests. The larger Guaraní tribes had a tradition of horticulture and fairly sedentary residences, and in fact by this time most formerly semi-nomadic groups lived and worked on ranches. The Ache and Ayoreode, however, had recently attracted the attention of the media because of violent encounters with ranchers. It was these groups that the regime hoped to quickly and quietly settle in "organized" reservations. Moreover, the president considered indigenous people to be helpless minors incapable of improving their conditions or protecting themselves, so he paternalistically promised to defend them from harm.

During the 1960s the DAI focused on settling the indigenous groups that still hunted and gathered. In 1959 a small band of Southern Ache requested protection from a rancher in Guairá Department in eastern Paraguay.[10] The regime seized the opportunity to locate permanently the people who had been hunting, poaching on cattle, and raiding campesino gardens. While the DAI sent food and funds to the new settlement, overseer Manuel Pereira resold the supplies and embezzled the money. Consequently the Ache had no health care for the respiratory diseases they contracted and many starved. The regime knew that Pereira was a drunkard and abused Indian women, but it was still very eager to settle the Ache.

The regime's settlement program grew steadily until the winter of 1971, when Mark Münzel, an anthropologist, arrived at the reservation to study Ache culture. He could not help noticing the poor living conditions and the ill effects of initial contact on the new arrivals. Münzel saw Pereira and armed native assistants bring Northern Ache to the camp by truck and keep them as prisoners, guarding them with machetes. The rancher denied medicine to the arrivals and threatened to kill them if they spoke with the German scholar.[11] "During my stay on the reservation," Münzel wrote, "I was physically prevented . . . from offering Indians medicine or nourishment."[12] By 1972, Pereira and his Ache assistants had brought nearly 200 Ache back to the reserve.

Münzel's account suggests a highly coercive but well-concealed plan to remove the indigenous people from their ancestral habitat. Once at the reservation, moreover, Pereira kept the Ache from hunting and also changed their tribal names to Christian designations.[13] Pereira forbade the natives from observing their traditional ceremonies and speaking their particular dialect, forced them to change their hairstyles, and made the men remove their *betá*, or lip ornaments. "The Ache are being convinced that it is a shame to be an Ache," recounted Münzel, and "they are told that the only way to escape from this shame is to become a hunter of Indians like Jesús Pereira."[14]

It did not take long for outsiders to discover the abuses at the reservation. Filled with horror, Münzel informed authorities in Asunción about Pereira's tyranny, the terrible living conditions, and the hunts to secure more Ache. During the fall of 1972, influenza claimed the lives of at least fifty Ache, most of whom had arrived only months before.[15] Münzel advised high regime officials, but when no one stopped Pereira's expeditions, the German anthropologist tried to draw more attention to the Ache. In March, after Münzel again pressured the overseer, Pereira threatened him and pushed him off the reservation.[16]

The anthropologist found ample support among Paraguayan ethnologists and especially from the Catholic Church, which by this time was at serious odds with the dictatorship. Soon the scandalous news spread overseas, and human rights organizations took up the case. In March 1974, Senator James Abourezk denounced Stroessner for genocide in the U.S. Congress. Abourezk called for an end to aid to Asunción and accused the United States of pouring "massive amounts of foreign aid into Paraguay" to support Stroessner's "ruthless regime," despite the accusations of genocide.[17] Shortly thereafter, Washington recalled its ambassador and relations between the two countries cooled considerably.[18]

As the foreign investigation into the Ache situation escalated, the regime turned to its most common method of handling opposition and dissent: the use of *mbareté*, direct force or coercion. In May 1974, Minister of Defense Marcial Samaniego compelled regime cabinets, religious agencies, educational institutions, and even a U.S. diplomat to sign a statement that Münzel's accusations had been false.[19] The denial was a tenuous fabrication. As Samaniego explained, "although there are victims and victimizers, there is not the third element necessary to establish the crime of genocide—this is 'intent.' Therefore, since there is no intent, one cannot speak of 'genocide.' "[20]

Meanwhile, in Europe, Münzel continued his battle and accused the regime of planning to eliminate all indigenous peoples of the country: "The dispute is no longer about whether or not there are Indian groups being destroyed in Paraguay, but only about whether or not these destructions can be juridically defined as 'genocide.' The discussion now refers clearly not only to the Ache, but to other Indian groups as well."[21] In retrospect, it is clear that a corrupt reservation manager, backed by the regime, permitted conditions to deteriorate to the point where many Ache perished. The deaths resulted mainly from exposure to diseases against which native peoples had no immunity. Some foresight, medical attention, and even a small amount of anthropological awareness might certainly have prevented such dire results for the Ache. Still, even if the dictator tolerated such neglect, there is no solid evidence that the regime methodically and purposefully intended to kill the Ache people.

Paraguayan opposition leaders employed Münzel's charges to criticize the policy of integration and in the process altered its effects for the natives. The *indigenistas* magnified the case to assist the Indian peoples. Even though stretched, Paraguayan scholars and the Catholic Church added their voices to Münzel's charges in the belief that a concerted effort, with international support, might actually improve both the Ache situation and regime treatment of all indigenous peoples.

Concerned anthropologists created several NGOs that over the next years improved the natives' legal situation, their access to lands, and their educational and medical conditions. By October 1975, these NGO projects had begun to make a difference. The Marandú Project, funded by the Interamerican Foundation and the Catholic University of Asunción, had informed the largest indigenous concentrations that they had legal rights and deserved access to land. By creating an indigenous council, Marandú provided native leaders with a forum from which to explain their situation to the authorities.[22] The Paï Tavyterã, for instance, began to move back to traditional communities after a project on their behalf strengthened tribal economic, legal, educational, and medical conditions. A new Guaraní Project produced similar positive effects for the other groups in eastern Paraguay.

In October 1974 the Catholic University hosted thirty indigenous leaders from Argentina, Bolivia, Brazil, Venezuela, and Paraguay for the American Indian Parliament of the Southern Cone. The visiting leaders formed a pan-indigenous council and issued a strong call for improved attention by national governments.[23] The native delegates employed a distinct ethnic discourse to highlight their current economic difficulties, accused states and missionaries of perpetrating five centuries of abuse, and demanded health care and legal protection as minimal reparations. Their final statement demanded that non-Indians respect indigenous languages and cultures, grant them equality in education and labor, and allow them to own property communally.[24] The gathering exposed native leaders in Paraguay to tribal organizations from other countries who used a discourse of oppressed classes to describe their conditions. After the conference, chiefs began to refer to themselves as victims of colonization and abuse when submitting requests to the regime.[25]

Most important, indigenous leaders and the ongoing international accusations of genocide pressured the regime to present its *indigenista* plans in a much more positive light and reform the agency responsible for the mismanaged settlements. In neighboring Brazil, human rights advocates had in 1967 accused the Service for the Protection of Indigenous People (SPI) of exterminating tribes. Instead of trying the guilty officials, Brazil's dictatorship disbanded the SPI and replaced it with a new agency, the National Indian Foundation.[26] In Paraguay the DAI had borne the brunt of the failed state plan to quietly settle the Ache. The dictatorship decided that a new agency with more authority might once and for all effectively integrate native groups. On October 20, 1975, Stroessner created a new state bureau to replace the DAI. The regime endowed the National Indigenous Institute (INDI) with greater resources than the former agency and granted it the authority to oversee all private initiatives for native peoples. Given the rise in advocacy on behalf of indigenous rights, the regime clearly wished to firmly control all activities in rural areas that involved the Indians.

Most significant to the indigenous people was the new promise to tolerate distinctly native ways of life, communal landholding, religious rituals, and tribal government. The decree that created the INDI repeatedly pledged to respect native cultures. The regime had not abandoned its plans to integrate the indigenous population into the larger society. After critics accused Paraguay of genocide, however, the state promised to effect integration while respecting basic cultural differences. The inherent contradiction in this logic shows that the decree was meant to appease the regime's critics; the push for integration and respect for distinctly indigenous cultures were mutually exclusive goals. Still, as native activism grew, indigenous groups increasingly called on the regime to honor its pledge to respect pluralism, even amid continued efforts for integration.

Not content at being pressured, Stroessner next tried to crush native organization. Late in 1975, security forces arrested hundreds of peasant leaders, political dissidents, and radical priests and imprisoned social scientists and students. Security forces ended the Marandú Project, which had raised the animosity of the military and ranchers as it tried to counter the smooth integration of the indigenous peoples by arresting and torturing its leaders.[27] The Indigenous Council gained permission to continue meeting only by submitting to the new INDI. This move compromised the body's effectiveness in lobbying honestly on behalf of their communities. While native organization forced Stroessner to alter how he presented his *indigenista* goals, repression also hampered the potential for pan-indigenous organization.

Direct force, however, could not quiet the ongoing accusations over the Ache. When Jimmy Carter probed allegations of human rights abuses, the International League for the Rights of Man highlighted the Marandú Project, criticized the United States, and alleged again that Stroessner intended to annihilate the indigenous population.[28] In response, Washington slashed its military aid to Paraguay from U.S.$2.4 million in 1976 to a token $700,000 in 1977, down significantly from $16.7 million in 1971. That same year U.S. economic assistance declined to $3.2 million from $12.6 million in 1971. When Washington inquired repeatedly in 1977 whether the situation had improved, Stroessner buckled under and promised to respect native cultures.

Growing Indigenous Organization in the Countryside

After the Stroessner regime pledged to respect their rights but also to continue the integration program, native groups stepped up their protests. The first to organize itself and press the state to return its territory was the Toba-Qom band, whom the DAI had expelled by force from a private ranch in 1969.[29] Over 600 Toba people now lived on a Franciscan mission forty kilometers west of Asunción. As most of their land was swampy and ranchers forbid them from trespassing to hunt, the Toba sold crafts or worked for *paraguayos* for a living. In February 1977, Toba leaders finally went to opposition newspapers and declared that their situation was critical and desperate.[30] In the earliest deliberate native attempt to influence the regime through the media, the Toba showed that with ancestral lands they could oppose regime plans to force them into the wider labor force.

Soon after the Toba began to press for land, an Enenlhit group that Mennonite immigrants had evicted late in 1971 also increased demands for their ancestral territory. This group had originally hunted and raised subsistence crops at Casanillo, in the northern Chaco. Over the next years the Enenlhit made public their displeasure by intoxicating themselves and disruptively wandering the streets of the largest Mennonite town. Women from this group went so far as to abort unborn infants to show their displeasure.[31] By aborting fetuses, the Enenlhit used an extreme form of resistance to protest the loss of tribal autonomy. As these protests produced no results, in 1977 the group defied explicit Mennonite orders and sent leaders to Asunción.

At nearly the same time a related Enenlhit group, which for years had endured difficult situations as workers in tannin factories along the northern Paraguay River at Puerto Casado, began to pressure the state to return their ancestral territory. Before coming to depend on debt peonage, this group had gathered and hunted along the Riacho Mosquito. Like their relatives, conditions for the Enenlhit had grown severe, and in 1977 the group took action. Over the next two years both Enenlhit groups sent chiefs several times per year on the expensive trip by boat and truck to the capital, where they secured support from NGOs and religious organizations by expressing their desperate need to recuperate tribal lands.

When by the end of the decade both cases were stalled in state bureaucracy, Toba chiefs visited opposition newspapers and made poignant pleas to the public. Speaking in Guaraní rather than their native language, the leaders threatened that if they did not regain their territory the tribe would all perish. The Toba adroitly employed the threat of genocide as a trump card, building on the regime's fear of further accusations à la Münzel. Ultimately their persistence paid off. In 1979, Colonel Oscar Centurión, director of the INDI, promised all three groups that he would work assiduously to return their lands. The director's pledge had a dramatic effect on the Enenlhit, who almost immediately stopped their drunkenness and began to give birth normally once again.[32] During the late 1970s, public opinion in Paraguay had shifted against the regime, and people in academic circles had come to believe that natives had a historical right to own land and to choose their own way of life. Now the three groups found advocates within the Catholic Church and higher education.[33]

While at this point the Church was less critical of the state, native rights was an area where the Catholic hierarchy could still portray itself as socially involved without further endangering tenuous relations with President Stroessner. The Church embraced indigenous land claims and publicly challenged the regime to improve the natives' situation. In August 1979 the Bishops' Conference urged the dictatorship to rapidly solve the Toba quest for land: "The missionaries among indigenous peoples . . . appeal to the corresponding institutions for them to quickly resolve the indigenous Tobas' anguished search for land. We trust that authorities do not seek the Tobas' deaths when they do not pay attention to their appeals. We reaffirm our firm support of the Tobas in their many-years-old continuous appeal for these lands that they need for their habitat."[34] The letter again employed Münzel's successful method for drawing attention to native affairs; the bishops threatened that if the state did not answer the Toba request, it would be directly responsible for their extinction.[35]

Leery of further scrutiny and anxious to reclaim foreign aid, Stroessner quickly addressed the Toba requests. In 1980 the INDI tried on several occasions to purchase the native territory from La Gauloise ranch.[36] Despite these threats, on every attempt the regime acquiesced to the powerful business and canceled the expropriations. Major newspapers publicized the Toba plight widely and sided against the regime. But the business played a final trump card when it argued that the state should not give lands to "*indígenas* encouraged by international organizations."[37] This appeal to Stroessner's phobia against a foreign Communist threat was successful: by the New Year, La Gauloise had defeated the Toba claim.

It was growing collective pressure from indigenous communities throughout the country that ultimately gave the Enenlhit more success than the Toba. The Enenlhit used several critical strategies to buttress their struggle. The most important was a steady lobby at the INDI. Oscar Centurión recalled that it was the persistent Enenlhit leaders who forced him to act on their behalf. At considerable risk to his job, Centurión argued that the Enenlhit had the right to reclaim ancestral territories and tried to purchase the land from the Casado Company.[38] In October 1980 the INDI pressured Stroessner to expropriate the natives' land, arguing that Casado was not using the territory to its fullest potential.[39] Clearly, the threat of a social uprising also weighed heavily on the state; the INDI claimed the takeover was necessary to "prevent the threat of serious social problems" from the socially marginated Enenlhit people.[40] When they learned of the expropriation decree, 300 Enenlhit moved to Casanillo to emphasize their demands and erected shelters outside the gates.

Centurión resorted to the police to force Casado to comply. When on December 26 the company finally opened the gates, the natives rushed in and cleared a road to where they planned to build their houses. The people were ecstatic. Father José Seelwische experienced the dramatic event and recalled their great joy at finally being able to occupy Casanillo.[41] Enenlhit leader Julio Esquivel publicly thanked those who had negotiated on his people's behalf and promised not to disappoint them.[42] By the close of 1980, the Enenlhit attempt was the first successful native effort to reclaim ancestral lands. The people's persistent lobbying had finally succeeded.

There was no escaping, however, that Enenlhit success flew in the face of plans for integration. Thus, the regime fired Centurión late in December. Colonel Machuca Godoy, his replacement, had voted against the expropriation and immediately promised to follow the "established line" of state indigenous policy.[43] Native leaders publicly expressed strong disapproval of national political affairs and Centurión's removal. The Indigenous Council, despite its pro-regime position, charged that the replacement was a direct result of Centurión's action on behalf of the Enenlhit.[44] Western Guaraní chief Severo Flores at the Indigenous Council declared natives to be part of a "peaceful revolution, which claimed land to work and survive" and which in this way would "meet officials' expectation that we contribute to the progress of the nation."[45] The reference to the de facto revolution shows the events' monumental importance in the leader's mind.

Another important conflict over land started when prosperous and conservative settlers from Manitoba tried to expel three Mbyá communities from within their Sommerfeld colony. These Mennonites had in 1946 purchased 33,000 hectares in Caaguazú from the federal government. The indigenous groups within the large property had helped them to build farms.[46] By the late 1970s, however, the settlers had grown to 1,400 and tried to clear land for ranching by evicting the Mbyá. In August 1981, Mennonite administrator Willie Hildebrand torched Mbyá homes and ordered them to leave. When Mennonite employers fired their indigenous workers and destroyed fifteen hectares of Mbyá crops with heavy equipment, the natives at Yhovy lost their food supply for the year.

Even more than other Guaraní groups, the Mbyá had depended on horticulture for a living. Indigenous groups immediately denounced the intrusions to *indigenista* agencies because the loss of their farmland promised an abrupt cultural change. Leader Anselmo Miranda declared: "Soon they will bring loaders to clear the woods. With them they will destroy our clearings and crops. This is because they want to bring cattle, but for that they will need to pass over our houses."[47] Other leaders denounced the eviction in the departmental capital of Villarrica, where a judge ordered the Mennonites to halt the destruction of indigenous crops and homes. Chief Máximo González reported: "It has been over twenty years that I am on this land and it is mine; I will cultivate it, even if it bothers these Mennonites. They are not even Paraguayans, but they carry more weight than a Paraguayan. Even the police fear them, because they have money. What is their Christ for, if they leave their neighbor without food? That is an evil religion, if it teaches evil and hatred."[48]

González's outburst was a calculated attempt to secure support within the wider population. Not only did González build on local jealousy of Mennonite prosperity, but he also appealed to patriotism and reminded campesinos that their own government had welcomed the outsiders, who had grown to exert significant political weight. Finally, the leader appealed to the anti-Protestant sentiment so prevalent among Catholic *paraguayos*, especially in rural areas. Within months the Mbyá had convinced the Institute of Rural Welfare (IBR) to order Mennonites to leave them in peace.[49]

The rise of conflicts in eastern Paraguay focused attention on the social effects of the regime's plans to extend cash crops and ranching into undeveloped areas. The press took up the cause with a vengeance and began to criticize state programs for their pernicious effects on indigenous communities. *La Tribuna*, critical of the regime, reported: "the indigenous people find themselves exposed to constant dislocation from their lands . . . [they are] separated from their means of subsistence and the worst of it all is that those responsible for these situations are large businesses."[50]

To quiet both rural native protests and the international charges of genocide, in 1981 the dictator finally approved of an indigenous rights law, called Law 904, that had for several years remained only in draft stage. The new legislation was unique in Latin America because it promised to respect indigenous cultures and the natives' right to own ancestral lands. Colorado Party politicians realized that the regime might use the proposed bill to counter growing popular criticism of the regime.[51] In addition, foreign relief agencies had promised to assist native groups only after such a law was in place.[52] The regime crafted the bill so it appeased some critics but did not change the *indigenista* model.[53] Stroessner first rejected the bill but later signed it in hopes that it would improve Paraguay's human rights record overseas.[54]

While the law seemed hopelessly delayed in Congress, the Toba-Qom and Enenlhit convinced the Catholic Church to step in on their behalf. In October the Church covertly purchased 15,000 hectares at Casanillo for the Enenlhit and 7,700 hectares for the Toba.[55] The cooperation between the Church and indigenous groups made the regime worry it might lose control of integration. That same month, deputies dramatically increased the INDI's power within the new law even as they curtailed its potential benefits to natives.[56] Congress elevated the INDI to the same level as state-run energy companies and authorized it to control all native peoples and non-Indian advocates.[57] When he learned that the Church had purchased land for the Enenlhit, Samaniego actually congratulated the bishop: "The INDI cannot help but congratulate the Paraguayan Bishops' Conference for this act, which shows its spirit of cooperation in the positive solution to the problems that trouble the indigenous communities in the country, adding itself in this manner to the national *indigenista* policy, which today has been strengthened by Law 904, which as a legal and philosophic tool is an example in America."[58] The defense minister's correspondence shows that while unwilling to enforce the new law, the INDI used the legislation in an effort to gloss over the detrimental effects of its integration agenda and as part of its constant attempt to improve its public image and keep the facade of popular legitimacy.

The extension of cash crops and state development projects, however, threatened native lands even more than misused legislation. Natives now joined forces to discuss how outside attacks had changed their lives. In September 1982 religious leaders from four Ava Guaraní communities in Alto Paraná and Canendiyú issued the following manifesto:

> We are going to pray (*ñembo'é*), we will improve our lives, but we have undocumented lands and need lands in order to improve. They promise us lands and ask us for patience and we see how each time they take more from us and what they originally promised us grows smaller. We are many and the land is small. This problem we present to you. This is our concern: to know whether you can do something to help. In the four communities . . . we have problems, because we are in a dire situation. We ourselves have to be respected, starting by respecting ourselves as we are and for what we are. We desire that no one disturb our prayers and take seriously our community (*yeroky*) that is sacred.[59]

The Guaraní request for assistance shows not only that natives were well aware that state promises carried very little weight. The call for outsiders to respect and honor communal religious expressions indicates that the struggle with Paraguayans had led the Guaraní to greater assertion of their ethnic distinction and self-worth. Guaraní groups disagreed with the state integration program, especially when it severed them from their lands.

In effect, indigenous groups used the native rights bill to focus their own resistance and to push the regime to honor its promises.[60] Catholic legal advisers informed the Enenlhit struggling to regain Riacho Mosquito that the new law could assist them in land claims.[61] Five Enenlhit chiefs began making the arduous boat trip to Asunción to press the INDI to honor Law 904, especially when the Casado Company offered the ancestral sites for sale in the United States and Europe.[62] This time, leaders directly addressed high regime authorities:

> We urgently need these lands. Our people cannot continue to exist. The difficulties that our brothers at Puerto Casado must endure are many and serious, such as the lack of food and work, illness, and severe treatment. Many brothers work only to get a bit of meat to feed their family. That is to say, with Gs.18,000 per month [U.S.$36] they must feed and dress an entire family. But even more do not even have work and must resort to hunting and fishing . . . in order to subsist. If they give us lands, our ancestors' territory, we will cultivate and live on them as did our fathers and grandfathers. . . . Given our situation of extreme need, we come to request that we be allowed to take ownership of these lands and begin to farm and raise cattle on them.[63]

The urgent Enenlhit plea was a desperate one. The leaders gained general sympathy by reviewing their critical economic condition and legitimated their pleas by promising to contribute to local production. Their efforts finally bore fruit. In November 1983 the IBR asked Casado to sell Riacho Mosquito for the Enenlhit. The company refused.

Widespread opposition to state integration clearly had altered native groups, uniting diverse tribes with a common resistance and cause. In November, at the Catholic University, Western Guaraní leader Severo Flores explained rising native unity:

> In general we perceive the whites as trying to satisfy themselves, taking advantage of indigenous people in every possible way, when it suits them, as they did in times of the Conquest . . . the native sees or perceives . . . that they came to take indigenous lands, to steal what we owned on this continent, . . . this is clear enough evidence for *indigenas* to have a clear understanding of the surrounding society. . . . Native groups that still survive today . . . [oppose] the paternalistic tutelage and every acculturation plan put forth by the enveloping society. And for the whites, it is no longer the time to speak in place of the *indígenas*, . . . because they have much to learn from us if they are in the business of building an American culture or culture of a specific nation. Because

indigenous persons today know what they want, know what they do, know what they ask for and, with even greater clarity, what they do not want. The indigenous person always respects another group's culture, and for this reason wishes that their own culture be respected.[64]

Flores showed that increased resistance was transforming indigenous consciousness. He situated indigenous groups securely outside of national society. Natives adopted a discourse that presented *paraguayos* as oppressors and tied them directly to the European conquest and depredations. More important, Flores argued that Indian protests had specific agendas that differed from the state plans for cultural integration and economic development. Indigenous people were aware that by opposing the regime's plans, they were proposing distinct models for society based on their own ways of life and worldviews.

These protests notwithstanding, the pace of state development continued unabated. In 1983 a government development project in Caazapá started to build roads and clear land. Paraguayan and Brazilian settlers by the dozens moved into the area with their cattle, thus raising the cost of the land and placing even more pressure on the Mbyá to abandon their ancestral holdings.[65] Hunters and collectors of *yerba maté* overran the native territories in search of a quick profit. Unlike the Enxet, Enenlhit, or the Ava Guaraní, who aggressively countered outside threats as a group, the Mbyá retreated and isolated themselves in reaction to the invasion. Such a strategy had allowed 2,000 Mbyá to live in ten tightly knit communities and continue a high degree of cultural integrity for centuries despite close proximity to campesinos.[66]

As native groups throughout the countryside worked to oppose threats to their lands, the regime tried to divide and discourage indigenous organization. Rather than back Enenlhit demands for Riacho Mosquito, the INDI sided with the Casado Company and tried to manipulate, coerce, and divide the native leaders. The INDI repeatedly encouraged the Enenlhit to accept offers that did not include any of their ancestral claims and even tried to divide the natives from the Catholic lawyers who represented them.[67] The natives themselves, meanwhile, continued to elicit assistance from regime opponents. National support for the native group reached unprecedented proportions. Never before had an indigenous movement attracted so much attention, and even the pro-regime newspapers supported the Enenlhit.[68] In 1984, 250 citizens, the Paraguayan Lawyers College, and the Catholic University signed a statement that asked the state to expropriate Riacho Mosquito.[69]

Other native struggles also assumed desperate proportions. In June 1984, Mennonites at Sommerfeld shoved down indigenous homes with tractors and bulldozers in a final attempt to evict them. Severo Flores again denounced the violence at the INDI: "My people are very afraid.

Some could no longer stand the threats and left. I have no idea where they have gone."[70] In July, Flores added that "the Mennonites want us to leave, but we will not go. We were born here and will stay where we are. Long before they arrived, our fathers and grandparents hunted and raised crops on this land and they have no right to evict us now."[71] The Mbyá claimed ancestral occupation as sufficient legal validation. Their protests must have moved some sympathetic authorities, for in August local police arrested Mennonite leader Willie Hildebrand and held him for burning Mbyá crops.[72]

The Mbyá struggle can be best explained when situated within the larger context of the protests growing daily against the dictator and his failing economic agenda. By 1984, Stroessner had started to lose his grip over the nation as his long economic boom came to an end. Paraguay had experienced its first balance-of-payments deficit in 1982, after a long decade of growth, and there was little the dictator could do to keep public support except to suppress opposition with vigor.[73] As the natives lost more land, in 1985 their protests became more demanding, focused, and desperate. The Mbyá in Caazapá, for instance, faced a land grab after the regime parceled out their communities for intensive commercial agriculture and ranching. The project laid 230 kilometers of new roads, and logging companies cut into the steepest terrain.[74] The rush of colonists in search of forest commodities forced fourteen Mbyá communities to abandon their ancestral lands throughout the year.[75] State promises of titles only made the depredations worse, as entrepreneurs tried to strip the forest before it was surveyed. Carlino Núñez from Ranchito described his people's loss after a rancher had sold their land and campesinos overran his community:

> We live in these woods that belong to us, that the Creator gave us. The authorities also say that the land we use belongs to us, but the owner wants to sell his lands to Brazilians and Paraguayans, and they want to evict us because we are poor, we do not have money. It is money that is now the boss, and poor people cannot have land. All that is left to the poor is to die. As the Brazilian colonists clear the woods, the animals disappear. For all these reasons I was traveling to Asunción, to speak with officials at the INDI. They assured me that the land problem was already resolved; they gave us hope, but we continue to wait. Already two months have passed and they do not appear.[76]

The Mbyá were desperate because their livelihood had disappeared along with the trees; the state program had destroyed their economic self-sufficiency. Still, Núñez showed a glimmer of hope: he had appealed for understanding and still awaited regime assistance.

The most widely publicized indigenous struggle for land in 1985 occurred in Alto Paraná Department, near Itakyrý. Over one hundred Mbyá lived at Paso Romero, part of the 75,000-hectare La Golondrina ranch. Owner Blas Riquelme, former president of the Chamber of Industry, had for years urged the Mbyá to leave their ancestral territory.[77] Early in October, manager Antonio Rotelo dragged the tribe's religious healer from his home and pushed him onto a narrow log bridge, shouting that his people were to quit the ranch. The manager hit Porfirio Fariña repeatedly with his rifle butt, fired shots close to his head, and finally, tearing off his clothing, threatened to castrate the shaman with his machete.[78] The next day Riquelme himself, accompanied by armed thugs on horseback, arrived and beat the Mbyá men, raped several women, and toppled the people's houses with tractors and torched them. The people fled in terror to the adjacent woods. When one couple returned to collect their possessions, Rotelo raped the wife in front of her husband.[79] United by the expulsion, natives immediately sent chiefs to opposition groups in the capital.[80] Graphic and emotional reports of such abuses raised public support. The popular outcry over the case attracted the attention of foreign human rights agencies and forced the INDI to purchase 1,500 hectares for the Mbyá adjacent to Riquelme's ranch.[81]

As abuses also continued at Sommerfeld, in 1986 the Mbyá resorted to desperate measures. In July the Mennonites' *paraguayo* peons began to cut down the last native trees.[82] Next, workers divided Mbyá settlements with barbed-wire fences to cut off their access to water.[83] Finally, peons began to rape the Mbyá women to intensify the harassment. Mennonite ranchers had promised to free their workers if by some chance the authorities ever arrested them.[84] Clearly the last straw, two Mbyá reported the violent mistreatment to Asunción. When the INDI ignored them, they denounced both the institute and the settlers: "The people from the INDI tried to mislead us; they always ask us to leave because, according to them, we have nothing to do here. They are always on the side of those who have money. I do not understand how foreigners could evict us from our lands; if we are in our traditional place, in our country, we have rights to this place."[85]

Critics of the dictatorship took up the Sommerfeld case. *Última Hora* accused the regime's development plans of "converting Paraguay's beautiful countryside into a desert."[86] The Church asked the regime to either expropriate the lands or to purchase them for the Mbyá.[87] By 1986, Paraguayans were fed up with the worsening economy, evidence of widespread corruption, and the regime's constant, heavy-handed repression. Rallies that demanded a democratic opening shook the country. In March and April, when the Authentic Liberal Radical Party held meetings in the interior, hundreds of peasants risked arrest to show their support. The ruling party mobilized the Macheteros de Santaní, the feared Colorado peasant militia, to repress the rural uprisings. The Church helped to organize large demonstrations against the continued repression. At the end of May, 2,500 priests and lay workers paraded through Asunción to demand social justice and a political opening.[88]

The protesters used forced indigenous integration to criticize the regime for abusing human rights. In 1986 the Catholic Church launched a national campaign on behalf of the Enenlhit. Base ecclesiastic communities, labor unions, and even peasant organizations added their support. Nearly 10,000 people signed a petition demanding the expropriation of Riacho Mosquito. Lawyers clinched the case by showing that the Casado Company had defrauded the government of U.S.$ 3.7 million and had never paid for many of its 5.5 million hectares in the Chaco.[89] Given repression and popular prejudice, such support for a native claim was outstanding.[90]

The Stroessner regime's response to indigenous demands for land was unambiguous as the dictator held fast to plans for integration. Although the weakened regime could not simply make the protests disappear, it did try to destabilize communities that continued some measure of economic independence. By 1986, the Paï Tavyterã had regrouped into more than thirty communities, secured provisional land titles, and regained enough economic independence so that most of them no longer depended on peon wage labor.[91] This type of rural peasant organization directly threatened the dictator's plans for inclusion and dependency. In December 1986 an INDI employee, María Elva González, moved to Amambay and distributed alcohol and clothes in Paï Tavyterã communities. The INDI co-opted native leaders with vehicles, alcohol, and clothing, promising to develop communities and to supply them with consumer goods.[92] Next, in a clear attempt to undermine indigenous autonomy and in the process to make a profit, the INDI extracted truckloads of wood from Paï Tavyterã, Mbyá, and Ava communities.[93]

By this time, however, indigenous activism had gained momentum as it joined the wider social protest against the regime. In July 1987, Paï leaders met with the INDI's president, accused him of ignoring earlier promises, and forbade the regime from ever returning to their communities.[94] The Paï Tavyterã took INDI employees to court, sending González into hiding and her colleague Ignacio Almirón to jail. Regime intervention led to alcoholism and disease as well as to a crisis in leadership and in agricultural production.[95] Still, natives from Amambay had defended their tribal lands, resources, and autonomy.

Native organization only increased. Early in 1987 the Enenlhit took advantage of the unstable political climate and demanded the expropriation of their homeland. They took their request directly to the Senate in June, where leader René Ramírez demanded retribution.[96] As protests mounted, the regime finally lifted the state of siege that had been in effect since 1954, and on July 16 the legislature promised to expropriate Riacho Mosquito.[97] The Enenlhit raised the stakes and presented Congress with 3,000 more non-Indian signatures on their behalf.[98] On July 30 the Senate unanimously expropriated 30,103 hectares from the Casado Company for 300 Enenlhit families, citing the "long and painful indigenous process."[99] As it had at Casanillo, the regime granted land to the Enenlhit to slow growing antigovernment opposition.

While the Enenlhit had recuperated ancestral lands, more native groups were unable to thwart integration. Throughout 1987, Sommerfeld continued to sow Mbyá lands with grass for cattle and crops. Community Km. 225 could use only twenty of their 400 original hectares. In October, Juán Gauto from Yaguary denounced his people's situation: "The cutting of trees continues without ceasing. The place that earlier had many woods is today an empty place because they have cut down all the trees. With this new interference our lands are constantly reduced, and our needs augmented. To continue surviving we urgently need for them to give us lands."[100] The Mbyá had reached a critical stage in their struggle to keep out the immigrants and were clearly aware that their chances of success diminished with increasing speed.

Time had also run out for the Mbyá in Caazapá. In 1987 the World Bank finally suspended loans due to abuses against the natives. This move, however, was an ineffectual slap on the wrist for Stroessner because by this time most native communities were devoid of the forest cover that had been their vital resource. The destruction continued unabated.[101] While clear-cutting in Caazapá was harmful to indigenous groups, it was disastrous for the environment. The extraction of hardwoods removed the highest tree canopy that supported the undergrowth and thus destroyed the forests.[102] Development upset natives' society by forcing them into new productive activities. Through agroforestry, the Guaraní had once employed tens of thousands of hectares through sustainable extraction. The loss of lands forced native groups onto increasingly smaller plots, where they lost critical protein as the animals and the jungle cushion for difficult agricultural years disappeared. As the wild cats and foxes left, the Guaraní lost additional income from the sale of pelts. Natives turned to commercial agriculture and cleared land to plant cotton and tobacco, but unlike agroforestry, this arrangement provided them only with a single crop at harvest and led to hunger during the long growing season. The Mbyá went into debt to support their families and to purchase foodstuffs, tools, herbicides, and insecticides. The primary cultural change was their loss of economic independence to local merchants.[103]

The unresolved indigenous conflicts only added fuel to growing demonstrations in the capital. The Church gained political mileage in August when it announced that Pope John Paul II would visit Paraguay in 1988 and meet with indigenous groups in the Chaco.[104] This message encouraged further demonstrations, and on October 30 the Church united the opposition into a massive show of strength. Archbishop Ismael B. Rolón led 35,000 workers, students, laypersons, and priests on a silent march through the capital in the largest demonstration against Stroessner in thirty-four years. The regime's collapse was in sight.

Contradictions: Indigenous Organization and Stroessner's Demise

In Stroessner's last year, indigenous struggles for land became desperate. In eastern Paraguay especially, non-Indians displaced over two dozen Guaraní communities. Native groups joined forces, and their protests drew attention to the regime's corruption and human rights abuses. Ranching businesses again threatened indigenous lands. On January 19, 1988, Campos Morombí S.A. tried to evict a group of Mbyá from Arroyo Mbói, within the ranch property. Morombí's owner was again Blas Riquelme, and when this time burning their homes to the ground did not force off the Mbyá, the rancher tried to bribe the natives into leaving his property. Instead of accepting the offers, Mbyá chiefs joined neighboring leaders and denounced Riquelme to the IBR, the INDI, NGOs, and finally the Catholic Church.[105] The situation had clearly changed since Riquelme's violent expulsion in 1985 of Mbyá from La Golondrina. The regime was weak enough for a brief but intense lobby to convince the dictator to expropriate the natives' land.[106] Congress granted 1,200 hectares to the Mbyá, and the following day Stroessner left for New York to speak at the United Nations on human rights, with a recent example in hand of his actions on behalf of indigenous rights.[107]

In fact, news about the eviction of indigenous groups clearly influenced opposition political groups in Asunción. In preparation for national elections in February, the Catholic Church published the *Diálogo Nacional*, a call for a democratic opening in which native rights figured prominently: "The indigenous communities aspire to freely choose their future, and to be allowed to create their own human development based on their own life choices as a people." Indigenous leaders had asked to be considered legitimate "authentic nations" within a free Paraguay.[108] The vision of a more equitable society showed a clear indigenous desire to participate more fully within national society. Despite opposition efforts, in February 1988, Stroessner swept the elections in Paraguay for the eighth consecutive time. At age seventy-five, the dictator was the longest-serving head of state in Latin America and the third longest-serving political leader in the world.

Despite the reelection, anticipation of the papal visit rattled the regime. The prospect of such an important meeting, however, was even more significant for the native people. Indigenous communities quickly took advantage of the relaxing political climate to demand that the dictatorship extend greater political protection. The Mbyá at Sommerfeld complained that the Mennonites continued to harass them. The INDI blocked the Mbyá's request.[109] The institute next tried to cancel the meeting between the indigenous people and the pope but ultimately bowed to the Church's popular authority.[110]

Late on May 17, 1988, 700 indigenous people welcomed Pope John Paul II to a Catholic mission in the Chaco. They had chosen Enenlhit leader René Ramírez from Riacho Mosquito to deliver their message. One part stressed native desires: "Whites say we should become civilized. We invite the whites to be civilized and respect us as people, respect our communities and our leaders, respect our lands and our woods, and that they return even a small part of what they have taken from us. Indigenous people want to be friends with all Paraguayans. We want them to let us live in peace and without inconveniences."[111] The loss of tribal lands featured prominently in his speech, and Ramírez accused the INDI of failing to defend indigenous properties: "The white authorities who should defend us, instead defend those who purchased our land with us still living there. The whites have created a law in our favor. The law is good, but they do not apply it in our favor."[112] The presentation was a strong repudiation of the regime's attempt to clear native peoples off their lands and integrate them into *paraguayo* society.

The native people's encounter with the pope scored several victories for their cause. Not only did the pontiff offer them his encouragement and sympathy, but he also recognized their struggle for land and called on those "responsible" to respect the "most dispossessed."[113] When the dictator bid the pope farewell the following day at the President Stroessner International Airport, he referred to the "special attention" his government had given to the native population. John Paul II responded, in front of the television cameras, with a distinct gesture of surprise that clearly showed his disbelief. By indicating his displeasure the pope added fuel to the dictator's critics' fire.[114] As if to confirm the loss of support, the INDI tried immediately to discredit the native message to the pope.[115]

If indeed the papal visit had encouraged the indigenous people, it should not be surprising that native groups promptly intensified their struggles. The Mbyá within Sommerfeld took advantage of heightened attention to native affairs and once again pressed their case against the Canadian immigrants. Clearly desperate, as a last recourse the natives took the INDI to court for not defending their interests. Indigenous people were by this time clearly aware of both their legal rights and the state's refusal to enforce its own laws: "We realize that Law 904 does not serve the indigenous people, but instead only the Mennonites, because it seems as if only they have rights here."[116]

North of Sommerfeld, state integration and development programs devastated native communities. On August 18, 1988, a cavalry division suddenly arrived at the Paï Tavyterã settlement of Takuaguy Oygue, a community in Amambay with one of the last remaining virgin forests. Colonel Lino Oviedo and a band of eight soldiers bearing automatic weapons and dressed in camouflage threatened to shoot the frightened people if they left the community to seek help. A group of army peons began to cut trees with chain saws and drag them out of the woods with bulldozers. Within seven days the group had razed so many trees that five army trucks transported the logs two times per day to the regional capital of Pedro Juán Caballero.[117] Under cover of darkness, community leaders defied Oviedo's threats and escaped to the capital, where they denounced the incursion.[118] The Paï Tavyterã reported that the army had sixty campesinos cutting down their trees with chain saws and twenty trucks removing the logs every day. Within only a few weeks, in fact, soldiers and workers had also completely ravaged indigenous fields of corn, manioc, and beans.[119]

After the regime gave the indigenous protests a cold shoulder, the Paï Tavyterã took their case to neighboring native groups. Late in September, sixteen communities gathered to support Takuaguay Oygue. "On that occasion," the chiefs recalled, "we affirmed, 'either us or the end of the world,' and we decided, given the authorities' indifference, to expel the invaders from our lands."[120] Out of desperation, on October 3, seventy Paï Tavyterã painted themselves for battle and with bows and arrows fell upon the *paraguayos* who were clearing their forest. Most of the soldiers fled in disarray, frightened to death by the sight of the yelling warriors. The Paï Tavyterã took several prisoners but released them when the army pledged to leave the natives in peace.[121]

The regime promises, however, proved once again to be an illusory excuse, simple attempts to defuse indigenous protests. Even in his weakened state, Stroessner was not about to give up a chance to destroy another native community. Six days later a militia troop entered Takuaguay Oygue again, this time firing into the air with automatic weapons. The soldiers detained seven indigenous men and threatened to kill the troublesome community leaders if they ever laid hands on them. Next, the invaders destroyed plantations of corn and watermelon and burned down houses. The entire Paï Tavyterã group fled to the woods in fear, never to return. Within days the army brought in heavy earth-moving equipment and by the end of October had leveled the community woods and sold the lumber, assessed at Gs.324,000,000, or U.S.$400,000, to Brazilian businesses.[122] Native appeals came to naught, and Takuaguay Oygue lost its property.

If the occupation of Takuaguay Oygue was disastrous for the Paï Tavyterã, it gave other groups the incentive to cling even more tenaciously to their lands. The Mbyá were determined to stay on their ancestral properties at Sommerfeld. The decision to remain shows that the Mbyá were keenly aware of the ongoing negotiations. To build public support, the indigenous people played off nationals against the immigrants. Ignoring the Mbyá's own historical separation from national society, Máximo González reminded *paraguayos* that the Mennonites were new arrivals: "This place has always been our site. My grandparents and my parents have lived here since time inmemorial. . . . It should not be possible to give priority to the *mennonitas* who moved here long after we did, but instead we should be considered as equals."[123] This developing consciousness, through which indigenous people identified themselves as having a greater right to the land than the new immigrants, appealed to those *paraguayos* who resented the wealthy Mennonites. When the Catholic Church took the Mbyá case directly to the legislature early in November, lawyers employed this new indigenous strategy: "These privileges today create an irritating inequality for the impoverished masses submerged in backwardness and misery, and we think that the *menonitas* [*sic*] should be incorporated immediately into the class that contributes to the nation, to begin paying back Paraguayan society for all the benefits they have received from it."[124] By casting native groups as part of the larger lower classes, the Church showed that the Mbyá were, in fact, integrated enough to deserve full legal protection and rights. Their lawyers upset the regime's case by throwing back at the state its very plans to include the native peoples.

The logic of this argument was not lost on the dictatorship, which by this time was unraveling from the inside and was under widespread attacks from its opposition. In December, Minister of Defense Germán Gaspar Martínez again employed indigenous rights to praise the dictator: "The Indians of the country are active subjects of a government policy from a patriotic and nationalist administration, presided over by Alfredo Stroessner." Every year, General Martínez claimed, state *indigenista* policy "enriches and vindicates indigenous cultures again, integrating them into national society. In this way by every year's end we have more lands, more schools, more indigenous professionals, more health [care], and a sustained increase in the aboriginal population . . . inserted today in the great fatherland, which belongs to everyone as the Republic of Paraguay."[125] Indeed, the indigenous people by this time had forced their way into national affairs to the extent that they were more a part of wider society than ever before. Curiously, however, as native testimonies indicate, they did so in order to perpetuate what they understood to be distinct cultural and spatial barriers between themselves and the national majority. Thus, even as they helped to undermine the dictatorship by demanding economic autonomy and ancestral lands, the native peoples had forged a wider pan-indigenous unity and sense of ethnic distinction. This new consciousness became the foundation for native struggles.

Conclusion: Indigenous People and the Fall of the Stroessner Dictatorship

Indigenous groups had helped to weaken the disintegrating regime by challenging the integration program, by demanding their ancestral lands, and by calling attention to the dictator's poor record on human rights. These actions contributed to widespread popular discontent against the endemic corruption and Stroessner's failed economic program. Indigenous protests had also forced the dictatorship to change the way it portrayed its economic and social policies. Growing native organization and protests in rural areas were a thorn in the regime's side, but they alone were not capable of overthrowing the regime. Despite widespread protests, the dictator clung to power through a combination of repression and deception. Ultimately it was his second in command, General Andrés Rodríguez, who overthrew Stroessner in February 1989 when he saw his chance at the presidency disappearing.[126] The new leader immediately pledged to preside over the transition to a full democracy, including freedom of assembly and press, widespread political organization, and even a new constitution.

Not to be left out of the new democratic opening after such a struggle, indigenous people pushed the new government to respect their organized and united front. Life following the regime continued to be difficult, and natives faced an uphill battle given the continuation of many authoritarian structures and personalities. Still, after a determined effort, indigenous people successfully lobbied until the new state dedicated an entire chapter of the 1992 national constitution to native rights. This formal inclusion in the new body of law made clear their important role in Stroessner's overthrow. The struggle with the Stroessner regime had changed indigenous consciousness until they identified themselves as a concerted lobby bloc opposed to a non-Indian economic and social agenda. The contradiction inherent in this successful struggle, however, was that pressing their demands for autonomy and protection actually integrated the natives into national society and culture further than they had ever expected. While indigenous people actually helped to undermine and bring down the regime, then, Stroessner's plans for integration to a large degree succeeded.

Seven years later, General Lino Oviedo tried to overthrow President Raúl Cubas Grau. Critics had already charged for years that Cubas was only a puppet for the ambitious general. Backed by the police and the army, in March 1999, Oviedo saw the opportunity to finally assume the role of dictator. To his surprise, thousands of students and workers took to the streets of the capital and prevented the strongman from seizing control. Again, the Indians helped the protestors, reprising a role they had played ten years earlier in the establishment of democracy. This role, as in 1989, was unappreciated but helped to end and prevent authoritarian rule.

Notes

1. See Andrew Nickson, "Tyranny and Longevity: Stroessner's Paraguay," *Third World Quarterly* 10, no. 1 (January 1988): 237–59; and John Hoyt Williams, "Paraguay's Stroessner: Losing Control?" *Current History* 86, no. 516 (January 1987): 25–35. Esther Prieto, in her article "Indigenous Peoples in Paraguay" (Van Cott, ed., *Indigenous Peoples and Democracy*, 1994) argued that natives had contributed to democratic change but did not show how they had concretely done so.

2. See, for example, Kevin Middlebrook on Mexico, Thomas Skidmore and Maria Elena Moreira Alves on Brazil, and Marguerite Bouvard on Argentina.

3. One exception is some articles in Donna Lee Van Cott, ed., *Indigenous Peoples and Democracy in Latin America* (New York, 1994).

4. For a detailed analysis of Stroessner's rise to power see Paul Lewis, *Paraguay under Stroessner* (Chapel Hill, 1980), 63–72.

5. Hugh M. Hamill, "Introduction," in his *Caudillos: Dictators in Spanish America* (Norman, OK, 1992).

6. Lewis, *Paraguay under Stroessner*, 64.

7. Benedict Anderson, *Imagined Communities* (New York, 1987), 16, 37, 140.

8. James D. Cockcroft, "Paraguay's Stroessner: The Ultimate Caudillo?" in Hugh M. Hamill, *Caudillos: Dictators in Spanish America* (Norman, OK, 1992), 339.

9. Decreto 1,343, *Por el cual se crea el Departamento de Asuntos Indígenas dependiente del Ministerio de Defensa Nacional* (Asunción, 1958), 1; DAI documents, 20, INDI. See also the appendix to Decreto 1,343, DAI documents, n.p., INDI.

10. "Grupos de Indios Guayaquíes aparecieron en Zona de Abaí," *La Tribuna*, October 17, 1959, 7; Kim Hill and Magdalena Hurtado, *Aché Life History: The Ecology and Demography of a Foraging People* (n.p., 1996), 49.

11. Mark Münzel, *The Aché Indians: Genocide in Paraguay* (Copenhagen, 1973), 52.

12. Mark Münzel, "Manhunt," in Richard Arens, *Genocide in Paraguay* (Philadelphia, 1976), 29.

13. Ibid., 32.

14. Ibid.

15. Miguel Chase Sardi, Augusto Brun, and Miguel Angel Enciso, *Situación sociocultural, económica, juridico-política actual de las comunidades indígenas del Paraguay* (Asunción, 1990), 41.

16. Chase Sardi et al., *Situación sociocultural*, 225.

17. James Abourezk, Senator for South Dakota, "Genocide Activities in Paraguay," *Congressional Record–Senate*, March 8, 1974, 5941–45.

18. Dennis Hanratty and Sandra W. Meditz, eds., *Paraguay: A Country Study* (Washington, DC, 1990), 196.

19. Infanzon to Bartomeu Melià, Asunción, April 17, 1974, INDI, File 110, CEE, 1974; "No hay genocidio en el Paraguay porque no hay intención de destruir grupos indígenas," *ABC*, March 9, 1974, 7.

20. Marcial Samaniego, *ABC Color*, May 9, 1974.

21. Münzel, *The Ache: Genocide Continues in Paraguay*, International Work Group for Indigenous Affairs document 17 (Copenhagen, 1974), 26.

22. *Marandú* is Guaraní for "information." The NGO informed indigenous people about their legal rights.

23. "Se inició ayer en San Bernadino reunión de líderes indígenas de la selva tropical," *ABC*, October 9, 1974, 14. See also Adolfo Colombres, *Por la liberación del indígena* (n.p., n.d.), 248.

24. "Parlamento Indio pidió se devuelva tierras a tribus con títulos de propiedad de las mismas," *ABC*, October 15, 1974, 9.

25. Angel Llorente and Antonio Carmona, *Parte crónica de el Proyecto Maranú*, "Proyecto de la Interamericana Fundation [*sic*]," Unpublished monograph, Miguel Chase Sardi Personal Archive, Asunción, 1973–1976, 24.

26. David Maybury-Lewis, "Becoming Indian in Lowland South America," in Greg Urban and Joel Sherzer, eds., *Nation-States and Indians in Latin America* (Austin, 1991), 222.

27. Llorente and Carmona, *Parte crónica de el Proyecto Maranú*, 30.

28. Kathleen Teltsch, "UN Body Accuses U.S. on Paraguay," *New York Times*, April 6, 1976, 5.

29. Francísco Cáceres, Toba Qom leader, interview, Cerrito, July 6, 1995.

30. "Los Tobas-Lenguas viven el sueño de la tierra propia," *Última Hora*, February 14, 1977, 20.

31. Father José Seelwische, interview, Asunción, June 29, 1995.

32. Ibid.

33. P. W. Stunnenberg, *Entitled to Land: The Incorporation of the Paraguayan and Argentinean Gran Chaco and the Spatial Marginalization of the Indian People* (Fort Lauderdale, 1993), 105.

34. Paraguayan Episcopal Conference to Marcial Samaniego, Juan M. Frutos, and Gauloise S.A., Asunción, August 31, 1979, INDI, File 122.2, CER, 1979.

35. Ibid.

36. "Tobas reclaman devolución de tierras que constituyeran su habitat original," *Última Hora*, March 15, 1980, 16.

37. "La Gauloise informa a la opinión pública," *ABC*, November 16, 1980, n.p.

38. Colonel Oscar Centurión, former director of the INDI, interview, Asunción, March 13, 1995.

39. Encouraged by Centurión, the Institute of Rural Welfare (IBR) based its right to expropriate the land on the Agrarian Statute of 1963, whose 16th article assigned the IBR with securing land to create indigenous settlements. See also "Decretan ocupación de tierras para asentamiento de indígenas," *Última Hora*, October 11, 1980, 11.

40. "Tobas-Maskoy esperan ocupar los terrenos de Casanillo," *ABC*, November 24, 1980, 18. The press and national authorities always referred to the Enenlhit as Toba-Maskoy.

41. Seelwische, interview. See also "Mañana ocuparán tierras de Casado, en Casanillo," *ABC*, December 14, 1980, 18.

42. "Tobas-Maskoy podrán ocupar tierras," *Última Hora*, December 27, 1980, 6.

43. "Asumió director del INDI: Extrañeza y malestar en indígenas," *Última Hora*, December 23, 1980, 12.

44. "Causa protesta la destitución del director del INDI," *ABC*, December 21, 1980, 19.

45. "Nos preocupa cambio en INDI," *Última Hora*, December 24, 1980, n.p.

46. Joseph Winfield Fretz, *Pilgrims in Paraguay* (Scottsdale, 1953), 48, 50.

47. "Mbyá denunciarón presiones de colonos Mennonitas," *Diálogo Indígena Misionero* 2, no. 6 (November 1981): 5.

48. "Desalojo de Mbyá en Sommerfeld, Le Rezan a su Diós pero nos dejan sin pan," *Hoy*, September 8, 1981, 16.

49. Chase Sardi et al., *Situación sociocultural*, 373.

50. "Los indígenas siguen siendo despojados de sus tierras," *La Tribuna*, September 3, 1981, 3.

51. "Desean elaborar una 'ley completa' para el indígena," *ABC*, May 10, 1981, 19.

52. "Existiría premura para el estudio del proyecto de ley," *ABC*, May 12, 1981, 27.

53. "Proyecto de ley que establece el 'Estatuto del Indígena,'" *Hoy*, September 2, 1981, 10.

54. Deputy Julio César Frutos, interview, Asunción, November 9, 1994.

55. Seelwische, interview; "Nuevo Horizonte para los Toba Qom," *Diálogo Indígena Misionero* 2, no. 6 (November 1981): 12.

56. Julio César Frutos, "El Estatuto del Indígena: Sus antecedentes cercanos," *Suplemento Antropológico* 17, no. 2 (December 1981): 74.

57. "Anteproyecto de Ley que Establece Régimen Jurídico de las Comunidades Indígenas del Paraguay," INDI, July 1980, 11, 13; "El Senado aprobó la creación del estatuto de los indígenas," *Hoy*, December 11, 1981, 8.

58. Marcial Samaniego to Bishop Olevar, CEP, Asunción, January 27, 1982, S.I. 019, INDI, CER, 1982.

59. "Nuestro Yerok es sagrado," *Diálogo Indígena Misionero* 3, no. 8 (December 1982): 12.

60. See, for example, "Estatuto de las comunidades indígenas, un instrumento válido?" *Diálogo Indígena Misionero* 3, no. 8 (December 1982): 10.

61. Mirna Vázquez, interview, Asunción, October 20, 1994.

62. Gladys Casaccia and Mirna Vázquez, *La lucha por la tierra en defensa de la vida: El Pueblo Maskoy frente a Carlos Casado S.A.* (Asunción, 1986), 40.

63. "Nuestro pueblo no puede seguir así," *Última Hora,* January 5, 1984, 10.

64. Severo Flores, "Las comunidades indígenas frente a la sociedad nacional," *Suplemento Antropológico* 19, no. 1 (June 1984): 98–99.

65. "Proyecto de desarrollo de Caazapá," *Dialogo Indígena Misionero* 5, no. 13 (June 1984): 13.

66. Esther Prieto, *Entre la resignación y la esperanza* (Asunción, 1989), 48; Robert Smith and Ramón Fogel, "The Invisible Guaraní: The Effects of Development Projects on the Chiripá and Mbyá of Paraguay," unpublished manuscript, Lawrence, Kansas, 1982, 34. See also Ramón Fogel, *El proceso de modernización y el deterioro de las comunidades indígenas* (Asunción, 1989), 64.

67. Mirna Vázquez, interview.

68. See, for example, "Maskoy: No ejecutaron hasta ahora la mensura," *Noticias*, April 27, 1985, 13.

69. Two Hundred Public Citizens to General Martínez, INDI, Asunción, October 4, 1984, Archivo Equipo Nacional de Misiones.

70. "Continúan presiones para desalojo de los Mbyá," *Diálogo Indígena Misionero* 5, no. 13 (June 1984): 6.

71. "Mennonitas ingresaron con topadoras a un asentamiento: Nuevamente hostigan a indígenas Mbyá," *Hoy*, July 10, 1984, 19.

72. Miguel Chase Sardi, "Paraguay: Situación de los indígenas," *América Indígena* 49, no. 3 (July–September 1989): 424.

73. Nickson, "Tyranny and Longevity," 248.

74. Richard Reed, *Forest Dwellers, Forest Protectors: Indigenous Models for International Development* (Needham Heights, 1997), 83.

75. "Indígenas en áreas del Proyecto Caazapá," *Diálogo Indígena Misionero* 6, no. 17 (April 1985): 3.

76. Fogel, *El proceso de modernización*, 91.

77. "Denuncian quema de capueras en Paso Romero," *Hoy*, September 24, 1985, 19.

78. Americas Watch, *Paraguay: Latin America's Oldest Dictatorship under Pressure* (Washington, DC, 1986).

79. Ibid., 60.

80. "A la Opinión Pública," *El Diario*, November 3, 1985, 6.

81. "Comunidad 'Mbyá' aceptó el asentamiento de 1.500 Has," *Última Hora*, May 30, 1986, 16.

82. "Mennonitas hostigan a comunidad Mbyá," *Diálogo Indígena Misionero* 7, no. 22 (July 1986): 4.

83. "Mennonitas: De perseguidos a perseguidores," *Nuestro Tiempo* 14 (October 1986): 41.

84. "Prosigue conflicto Mbyá en Sommerfeld," *Diálogo Indígena Misionero* 7, no. 23 (August 1986): 4.

85. "Comunidad Mbyá-Apyteré denuncia a menonitas [*sic*]," *Última Hora*, July 23, 1986, 16.

86. "Los Mbyá Apyteré defienden su derecho a la vida," *Última Hora*, July 26, 1986, 12.

87. "Menonitas [*sic*] hostigan a los indígenas en Sommerfeld," *Sendero*, August 1, 1986, 10.

88. Williams, "Paraguay's Stroessner," 26.

89. "Más firmas incurrieron en fraude," *El Diario*, November 28, 1985, 11.

90. In 1986 and 1987, for example, the government reported 162 arrests in cases relating to land disputes. Human rights and peasant organizations reported that more arrests, usually involving torture, also took place. Americas Watch, *Paraguay: Repression in the Countryside* (New York and Washington, 1988), 17.

91. "Estudio sobre el proceso de los Paï Tavyterã de 1972 a 1988," unpublished mimeograph, Servicios Profesionales Antropológicos y Jurídicos, Asunción, March 1988, 4.

92. "Recuento histórico-analítico de los trabajos con los Paï Tavyterã," Unpublished manuscript, Asociación Indigenista del Paraguay (AIP), 88.

93. "Denuncian venta ilegal de madera de colonos indígenas," *El Diario*, March 21, 1987, 23; Crispín Torres, Yvykatú, to Dr. Gadea, Coronel Oviedo, September 3, 1987, Guaraní Project files, AIP.

94. Friedl Grünberg, "Estudio sobre el proceso de los Paï Tavyterã de 1972 a 1988, evaluación de las consecuencias . . . ," SEPSAJ (Asunción, 1988), 24.

95. "Denuncian a dos supuestos funcionarios de la entidad," *La Tarde*, March 24, 1987, 26; "Recuento histórico-analítico de los trabajos con los Paï Tavyterã," 95.

96. "Los sufrimientos aumentan y no tenemos tierras donde vivir," *Última Hora*, June 6, 1987, 11.

97. "Los Maskoy solicitan expropiar tierras," *La Tarde*, June 4, 1987, 26. See also, "El Pueblo Maskoy frente a Carlos Casado S.A.," *El Pueblo*, January 28, 1987, 11.

98. "Nuevas muestras de solidaridad para con Maskoy," *Hoy*, July 22, 1987, 21; "Otras 3,000 firmas dan su apoyo a los maskoy [*sic*]," *Última Hora*, August 21, 1987, 16.

99. "Senado aprobó expropiación," *El Diario*, July 31, 1987, 11.

100. "Se agudiza un problema de tierra con indígenas," *Hoy*, October 15, 1987, 26.

101. Reed, *Forest Dwellers, Forest Protectors*, 84.

102. Ibid., 89.

103. Ibid., 93–98.

104. Seelwische, interview; "El Papa estará con los indios," *El Diario*, August 31, 1987, 18.

105. "Reclaman cese de presiones a comunidades Mbyá-Apyteré," *Última Hora*, April 9, 1988, 20.

106. "IBR solicitará 1,200 Has. para indígenas Mbyá Apyteré," *Patria*, April 18, 1988, 14.

107. "Expropian tierras para indígenas Mbyá Apyteré," *Última Hora*, June 4, 1988, 10.

108. "Conclusiones del Diálogo Nacional: Indígenas aspiran a que se reconozca su presencia," *Última Hora*, January 21, 1988, 16.

109. "Posiciones encontradas, del IBR y del INDI, ante el caso," *Última Hora*, June 30, 1988, 22.

110. "INDI no organiza reunión de indígenas con el Papa," *La Tarde*, January 27, 1988, 15.

111. "Discurso de bienvenida dirigida a su santidad Juán Pablo Segundo," unpublished mimeograph, Mariscal Estigarribia, May 17, 1988, AENM.

112. Ibid.

113. "Juan Pablo II se pronuncio a los indígenas," *Diálogo Indígena Misionero* 9, no. 29 (July 1988): 15.

114. Miguel Carter, *El Papel de la Iglesia en la Caida de Stroessner* (Asunción, 1989), 123.

115. "Le hicieron leer el mensaje al cacique," *El Diario*, May 21, 1988, 10.

116. "Nos quieren dar tierras feas y con muchos esteros," *Última Hora*, July 1, 1988, n.p.

117. "Denuncia del Ecocidio Cometido en el Tekoha Paï Tavyterã de Takuaguay-Oygue," *Suplemento Antropológico* 23, no. 2 (December 1988): 225.

118. The Paï leaders presented their case to the INDI, the Institute of Rural Welfare, the Legislative branch, and the Supreme Court without receiving any help. *Dialogo Indígena Misionero* 9, no. 30 (October 1988): 3. See also "Denuncia del Ecocidio Cometido," 225.

119. "Denuncia del Ecocidio Cometido," 226.

120. Ibid.

121. "Se saben más detalles del incidente con los nativos Pai," *Última Hora*, October 14, 1988, 28.

122. "Denuncia del Ecocidio Cometido," 227.

123. Ibid., 15.

124. "Privilegios de menonitas [*sic*] van en detrimento de indígenas," *Última Hora,* November 8, 1988, 21.

125. "Un saldo a favor del indigenismo," *Última Hora*, December 27, 1988, 16.

126. "Paraguay Coup: Battle for Succession," *New York Times*, February 4, 1989, A5.

III

Indians and Guerrillas

7

Villagers at Arms: War and Counterrevolution in the Central-South Andes

Orin Starn

It is ironic that Peru, one of the countries with the largest number of native people in Latin America, both as a percentage of the population and in terms of absolute numbers, has not had a significant indigenous movement while its Andean neighbors, Ecuador and Bolivia, have had numerous very strong ones. This fact is in large part due to the guerrilla war that began in Peru in 1980, when the Maoist Shining Path (Sendero Luminoso) made its appearance. At first, it seemed that the Shining Path would be able to hook into Andean culture and seduce the highland Indians into following their ideology. Shining Path adherents thought that their plan for autarky would be popular among the peasants, because they assumed that thus they would be able to return to their Andean roots and be free of the European influence.

The Shining Path was wrong. As Orin Starn shows, its totalitarian violent ways turned off the peasants. Moreover, the Peruvian army, after behaving in many ways like their guerrilla enemies, wisely began to offer concrete benefits to the villagers, though even so within a context fraught with violence. They used their superior resources to force the peasants to create militias that fought the Senderistas. In the end, this strategy proved to be successful, though at a high cost to the peasants. Nevertheless, this history of repression and organization of and by the army helps to explain why Peru did not develop a significant indigenous movement. Now that the guerrillas are virtually gone, will the indigenous people organize as such? It is too early to tell, although the 2001 election of Alejandro

From Orin Starn, "Villagers at Arms: War and Counterrevolution in the Central-South Andes," *Shining and Other Paths: War and Society in Peru, 1980–1995*, ed. Steve J. Stern (Durham: Duke University Press, 1998), 224–57. Reprinted by permission of Duke University Press.

Toledo, who billed himself as the first Indian president, suggests that the Indianist movement might have a future in Peru.
  Orin Starn is a cultural anthropologist who teaches at Duke University.

> His laughter shatters . . . all the familiar land-
> marks of my thought—our thought, the thought
> that bears the stamp of our age and our geogra-
> phy—breaking all the ordered surfaces and
> planes with which we are accustomed to tame
> the wild profusion of existing things.
> —Michel Foucault on the Argentine writer Jorge
> Luis Borges[1]

In 1993, I gave a lecture at Ayacucho's Huamanga University. Ayacucho is a city of contrasts, of ponchoed peasants and mini-skirted teenagers and colonial churches and cement-block houses, set against the painful beauty of dry mountains and a turquoise Andean sky. Originally founded under the Spanish Viceroyalty, the university reopened in 1959 as part of the Peruvian government's push to "modernize" the "backward" interiors of the national territory. But the school is best known as the birthplace of the Communist Party of Peru-Shining Path, the Maoist revolutionaries who have fought a thirteen-year war to topple the Peruvian state.[2] The Shining Path founder, Abimael Guzmán, now imprisoned, taught philoso-phy there in the 1960s, and the core of his cadre were students. After the occupation of Ayacucho in late 1982, army troops made frequent raids into the university to murder and kidnap suspected rebels. Soon, the Shin-ing Path also began to kill students and staff on charges of collaboration with the military, including seven professors. Fear hung over the entire city of Ayacucho, whose name in Quechua means "Corner of the Dead," as the terror of the dirty war between the army and the guerrillas engulfed the highlands.

Now, however, my friend, a young history professor, assured me that it was calm enough for even a visiting *gringo* to lecture. Before a packed hall (the talk was mandatory for students in the social sciences), I gave a spiel about anthropology in the United States. Still, I was uneasy when question time arrived. A few years before, when I spoke at Lima's San Marcos University, a Shining Path militant stood to denounce "Yankee imperialism" and called for renewed commitment to the "people's war," triggering a chair-throwing melee with his classmates. This time, how-ever, the climate was completely different. One student asked about Clifford Geertz; another about recent debates in Andeanist anthropology. After the class, people had more urgent questions. How hard is it to get a visa to the United States? And had I ever met Yoko Ono or John Lennon?

Leninism displaced by Lennonism? This was how another Peruvian friend described it when I told him the story. To be sure, the recent and violent past has not vanished. Many Ayacuchans, including students, seem to sense the truth of Walter Benjamin's famous injunction that "even the dead will not be safe from the enemy if he wins" and the consequent urgency of "seiz[ing] hold of a memory as it flashes up at a moment of danger."[3] Tales circulate in living rooms and on street corners of loved ones tortured or disappeared by the military, a stubborn refusal to acquiesce to the state's desire to erase the use of terror from collective memory. At the same time, however, few Ayacuchans are attracted any longer by the Shining Path, which has left a grisly trail of massacred villagers, murdered mayors, and burned crops in the name of the fight for a Maoist utopia. With none of the original romance of a popular uprising, and as Marxism and the dream of revolution have unraveled across Latin America, the Shining Path barely survives across the arid mesas and blue-gray peaks of this Andean department of half a million people. Many Ayacuchans from all walks of life speak of a sense that *"hemos pasado lo peor*—the worst has passed," and even proffer a guarded optimism about the future.

Much of the talk about the war's ebb has centered on the capture in 1992 of Abimael Guzmán. What went far less noticed in the hubbub over the arrest of the man regarded by his followers as "the greatest living Marxist-Leninist" was that the Shining Path's influence had already declined over much of the rural Andes. Their Maoist blueprint projected the encirclement of Peru's cities from the countryside to "put the noose around the neck of imperialism and the reactionaries . . . and garrot[ing] them by the throat," in Guzmán's words.[4] By the start of this decade, however, more than 3,500 villages in the departments of Apurímac, Ayacucho, Huancavelica, and Junín had organized what came to be known as *rondas campesinas*, or peasant patrols, to fight the Shining Path.[5] Despite the assassinations of hundreds of patrollers, or *ronderos*, the alliance of the peasants and the military pushed the Maoists almost completely out of former strongholds, from the stony canyons of Huanta and snowy peaks of Comas to the rainy valley of the Apurímac River. How to deal with the *rondas* was reportedly a main question at the December 1991 Lima meeting of the Shining Path's Central Committee. The "scientifically guaranteed" logic of Guzmán's plan was upended in a reversal as startling as a *pachakuti*, the inversion of heaven and earth predicted in Andean mythology, as peasants rose in arms against a revolution waged in their name.

This essay examines the history of the rondas campesinas.[6] Easy characterizations of the patrollers as either brutish Hobbesian thugs or noble Tolstoian defenders of pastoral traditions or national sovereignty collapse in the face of this unanticipated turn in Peru's war. "Swings from noble savage to murderous savage, from shattered victim to heroic resister," as anthropologist Irene Silverblatt affirms about representations of Peru's indigenous peoples in the seventeenth century, "have drained the life and lessons" of Andean history under colonialism. To avoid the same mistake with Peru's postcolonial peasants, we need to grapple with the compromised histories—the stiff limits and unintended consequences, split allegiances, missed chances and complicities—that make us "contradictory selves, part of contradictory worlds."[7] The need to push against the confines of dualism and linear thinking is manifest not only in the fragmentation, intertextuality, and massive commodification of the postindustrial megalopolises of Latin America or the United States. In the countryside of the Third World, precisely in those "isolated" and "remote" villages that remain the targets of so much metropolitan discourse of authenticity and Otherness, the wild contours of the social landscape turn out to be just as defiant of our preconceived categories and models, and the world also to be moving in more than one direction.

The Cultural Politics of War and the Rondas Campesinas

"Medieval Villages" and Andeanism

As I found it in 1993, Cangari-Viru Viru perched on a dry ridge above the Cachi River.[8] The villagers had built eighteen guard towers of adobe brick and red tile into the mud wall that enclosed their fortified settlement of ninety families, five miles to the southwest of the town of Huanta. In the crisp light of the Andean dawn, a stream of women and men headed down to the riverplain's patchwork quilt of green and brown fields to tend crops and animals. They returned in the evening, herding goats and cows up the winding footpath and inside the walls. By eight P.M., the men on the ronda for the night took their posts with one-shot homemade guns of iron pipe, called *hechizos*, shotguns, and Mauser rifles, ready to defend against raids from across the shallow river. Except for the rifles, the most immediate comparison might have been with a hilltown of Medieval Europe, perhaps San Gimignano or Rocamadour, where the inhabitants of eleventh-century agrarian societies also withdrew at night into walled enclaves to protect against what the Jewish historian Marc Bloch, himself later assassinated by the Gestapo, called the "disorder and havoc" of dangerous times.[9]

Of course, many outsiders have compared the Andes to Medieval Europe. "Feudal," "archaic," and "superstitious" are just some of the adjectives in novelist Mario Vargas Llosa's well-known report on the 1983 massacre of seven journalists in Uchuraccay, just eight hours uphill from Cangari-Viru Viru.[10] Whether as praiseworthy defenders of indigenous ways or, as for Vargas Llosa, backward brutes, villagers figure in the broad tradition of Andeanism as the inhabitants of a primordial "Andean world" isolated from the fast pace and advanced technology of the present-day West. In Peru, this vision maps onto an imagined geography that presents the coast, and especially Spanish-settled Lima, as "modern," "official," and "Western" in contrast with the "premodern," "deep," and "non-Western" Andes. As Vargas Llosa puts it about Uchuraccay's villagers, "they come from a Peru different from the . . . modern European Peru . . . in which I live, an ancient archaic Peru that has survived in these sacred mountains despite centuries of isolation and adversity."[11]

A great deal of recent scholarship emphasizes the need to avoid the trap of the representation of village societies in the Third World as a moribund artifact of a bygone epoch. In fact, the Medieval analogy unravels on a closer look at Cangari-Viru Viru. This village was settled only in 1990. Then-commander of Huanta's Eighth Battalion, Lt. Col. Alfonso Hurtado Robles, known as "El Platanazo—the Big Banana" for his pale skin and unusual height—along with his main lieutenant, Sergeant Jhonny (*sic*) Zapata, or "Centurión," spearheaded an aggressive campaign to organize the 56,000 inhabitants of the province's countryside against the Shining Path.[12] In the cactus hills of the lower valley, the army ordered the villagers to leave their scattered farmhouses for nucleated settlements, or *agrupaciones*, and to organize into a patrol system. "Centurión arrived and told us to [become] agruparnos and start rondas, or we'd see what happened," remembers Antonio Quispe, who owns an acre of land and works in construction in the town of Huanta.[13] The families of two scattered settlements along the Cachi River—Cangari and Viru Viru—built and moved into the hyphenated village. Everyone became a rondero under the command of the two villagers entrusted by the army with the titles of "commando" and "civil defense committee president." Another reminder of the flimsiness of the fiction of the timeless Other, and the untenability of the distinction between societies "with" and "without" history (see Wolf 1982), Cangari-Viru Viru proves a product of these last years of the twentieth century, and in particular of a military plan to block the Shining Path's bid for revolution.

So does Cangari-Viru Viru boil down to coercion? Critics have charged that the military organizes by force, placing unarmed peasants on the front line of a vicious war. "Peasants become cannon fodder for Shining Path reprisals," as one leftist senator told me in 1989.[14] Many journalists and scholars have pointed to the danger of the resettlements and patrols devolving into "paramilitary groups" that "extort," "blackmail," "rob," and "pillage," pitting the poor against the poor to quicken the disintegration of the delicate fabric of Andean life.[15] To these observers, the history of the rondas campesinas appears the same as the Guatemalan army's Vietnam-inspired "strategic hamlets" and civil patrols, an extension of the brutalization of the poor majorities by repressive Latin American regimes.[16]

It might be asserted that the Peruvian military's recruitment of peasants echoes the Spanish Conquest, when Pizarro's band of 150 adventurers used a mass of native auxiliaries to topple the Inca Empire.[17] Imposed resettlement also has a colonial genealogy. As part of a design to "civilize" Andeans, and to establish a steady labor supply for the giant mines of Potosí and Huancavelica, Viceroy Francisco Toledo forced the dispersed native population in the 1570s into Spanish-supervised villages, or *reducciones*.[18] Historian Alberto Flores Galindo invokes these historical antecedents in his 1987 description of the counterinsurgency forces as a "colonial army," the evil protagonists of a vicious war of disappearance and massacre of Quechua-speaking villagers in Ayacucho's impoverished countryside.[19] Then-commander Clemente Noel, who studied at the U.S.-run School of the Americas in Panama, relied mostly on outright intimidation, including the assassination of patrol opponents, to start the first rondas, then more commonly known as "Comités de Defensa Civil" (Civil Defense Committees).[20] Navy infantrymen controlled the first resettlements, or *"bases civiles"* (civil bases) like Ccarhuapampa outside the town of Tambo. Meanwhile, Shining Path columns assassinated suspected military collaborators with the troops, dubbing them *"yanaumas,"* or black heads, for the ski masks that some of the first patrollers wore to conceal their identities. The rebels also raided villages where rondas had started. In July 1986, for instance, they descended upon Ayacucho's Cochas, slitting the throats of eighteen villagers, including a four-year-old girl and an eighty-two-year-old woman, amid shouts of "Death to Wretches [collaborators with the rondas]" and "Long Live the Revolution and Gonzalo" (Guzmán's *nom de guerre*).[21] Much of the counterinsurgency's history backs a view of the rondas campesinas as furthering the suffering of Andean peasants, deepening what another of Peru's leading historians, Nelson Manrique, has called *"manchay tiempo"* (the time of fear).[22]

But Cangari-Viru Viru also undercuts this reduction of the rondas campesinas to simple coercion. Initially, the Shining Path won the sympathy of many Huantinos, including on the Cachi River, for its punishment of adultery and thievery, and appeal to the desires in an impoverished countryside for a more just order. Many of the high-school and university students who formed the bulk of the cadre came from rural families, and sometimes used local ties of kin and friendship to promote the revolutionary cause.[23] Mistakenly, if perhaps understandably, some U.S. scholars proclaimed the Shining Path a "peasant rebellion" or "agrarian revolt."[24] A view of the Maoists as an indigenous insurrection dovetailed with the Andeanist vision of the mountains as a primitive locale of perennial turmoil and rebellion as well as the concept of the insurrectionary villager that was a mainstay of U.S. scholarship on rural upheaval in the wake of the Vietnam War. But this portrayal overlooked that the Shining Path was begun by privileged intellectuals in the city of Ayacucho, and that the revolutionaries were, by 1983, as active in metropolitan Lima as in Andean villages. More broadly, it ignored that the party operated through a rigid hierarchy by race and class that replicated the social order it sought to overthrow. Dark-skinned kids born in poverty filled the bottom ranks under a leadership composed mostly of light-skinned elites.[25] Although it had the approval of some poor farmers in particular places over specific periods of time, the Shining Path was never an organic uprising of the downtrodden, much less one of what anthropologist Eric Wolf calls "the peasant wars of the 20th century."[26]

These tenuous roots help to explain the Shining Path's decline along the Cachi River. By 1990, most villagers realized that the military was not about to "collapse before the glorious advances of the people's war," as the first cadre in Cangari had promised in 1982. For example, Lidia Vásquez, who owns the "Emerald of the Andes" juice stand in Huanta's market, remembers how the rebels "fled like sheep" across the Cachi River when the army arrived in 1989, leaving villagers to face a house-by-house search by angry troops. Although it would be a mistake to present the rural poor as the makers of "rational choices" as if they were outside culture and ideology, historian Steve J. Stern rightly underscores that "peasant societies, to survive, are notoriously sensitive to changes in power balances." Mounting evidence of the Shining Path's weakness clearly lessened the luster of the revolution.[27] Vásquez and many others also tired of the Maoists' missionary zeal: for example, "Commander Percy's" order that the standard expression of "Ay, Jesus!" be replaced by "Ay, Gonzalo!"[28] The rebels angered more peasants still with forced recruitment, demands for food, and executions of suspected *soplones*, or stool pigeons.[29] A decade of revolutionary war only intensified the insecurity and impoverishment of an already harsh world, where no one knew whose mutilated body might appear on the dirt highway or at the bottom of a rocky canyon. No longer was the Shining Path a vessel of dreams for a more egalitarian future. To the contrary, many Huantinos blamed the revolutionaries for the nightmare of a war without apparent end. "All of us supported them at first, but all they have brought us is misery," says José Huamani, a stooped man of forty-five, who lived for many years in a jungle colonization in the Apurímac Valley before moving back to his native Cangari.[30]

Moreover, the military was positioned to exploit growing discontent with the revolution. Although the indiscriminate brutality of the counterinsurgency in 1983 and 1984 forced many peasants to reconsider the wisdom of backing the Shining Path, it also foreclosed the possibility of alliance with the troops. By 1990, however, the military had launched an uneven bid to improve relations with the peasantry. Thus the Big Banana went to birthday parties and holiday festivals in Huanta's countryside; and he delivered speeches about "peasant pride" and "the suffering of the poor" that harked back to Peru's so-called "military socialist" regime of the late 1960s and early 1970s, popular with many Andean villagers for breaking the grip of big landlords in the sweeping agrarian reform of 1969. To be sure, this was an authoritarian, and even fascist, populism. The Big Banana did not hesitate to blow apart with hand grenades captured rebel leaders. "Commander Raúl" and "Commander Percy's" remains were found in Huanta's Cáceres Square at dawn in July 1991, a reminder to the entire province of the grim price of support for the revolution. Still, the decline of indiscriminate violence by the army contributed to new cooperation of peasants in resisting the Shining Path. As the Huanta-born anthropologist José Coronel concludes, "many villagers were weary of war, ready to take any measure to end a revolution that had brought them only suffering and death."[31]

Thus many villagers in Cangari and Viru Viru were willing to move into a nucleated settlement in 1990, even though they knew it was a declaration of war against the Shining Path. It took less than a month for most families to build adobe houses on the hill. Over the next year, the Shining Path launched three nighttime raids. Once they catapulted hand grenades into the village from a stony outcrop. But villagers, dug in behind their earthen walls and an outer fence of brambles, suffered no casualties. Rather than spread fear, the attacks strengthened a feeling of common cause. Peasant society was reconstructed, as villagers built a chapel, school, health post, and a dusty plaza named "Lucas" after a Cangari patroller killed in 1989. The army donated five shotguns in 1992, and villagers held a barbecue to raise funds for a Mauser rifle with a longer range. "When Centurión arrived, we thought he was going to kill us all . . . but now we're very grateful to both him and the Big Banana, because we're living in more tranquility," affirms Juan Sinchitullo, who has returned to Cangari-Viru Viru to plant beans and corn on his riverside plot after six months as a watchman in a Lima paper factory.[32] In the improbable turn of this Andean history, a pair of army officers occupy a privileged place in the collective memory of hundreds of peasants in Huanta's countryside.

Andean Difference(s)

Cangari-Viru Viru should not be taken as a "typical" case. Even before the Incas, the mosaic of diverse ethnic polities already belied the concept of a single Andean culture or worldview. The rondas have proved to be no exception to this history of regional variety in the Peruvian Andes. The implementation of patrols coincided with resettlement in Cangari-Viru Viru and other villages on the Cachi River. In other areas, peasants built walls and mounted patrols in preexisting settlements, whether refugee camps or established hamlets or towns. The strength of the rondas also differs from the fledgling patrols in Ayacucho's Víctor Fajardo and Lucanas provinces to the paraprofessional armies of the Apurímac Valley. As we will see in a moment, however, disenchantment with the Shining Path, along with the new alliance with the military, mark the central themes in the explosive growth of the organizations throughout the south-central Andes. By 1993, almost every village had a ronda steering committee across hundreds of rugged miles from Andahuaylas to Junín. Every night, thousands of peasants head out into the uncertain darkness for their weekly or monthly turn on patrol. Sentry towers of wood or mud loom over hundreds of villages and towns, and ronderos staff hundreds of checkpoints along the pot-holed highways that criss-cross the interiors. Out of the harrowing matrix of blood and death, peasant resistance to the Shining Path had mushroomed into a powerful, and perhaps decisive, force in the conflict that ravaged Peru's rugged mountains for more than a decade.

Perhaps the most striking sign of the changing terms of the counter-insurgency came in 1991. The army began the massive distribution to Andean peasants of more than 10,000 Winchester Model 1300 shotguns. At ceremonies presided over by a general or even Peru's President Alberto Fujimori, and with the Winchesters blessed by a priest as if for a Holy War, the arms were handed over to peasants in little plazas of hamlets and towns across the war zone. During the Conquest, the Spaniards rigorously banned Indians, even trusted auxiliaries, from possessing either horses or swords, the instruments of Iberian supremacy in the deadly arts of war. Giving out guns would have been just as unthinkable for the Peruvian officers in the first years of the fight against the Shining Path, as the military was no more trustful than the original band of European conquerors of the real allegiance of the Andean villagers.[33] Many peasants, including those in Cangari-Viru Viru, complain about the inadequacy of the allotment of four or five guns per village. They also want automatic weapons, to match the Shining Path, with its Kalashnikovs and FALS stolen from the police, and radios to call the army. Nonetheless, the Winchesters were welcomed in hundreds of villages, the culmination of months and sometimes years of petitions to the authorities for the means to defend themselves, besides machetes, spears, hand-grenades of "Gloria"-brand evaporated milk tins, gunpowder, and nails, and the one-shot *tirachas*. A national law in 1992 recognized the right of the ronderos to arms, codifying the reversal of the colonial withholding of the technology of war from Andean peasants, and signaling the confidence of Fujimori and his generals in the strength of their unlikely alliance with the peasantry in the war against the Shining Path.[34]

Images of Otherness

Andean villagers have always made their lives within extensive structures of economic interchange and imperial rule. Already in the ethnic kingdoms of pre-Columbian Peru, and even more so after the Spanish Conquest, traffic was heavy across the permeable lines of local politics and state-making, provincial custom and official religion, village barter and regional commerce. These busy intersections have always belied the proclivity to imagine the separateness, in the parlance of American anthropology of the mid-twentieth century, of the "folk" and "urban," or "Little Tradition" and "Great Tradition." Undeniably, however, the incorporation of Peru's interiors into national and transnational life has intensified. Today, Andean villagers, the protagonists of the rondas, buy tennis shoes and Nescafé, tune in twenty-four-hour news from Lima on battered radios, and head to the national capital and even the United States or Europe to work for months, sometimes years, as maids, gardeners, construction workers, students, and streetsellers dreaming of the comforts of a middle-class life.[35] In the process, as the Peruvian anthropologist Carlos Iván Degregori underscores, the myth of the return of the Incas has given way to the myth of progress through roads, bridges, schools, and other markers of Western-style development.[36] To be sure, the advent of modernity has not meant the loss of a distinctive, sometimes fierce, sense of independent identity. Yet what it means to be Andean can no longer be understood, if it ever could, as the petrified inheritance of an "archaic" or "feudal" past. In the Andes, as elsewhere around the planet, identity and difference unfold in the charged context of the interlinked field of communities, classes, and nations in the contemporary global system.

Nevertheless, for many prosperous Peruvians in Lima, often more likely to have spent time in Miami or New York than Andahuaylas or Apurímac, the eruption of the Shining Path seemed only to confirm the eternal alterity of the provincial, the dispossessed, and the Andean. Most conversations in the wealthy enclaves of San Isidro and Casuarinas, as well as some of the first writing by U.S. pundits and policymakers in the nascent field of "Senderology," ignored that the Shining Path was a Marxist party, notable for its lack of appeal to "indigenous" or "Andean" roots, and that the leader was a white intellectual who cited Kant, Shakespeare, and Washington Irving in his most famous speeches. To the contrary, the Maoists were cast as primitive rebels from a "non-Western" world, as, in the sensationalizing exoticism of one British journalist, a child of the "magical world of the Indians" and the "cruelty" and "ferociousness" of "the Indian Mind."[37] Many in the privileged classes in Lima, largely of European descent, came to think of "*ayacuchano*" (Ayacuchan) or even "*serrano*" (mountain-born) as a synonym for "terrorist," as old anxieties about the irrationality of "the Andean" interlaced with new fears of "international terrorism" of the Reagan-Thatcher years in the stigmatization of the rebels as "crazed subversives" or "demented criminals."

By contrast, the Fujimori government uses the rondas to suggest it has rechanneled the dangerous energy of Peru's poorest inhabitants to the defense of democracy and nationhood. Each year, beginning in 1993, the army has trucked thousands of ronderos into Lima to march on July 28, Peru's Independence Day. Newspaper photos and television news footage overflow with the "exotic" imagery of ponchoed peasants, along with a sprinkling of Amazonian militiamen in jaguar-tooth necklaces and war paint. This coverage exhibits, and even reinforces, the old conviction of the perennial Otherness of Indians and peasants. In this context, however, the difference of the Other electrifies what Fujimori calls "our crusade to eradicate the scourge of terrorism," as legions of villagers, Winchesters over their shoulders, march through Lima's streets with columns of nurses, engineers, schoolchildren, doctors, and squadrons of policemen and soldiers. Despite, as we shall see, their marginalization from ronda leadership, women wearing the "traditional" garb of bowler hats and wool skirts also parade with spears and guns, an invocation of the popular image of the Andean woman warrior, which traces as far back as the pre-Columbian deity Mama Huaco, and an extension of the guarantee of the government's ability to harness the peculiar powers of multivocality and diversity, in this case the "female" as well as the "Andean." The extremes of violence and reason, male and female, "the Andean" and "the Western," "the primitive" and "the modern" converge in a public spectacle of national unity, staged by the government as part of the cultural politics of state-building in the wake of harsh years of political violence and economic crisis that have torn so deeply at the fiction of the imagined community of a united nation.

Marks of oppression and division hardly disappear, however. The triumphalism of the pageantry effaces the war's human costs, including the massive human rights violations under Fujimori and his two predecessors, Fernando Belaúnde and Alan García. Meanwhile, the Winchesters of the peasants look like pop-guns next to the rocket-launchers and bazookas of the regular troops, an obvious reminder of the military's ultimate supremacy. Sleek generals and ministers occupy the position of privilege on the reviewing stand, magisterially elevated above the marching columns of Andean peasants, in a straightforward reflection of the power of white over brown, rich over poor, and city over country. Indeed, the very existence of the rondas speaks of the second-class citizenship of peasants. Wealthy creoles pay for Dobermans, armed *guachimanes*, or watchmen, electric fences, and cement walls to protect themselves from crime and political violence. By contrast, Andean peasants possess only the option of collective organization, still another example of how the desperate inequalities of race and class govern the logic of survival in Peru. Even as it plays on the politics of inclusion and diversity, the spectacle underlines the subordinate terms of the incorporation of Andean and peasant identity into the fabric of nationhood.

After the march in 1993, most of Cangari-Viru Viru's fifteen marchers stayed in Lima to visit with relatives in the gray shantytowns of

Huaycán and Villa El Salvador. Eventually, Antonio Quispe and his fellow villagers trickled back to the mountains, to the animals and plots that offer a fragile livelihood. In Cangari-Viru Viru, life is hard: the rivalries of local politics, the worry about drought or floods, the danger of a Shining Path raid from the desert hills across the Cachi River. Still, and in a precarious security guaranteed in large measure by their own initiative in the rondas, villagers also carve moments of reprieve, whether the quiet excitement at a new baby's birth or the raucous energy of the San Juan's Day fiesta. Against the landscape of want and terror, the intertwining of desperation and hope, pain and delight, and loss and enjoyment stand as tenacious, if bittersweet, witness to the last line of a poem by Peru's greatest Quechua-speaking writer, José María Arguedas: "*kachiniraqmi*, I still exist."

Counterrevolution as Social Movement

Until recently, anyone who spoke about Peruvian "peasant mobilization" referred to left-allied federations, or the village patrols in the northern departments of Cajamarca and Piura, also known as rondas campesinas, which grew rapidly in the 1970s and 1980s to stop thievery and then to resolve disputes and supervise small public works projects.[38] Leftist journalists and scholars, myself included, framed the phenomenon of Andean self-defense committees in a contrast between the "grassroots" and "independent" patrols of the north and their "imposed" and "manipulated" namesakes in the south and center. Rondas campesinas has a grassroots sound because of its association with the antithievery movement in the north, mostly untouched by the war. When the military borrowed the name in the early 1980s for the anti-Shining Path patrols, this appeared as a blatant bid to gloss over the compulsory character, and very different mission, of the new organizations. No one imagined that these patrols, too, would turn into a massive movement with an important degree of popular participation and autonomy from the state. The entire existence of the rondas suggests the instability of the line between "grassroots" and "imposed," "autochthonous" and "forced," "autonomous" and "manipulated." This instability reiterates the imperative of openness to how activism from below can defy our expectations about and for the disenfranchised.

At the same time, flexibility ought not mean abandoning a rigorous effort to unpack the origins and consequences of any movement for change. A good place to start may be with the question of causality, already an axis of debate in the extensive literature on rural mobilization in the 1960s and 1970s. In retrospect, much of this scholarship was mired in an illusory quest to establish a single "model" to explain the outbreak of peasant revolt, as if the particular circumstances behind the multiplicity of uprisings could be summed up in a unitary formula. At the opposite extreme, the aura of indifference, and sometimes even contempt, towards "metanarratives" and "teleologies" in poststructuralist theory can lead into slipshod analysis that does more to mystify than illuminate the politics of protest. Instead of an abrupt dismissal of all concern for origins as "authoritarian" or "totalitarian," scholars might recognize the need for specificity and precision, and avoid the reduction of the study of social movements to a simple quest for "causes," yet without a wholesale abandonment of careful inquiry into the forces behind the fraught decision of people at a specific time and place to organize to alter's history course.

Disenchantment with the Shining Path represents a basic cause for the explosive expansion of the rondas. The insightful work of a number of journalists and scholars, mostly Peruvian, suggests a pattern of initial acceptance among the peasantry, or at least tolerance, followed by mounting disaffection.[39] Although this loss of support has much to do with the arrival of the military, and the realization of the price of opposition to the government, it also represents a reaction against the Shining Path's myopic inflexibility and planned use of mass violence. In the upper mountains of Huanta in 1983, and again to the north in 1988 and 1989 in the Mantaro Valley, the Maoists' order to stop the sale of surplus crops to towns and cities, part of the plan to "strangle" the cities, provoked angry discontent, as the marketing ban shut off a source of social interchange and economic income so long a fulcrum of Andean life.

Inflexibility also proved a problem in the guerrillas' refusal to stop forcibly recruiting children, some as young as eight or ten. The same was true of the fierce and unsuccessful campaign to wipe out Pentecostal churches in the Apurímac Valley in the mid-1980s. Rebel leaders saw the mushrooming of these congregations in Peru's interiors as a direct challenge, unlike the generally less organized and fervent Catholics, and burned churches and murdered pastors. In reaction, Protestants developed an apocalyptic view of Guzmán's followers as the armies of the Anti-Christ, and ultimately mobilized against them. In many areas, finally, villagers resented the Shining Path's "popular justice." The execution of a cattle rustler or corrupt mayor might be applauded at the start. Eventually, however, the increased number of killings, especially of suspected "collaborators" and "servants of the reaction," and the macabre means—often by stoning or slitting throats to heighten fear and save bullets—backfired against the Maoists in many areas. The murders often embittered the friends and relatives of the dead, and extended the erosion of the initial aura of the Maoists as beneficent champions of the peasantry. An absolute, even arrogant, certainty about the dictums of "Marxist-Leninist-Gonzalo Thought" and the infallibility of the revolution turned out to be a serious liability for the Shining Path, as the guerrillas were incapable of compromise with the peasantry. Instead of a progressive consolidation of rural backing after the fashion of the Chinese Red Army or Viet Cong, the Shining Path laid the foundation for the explosion of armed revolt against its revolutionary design.

The other key force was the improved relation between the military and the peasantry. Unlike its counterparts in, for instance, Argentina or Chile, the Peruvian military has a tradition of populism as well as authoritarianism. In particular, the army has served as a rare avenue of social mobility in Peru in the twentieth century, always with a sprinkling of dark-skinned generals of humble origins. This largest of the three branches spearheaded the agrarian reform and nationalization of foreign companies under General Velasco's presidency. Noel's counteroffensive of 1983 and 1984 displayed the most brutal and imperial side of the military. Torture, rape, and murder of suspected rebels remained a mainstay of the counterinsurgency in subsequent years, leaving Peru the world's highest number of "disappeared" from 1988 to 1991. Already by 1985, however, and especially with the evident ability of the rebels to survive the storm of violence, many officers recognized the need to combine intimidation and persuasion in a so-called "integral" strategy, including "sociopolitical development" and "civic action" to build support among the peasantry. Selective killing began to predominate over wholesale slaughter, as civilian deaths at the hands of the military declined by more than two-thirds after 1983–1984. More soldiers were recruited from local villages and provincial towns. Showy generals like Alberto Arciniega and Adriano Huamán played up their own peasant origins, posing for pictures with babies and dancing and drinking at parties and festivals.

Although some troops maintained a colonial posture of distance and superiority, the new ties were reflected in a rapid rise of requests from peasants in the late 1980s and early 1990s for garrisons to be stationed in their villages and towns, a graphic illustration of the partial shift of the military's image from occupiers to protectors. As historian Jaime Urrutia, himself kidnapped and tortured by the army at the start of the war, emphasized in a recent retrospective, the army "has changed . . . [officers] like the sadly celebrated Commander 'Butcher,' who headed the Cangallo garrison . . . are no more than a bitter memory, and peasants no longer live in terror of disappearances and arbitrary arrests."[40] The Shining Path still claimed, in 1988, to rest "on the poor peasants."[41] Ironically, however, the military, stern and forbidding, yet also able to compromise, outmaneuvered the Maoists in the battle for the countryside.

The rondas grew at the intersection of the new ties between peasants and the military. By 1990, Quechua-speaking officers travelled to the high moors of Ayacucho and Huancavelica, dressed in *chullos* and ponchos, to urge their "brother peasants" to take up arms against "the enemies of Peru."[42] "Ronderos and Armed Forces—Together We Will Make a Peru of Peace," proclaimed an army-manufactured pennant on the wall of the municipality in the Ayacucho village of Quinua, a ceramics center I visited in 1993. To cement the image of profitable partnership, the military also promised, and sometimes provided, donations of tools, medicine, and food as well as guns. In 1991, I attended a meeting of fifty leaders of the rondas in the walled army headquarters in the Mantaro Valley, where a general mixed in promises of tools and tractors with the exhortation to "continue in your rondas." The military later donated 200 Japanese trucks, as a reward, in the general's words, for their "collaboration" against the Shining Path. The threat of force hardly disappeared, and, in fact, some inhabitants of Quinua remember how a mustachioed lieutenant threatened in 1989 to take "drastic measures" against villagers who refused to participate in patrols. Still, the inclusive rhetoric and material incentives, along with hate for the Shining Path, encouraged the interest and sometimes even enthusiasm about resettlements and patrols on display in Cangari-Viru Viru, and dozens of other villages.

Finally, the rondas took on a self-reinforcing logic. At first, the Shining Path often succeeded in putting down the patrols by force, as in the 1983 massacre of 80 peasants in the Ayacucho village of Lucanamarca, justified by Guzmán as "annihilation in order to defend . . . the people's war . . . demolish the imperialist dominion . . . and wipe them from the face of the Earth."[43] By the 1990s, however, the rebels were increasingly on the defensive in many areas, in some cases almost entirely expelled, as in the Apurímac Valley. Success emboldened villagers to maintain rondas, and adjoining hamlets and towns to organize, all the more so with the news from Lima of Guzmán's capture. Resistance to the Shining Path snowballed with startling speed in 1991 and 1992, most notably in Huanta and the Mantaro Valley, where thousands of peasants across hundreds of mountainous miles organized into a strong network of patrols and resettlements in little more than a year. In many places, like Cangari-Viru Viru, attacks to put down resistance only deepened contempt for the rebels and strengthened the rondas. Shining Path propaganda promised the "miserable mercenaries . . . will be disinflated like a circus balloon."[44] To the contrary, the rondas expanded in 1993 into Vilcashuamán, Víctor Fajardo, Cangallo, and Huancasancos, the last Ayacucho provinces where the Shining Path had significant influence. The feeling of impotence in the countryside diminished as the rondas evolved into a movement that burst beyond the ability of Guzmán and his followers to contain or repress it.

The Consequence(s) of Mobilization

Many scholars of rural mobilization have emphasized the urgency of careful evaluation of the limits as well as achievements of any initiative for change. By the end of the 1980s, caution tempered the initial, and sometimes utopian, ebullience of progressive researchers about the emancipatory potential of social movements in Latin America. On close inspection, the ghosts of clientelism, factionalism, and bossism haunted even the most seemingly "democratic" and "grassroots" of popular initiatives, like Ecuadoran indigenous federations and Brazilian gay and lesbian coalitions, belying the proclivity of scholars to assume a clean break between the "old" and "new" politics of struggle. More broadly, it was difficult to ignore, in the short term at least, and with the possible exception of the Workers' Party in Brazil, the failure of movements from below to translate into national politics of structural transformation while the Left withered in the face of the avalanche of neoliberal victories in congressional and presidential elections. As political scientist Sonia Alvarez concludes, "a certain pessimism set in [by the late 1980s]" about the "seemingly limited gains of social movements in the face of political violence and economic crisis in Latin America."[45]

In the rondas, one of the most obvious problems centers on gender. Many women speak enthusiastically of a greater peace and security with the rondas. They do the cooking and childcare that allows their sons and husbands to patrol. Women, armed with clubs and kitchen knife-tipped spears, also act as sentries, and as a last line of defense. Yet the confluence of ideologies of public leadership and war as male domains have led the rondas to perpetuate and even fortify an old history of female subordination in village affairs and, more broadly, the national politics. Except in the public theater of Lima marches, only men carry guns, the supreme symbol of ronda power. No women are elected as commando or civil defense committee president. "The people got macho," villagers of both sexes will say in a masculinization of the patrols that writes out women's vital role. The Peruvian anthropologist Marisol de la Cadena asserts that peasant women tend to be viewed negatively as "more Indian" than men by virtue of the greater likelihood that they will not speak Spanish and remain more "traditional" in dress and duties, like herding and weaving.[46] The rondas reinforce the ideology of second-class status of women and "the female" in Andean societies.

A second and related problem involves corruption and bossism. Andean villages have always been far less egalitarian or harmonious than might be suggested by the organic-sounding label of "peasant community."[47] Rumors of misappropriation of funds or misuse of authority by local leaders, whether of irrigation committees or village councils, represent a familiar feature of the social landscape. "Small village, big hell," as a Spanish aphorism has it. The rondas have been no exception. Many commandos and civil defense committee presidents have faced accusations, in some cases justified, of everything from stealing money donated by the government to excusing relatives from patrol duty. The close ties of ronda leaders in some places to the military can give them undue leverage in local politics, as in Junín's Comas, where some village presidents complain of a decline in their authority. In the extreme case of the 1980s in the Apurímac Valley, where the rapid growth in the 1980s of coca cultivation into a source of dollars exacerbated the climate of uncertainty and volatility, the first leaders turned the rondas into personal fiefs. This was the case of schoolteacher-turned-denture-maker Pompeyo Rivera Torres, "Commander Huayhuaco," who operated as a jungle warlord before his 1989 arrest for drug trafficking.[48] All of these histories undercut the effort to reduce the rondas to a tidy tale of innocent peasants against evil guerrillas, or to imagine a uniform backing for the organizations.

Corruption and bossism extend to the relation of the rondas with civil and military authorities. Some politicians have used the organizations to, in effect, buy votes. For example, the current mayor of Huanta campaigned by handing out bullets in the countryside, and persuaded (reportedly promising future favors) some commandos and civil defense committee presidents to speak in his favor at village assemblies. More centrally, the military maintains a strong influence, an accountability codified into Legislative Decree No. 741, which stresses that every ronda committee "must be authorized by the Joint Command of the Armed Forces . . . and operate under the control of the respective Military Commands [in their region]."[49] In practice, the military's authority assumes a variety of forms in the day-to-day operation of the rondas, from mandatory barracks meetings to demands for overnight lodging in villages for soldiers. In all of these relations, examples exist of military corruption, like the sale of bullets supposedly donated by the government by officers to peasants. More broadly, as many ronderos do not hesitate to complain, the entire rise of the rondas exploits the unpaid labor of villagers, who must guarantee the public safety that was previously the duty of the state. "We sit out here in the dark waiting for the next attack, keeping the peace," the commando in Cangari-Viru Viru explains, "while the colonel and the brewery owner dance and drink in town." Far from an unambiguous tale of rural "initiative" or "agency," the rondas mark the partial reinscription of Peru's colonial hierarchy of town over country and state over peasantry.

Finally, the rondas do not tie into a broad program for change. If anything, their achievements have reinforced convictions about the worthlessness of "politics" and "the politicians." Some of the lowest turnout for recent regional and national elections have come in places where the rondas are strongest. Alberto Fujimori presents himself as a champion of the rondas, helicoptering into the backlands to preside over the distribution of food and medicine as well as guns to ronderos and praising them on television "as some of Peru's greatest patriots." But even this master of populism wins only a tepid backing from most peasants, signaling a widespread cynicism about the political system. The lack of enthusiasm about representative democracy is understandable given a history of flagrant government corruption and broken promises. Obviously, too, the intensity of the battle for survival can assume an overwhelming precedence over events in Lima. Yet indifference also points to the preeminently local thrust of the rondas that leaves the terrain of national politics to the populist authoritarianism of Fujimori and his military allies. Broadly congruent with the exhaustion with utopias in the post-Cold War world, the disinterest of the ronderos in electoral politics and national change may not last.[50] Perhaps the organizations will turn into a vehicle for a more articulated platform in the remaking of economic structures and state policies. Currently, however, the movement meshes with the end of the days of strikes, marches, and mass protests and the virtual absence of a collective response to the devastating policies of deregulation and austerity, which have disproportionately slashed into the already meager incomes of Peru's majorities. No challenge grows to what the Uruguayan novelist Eduardo Galeano labels the "structures of impotence" of Latin America in the teeth of economic neoliberalism.[51]

One of the obvious lessons of this survey of the limits of the rondas is to reiterate the heterogeneity of the makeup of any kind of social mobilization. Thus, as we have seen, women play a different, and mostly subordinate, role than men, while leaders are better situated than followers to gain from favors of politicians or army officers. The unified sound of the label of "movement," no more than the familiar standbys of "culture" or "society," should not conceal the inevitable differences in interest and standpoint of the differently positioned participants in popular initiatives. Instead of a unilateral focus on consensus of liberal and functionalist models or, conversely, on fragmentation and partiality in some brands of poststructuralist theory, the rondas suggest the urgency of a sensitivity to the delicate and sometimes explosive dialectic of difference and commonality, polyphony and solidarity, and conflict and consensus in every bid for change around the world.[52]

"No Longer Tame Lambs to the Slaughterhouse"

Stubborn contradictions and limits pervade rural mobilization against the Shining Path. Yet it would be just as wrong to ignore as to overplay the inroads of any social movement in Latin America or anywhere else, perhaps even more so in light of the tremendous, sometimes almost preposterous, courage demanded to make even modest gains against the grain of the savage dangers of the contemporary order. In dozens of cases, from shantytown soup kitchens in Honduras to indigenous federations in Ecuador to the rondas in northern as well as southern Peru, activism from below means the margin of survival in daily life as well as a challenge to the very terms of cultural domination and political exclusion between the elite and the dispossessed, the white and the brown, the rulers and the ruled. These challenges occur in subtle as well as open ways. More than just the glory of slaves, these dynamic initiatives remain a welcome sliver of hope in the struggle for justice and dignity in today's world.

A greater peace represents the most obvious achievement of the rondas. The Shining Path still attacks patrollers and resettlements, as in a September 1993 raid on the Ayacucho village of Matucana Alta, where twelve Quechua-speaking farmers were murdered, including five children. In general, however, the rondas have vastly reduced the Shining Path's ability to operate in the Andean countryside. In their former stronghold of Huanta, a ragged and hungry band only descends from the freezing moors of Razuhuillca to steal food and cattle in sporadic raids. Checkpoints and patrols have pushed the rebels out of the Upper and Lower Tulumayo Valleys in Junín, where peasants, in the words of one leader, began to fight in 1990 with "clubs, machetes, rocks and slings." With almost no help from the military, the rondas have also expelled Shining Path from another of the war's bloodiest battlegrounds, the Apurímac Valley. In these and many other war zones, many peasants confirm a greater, if by no means total, sense of security and calm with the rondas. "There are no more massacres, not even attacks, nothing," concludes Juan Pardo, the commando in the village of Vinchos, which lies on the windy grasslands above the city of Ayacucho.[53]

To be sure, many rondas have not shied away from recourse to deadly violence. In 1991, I cut a deal with a taxi driver to take me to the district of Comas, six hours above the city of Huancayo. Halfway up the winding track into the icy mountains, the muffler fell off the rusted Nissan, forcing us to turn around. On the way back down, we met a pickup filled with ronderos returning from a meeting at the Huancayo army headquarters. It stopped, blocking our path on a rocky curve. In the gray light of the mountain morning, I watched with a sinking feeling as twenty ronderos jumped off the bed, grabbed stones, crowbars, and shotguns, and moved, silently, to surround us. Fortunately, and at the last moment, one of the weatherbeaten farmers recognized the taxi driver as his cousin. Tension dissolved. "The terrorists ambush, and we have to be ready to defend ourselves," one of the gun-toting villagers explained, apologetically. My apprehension, however, had not been altogether a product of negative stereotypes about peasant ferocity. Just a year before, Comas peasants stoned thirteen suspected guerrillas, sliced off their heads, and took them in a blood-soaked burlap sack to army headquarters.[54]

Any discussion of violence by villagers risks a fall into the essentialist view of the intrinsic brutality of the Andean peasantry, displayed in one Peruvian historian's incautious claim about "the frequency of unrestrained cruelty in peasant wars." Yet it would also be irresponsible to ignore the ronda killings of "suspected subversives" from Huaychao in 1983 to Paccha in 1992. Understandable, if not justifiable, against the explosive background of fear, personal and village vendettas, and mass violence by the Shining Path and the military, these examples of ronda terror undermine the inverse, and ultimately just as condescending, essentialism of the view of Andean peasants as the universal bearers of a noble ethic of "punish, but do not kill."[55] Once again, the rondas defy easy judgment or sweeping generalization, in this case even of "life-giving" or "life-taking" or "violent" and "peaceful." Instead, they exemplify the mobile and multiple contours that shape any social movement.

I do not wish to minimize the problem of violence, but it should be emphasized that killings by ronderos have fallen substantially, and are now a relative rarity. The rondas resemble their northern Andean namesakes in this respect. There, the lynching of suspected rustlers, although never as frequent as that of suspected rebels in the center and south, also declined after a measure of order was reestablished and the threat to survival and livelihood diminished. In a surprising number of cases, former guerrilla supporters have even been reincorporated into village society, if willing to abandon the doctrine of revolution at any cost. "We lived in misery, and it was understandable that some would make the mistake of joining the Shining Path," as Hugo Huillca, the Apurímac leader, explains this strong, if not universal, ideology of forgiveness.[56] Several current commandos and civil defense committee presidents in the Apurímac and Huanta were former Shining Path collaborators, in striking testimony to the surprising elasticity of the rondas in the evolution into mass organizations.

In the broad view, an intricate array of factors lies behind declining violence in the war zones, including the capture of top guerrilla leaders and the drop in disappearances and massacres by the military. But a superficial look at the statistics of the last few years bears out the claims of Pardo, Huillca, and others about the patrols' significant role in restoring peace. The massive expansion of the organizations in 1990 and 1991 corresponded to a 30 percent decline in recorded casualties and deaths in the departments of Andahuaylas, Apurímac, Ayacucho, and Junín. As late as 1991, human rights organizations still asserted that "the patrols have contributed to the escalation of violence."[57] This position can no longer be sustained. By contrast to, say, the cases of Angola's Eastern Provinces or Colombia's Middle Magdalena, the militarization of the civilian population has become the precarious path out of one of the fiercest and bloodiest wars in late twentieth-century Latin America.

Today, many critics admit the rondas have contributed to a surprising resurrection of civil society, a second benefit of the organizations. There are regular meetings of the entire village to discuss ronda business, whether fundraisers for guns or scheduling patrols. As in the northern patrols, all men in the village must patrol and attend assemblies. Skulkers may be fined or even whipped. Nonetheless, in most places this participation no longer rests as much on military intimidation as on the collective conviction among villagers that rondas are desirable. Commandos and civil defense committee presidents are no longer named by army officials in most villages. Instead, open assemblies elect them like other village leaders, part of what historian Ponciano del Pino calls the *interiorización* (interiorization) of the rondas into the everyday fabric of Andean villages.[58]

A panoply of other civil organizations, such as parent-teacher associations, women's clubs, and irrigation committees, have also been reactivated with the new security provided by the patrols, expanding the room for local participation in village organizations shattered by war. Increasingly, too, the rondas themselves have expanded beyond a purely military mission. When cholera broke out in the Apurímac Valley's Palmapampa, for instance, a ronda delegation traveled to Ayacucho to request rehydration salts from development organizations and the government. Many rondas even incorporate old modes of village cooperation, holding *faenas*—or collective work parties—to build guard towers and walls, or, in the case of Chaca, a potable water project. A system of *chasquis*, or messengers, after the Incan communication system, links the villages in the upper reaches of Huanta so that word of guerrilla sightings and attacks is shared. In part, then, the rondas have been "Andeanized," "peasantized," and "villagized," reconfigured to local logics of necessity and tradition. Rather than hastening the demise of mountain traditions or institutions, they have become a vehicle for the defense of village interests and life, another chapter in the painful history of recomposition and transformation that has characterized Andean societies for so many centuries.

A final and interrelated achievement has been to restore a sense of agency among villagers in the war zones. The harshness of rural life in Apurímac, Ayacucho, and Huancavelica—three of the poorest departments in an impoverished country—partially explains the initial receptivity to the Shining Path's call for radical change. But the war spun the world into what peasants call *chaqwa*, Quechua for chaos and disorder. Massacres were routine by both sides. More than 600,000 were forced to flee for their lives.[59] By contrast, for many peasants the rondas have become a sign of their ability to be more than eternal war victims. "We're no longer tame lambs to be led to the slaughterhouse," says the Quechua-speaking civil defense committee president in Ayacucho's Vinchos.[60] In the Apurímac Valley, villagers even celebrate the anniversary of the founding of the local ronda with ballads, poems, and speeches. They speak of themselves with pride as "ronderos" as well as campesinos (peasants), comuneros (villagers), and peruanos (Peruvians). Common throughout the south-central Andes is talk of superiority even to the military. "We're able to do what they never could," says one man in Chaca, "that is, restore tranquility in these communities." Much of Peru's national culture still affixes the qualities of backwardness to "the peasant" and "the Andean." Despite its claim to represent villagers, the Shining Path's urban vanguard also presumes a superior understanding of "science" and historical destiny, arrogating to itself the obligation to "beat ideas into the heads of the masses through dramatic deeds," as one party document proclaims.[61] Against the stigma of ignorance and inferiority from the Maoists as well as national ideology, peasants have made the rondas into an affirmation of partial control over their hard world.

Wakeful Theory

It should be apparent that the "limits" and "achievements" of the rondas cannot be neatly disentangled. "Systems of power are multiple," as anthropologist Lila Abu-Lughod underlines, "overlapping and intersecting fields."[62] A social movement may reinforce the operation of oppression at one level, yet cut against the grain of domination and misery at another. The rondas remain caught within the disturbing logics of sexism, corruption, and bossism, and within a neoliberal offensive, even as they carve a promising stability out of the relentless fear and chaos of war. To be sure, the weave of the "negative" and the "positive" is especially dense in this unanticipated case of rural mobilization, even if my own feelings tilt toward admiration, even astonishment, at the achievements of the ronderos against the grain of a difficult history. Nevertheless, the multilayered and sometimes compromised trajectory of the rondas also stands as much as the norm as the exception in these unruly times at century's end, epistemologically and politically uncertain, emblematic of the world's willful reluctance to rest inside the categories we in the academy invent to contain and explain. It will not do to jettison the hope of understanding the interplay of culture, action, and political economy that defines human experience, much less to lose respect or empathy for the ingenuity and boldness of so many of the political initiatives of the disenfranchised. Surely, however, good analysis depends on the ability to press beyond the imperial legacy of stationary polarities and preconceived narratives. On this terrain, admittedly insecure and unstable, scholars will struggle to define the terms for the remaking of social thought.

In *Beyond Good and Evil*, Friedrich Nietzsche warns against a "solemn air of finality" in social theory, "no more than a noble childishness or tyrannism." This most trenchant of nineteenth-century critics of emptiness and pretension launches a savage attack on "audacious generalization" and "dogmatic philosophy." He imagines no pure place for the social analyst outside of history or politics, always insistent that we too are, as in the title of another of his most famous treatises, "Human, All Too Human." And yet, even Nietzsche refuses to relinquish the possibility of limited yet serious understanding. As the unexpected eruption of the revolt against the Shining Path reminds us with desperate poignancy, the "task is wakefulness itself" for a "philosophy of the future" to understand the beauty and agony of the workings of the world.[63]

The Politics of Postmodernism

Culture on the Frontiers

Some observers continue to paint the rondas in the old frame of the Peruvian Andes as a place of primordial and millenarian customs. "Time stands still in the Andean countryside," writes one Lima journalist, as another compares the ronderos to "Atahualpa's Inca warriors."[64] More productively, however, the rondas' particular history might be viewed as an indicator of Latin America's broader predicament at century's close. After all, many critics emphasize that themes of fragmentation, displacement, and transculturation have always been fundamental to millions of Latin Americans from East Los Angeles to Caracas and São Paulo. Already in the early eighteenth century, before anyone spoke of "intertextuality" or "pastiche," the young Topa Inca posed for a portrait in a Spanish waistcoat with an Inca royal tassel, or *llautu*, draped across his forehead. Two hundred years later, José María Arguedas linked his admiration for Western machinery with a celebration of the Andean *apus*, or mountain spirits, in his famous Quechua poem "An Ode to a Jet Plane." As literary theorist Alberto Moreiras concludes, "the marginality and deferment of all colonial societies with respect to what happens in the metropolises led Latin American culture, from its beginning, to be a culture of translation and transculturation."[65] Moreiras and a number of other scholars assert that postmodernity arrived in Latin America before it came to the First World. In this view, Latin America's past stands as continuous with its present and its future of flux and transculturation—the advent of instantaneous communications, rapid technological change, "flexible" capital accumulation, and the other hallmarks of what David Harvey calls "time-space compression" around the world.[66]

Even many Latin American critics leave out the countryside in their talk about the "postmodern" and the "postcolonial." In his otherwise fine *Culturas Híbridas*, for instance, Argentine Nestor García Canclini describes the subcontinent's condition in terms of "a multitemporal heterogeneity" of the "traditional" and the "modern." His link of the "traditional" to the "pastoral," the "rural," and the "folk" marks a partial return to the evolutionary chronology that denies the coevalness of Latin America's fifty million small farmers, presenting their customs and visions as the artifacts of a premodern past. As we saw in the case of Cangari-Viru Viru, an adobe village built only a few years ago amid war's heat, this thinking overlooks the fact that even the most ostensibly "traditional" Latin Americans do not live, as some of us anthropologists still put it not so long ago, "submerged by the tides of history."[67] To the contrary, as this essay has emphasized, Latin American peasants also build their lives at the volatile intersection of the local, regional, and global. Values and traditions in the countryside can only be understood within the same temporal and spatial networks that bind us all in the startling reality of interdependence on a global scale, no matter whether one chooses to call it "postmodernity," "postcolonialism," "post-Fordism," "late capitalism," or even, as one critic suggests, none of these labels that can become "so empty and sliding as signifiers . . . [as] to be taken to mean anything you like."[68]

If the countryside must be a part of our thinking about cultural mixture and political flux in Latin America, the rondas also underscore the dangers of presenting this condition as a blithe Rabelaisian carnival of polyphony. Perhaps because of their focus on the art, music, and literature of Latin America's cities, and scantier attention to rural areas and shantytowns where histories of poverty and terror are more likely to be the norm than the exception, many theorists slide towards a depiction of the heteronomous logic of kitsch and pastiche as a neatly positive development.[69] On display in the rondas is the spliced spectacle of "commandos" who speak Quechua and worship mountain spirits, even as they go by war names like "Jehovah" and "Rambo." Yet the stark predicament of these farmers warns against a "ludic postmodernism" where the politics of difference reduces to "play" and "pleasure," and highlights the need to avoid the neoregionalism of the "more-postmodern-than-thou-by-virtue-of-our-hybridity" syndrome of some Latin American scholars, as if plurality or hybridity were somehow by their very nature a sign of the good, the "subversive," the "transgressive," or the politically progressive.[70] The interactive, improvisational dimensions of contemporary life reflect joy and possibility, but also pain and destruction, especially for those at the precarious margins of global society.[71]

Still, García Canclini's axiom that "culture everywhere is on the frontiers" offers one way to reckon with the hard struggle of the ronderos.[72] On one of my last days in Ayacucho in June, I traveled a mountain highway with a journalist friend to the village of Chaca, at 11,000 feet in Ayacucho's Iquicha moors. Nineteenth-century priests and present-day observers have described the Iquichanos as part of an "ancient archaic Peru" of "strange customs" and "incomprehensible enigmas."[73] In the little plaza, a fierce sense of a distinctive past was on display in the "Indian" dress of men in chullos and ponchos and women in embroidered blouses and wool skirts. As usual, one did not have to look far for signs of invention and recombination. The bright aluminum linings of National-brand cigarette packages gleamed elegantly between the carnations and roses that single women have long pinned on their black bowler hats. Contrary to the view of the rootedness of Andean peasants to the land, three ponchoed men had just returned from Lima, eighteen hours away by truck and bus. Most of Chaca's peasants are refugees from higher up in the moors. Now, they want to repopulate their Andean hamlets, recreate the village life that has taken on a nostalgic glow after forced flight, poverty, and racism in the shantytowns of Ayacucho and Lima. Out of the space of terror, and through the rondas, the "traditional," the "peasant," the "Iquichan," and even the "Andean" may be recreated, as they have been so many times in this rugged region with its long history of periodic upheaval and displacement.[74] Culture and tradition, as the Peruvian critic José Carlos Maríategui already insisted in 1927, are "alive and mobile . . . always remold[ing] themselves before our eyes . . . [they are] suffocated by those who want them dead and inert, who want to stretch the past into an exhausted present."[75] Rather than a return to essential or primordial origins, the rebuilding of Iquichan society will unfold at the crossroads of old legacies and new influences, the weight of the past and the unpredictability of the future.

That night, the Chaca schoolteachers warned me to keep my tennis shoes close when I went to bed in their thatch-roofed adobe compound, and to run for the canyon if the Shining Path attacked. But the only sounds to break the night's still were Quechua hymns from a nearby Pentecostal church. In the frozen dawn, a group of ronderos from Puros arrived to take us up the winding trail to their now-abandoned village. The burned, stony ruins perch on a windy saddle that feels like the top of the world. There men and women spoke of their plans to return, to build a school and health clinic (along with guard towers to protect against the still-present danger of rebel raids), and to remake village society. Their journey embodies the fragile struggles of millions everywhere to gain a measure of control over their lives in the tumultuous violence of a world where so much that seemed solid has melted into air. "We are faced with a transitory landscape, where new ruins pile up on each other," concludes writer Celeste Olalquiaga, and "it is in these ruins that we look for ourselves."[76]

"Jeremiah" and "The Savage"

As I flew out of Ayacucho after my university lecture, the plane cruised between the clouds above the Mantaro Valley before its plunge down the Andes to Lima's grimy airport. The Mantaro's history offers a possible scenario for the rondas. Here the future Peruvian President Andrés Avelino Caceres rallied peasants to fight the Chileans in the War of the Pacific (1879–1883), as most of the Mantaro's aristocracy collaborated with the invaders. When the war ended, Caceres promptly sided with the elite to repress his former followers' demands for property rights. Four peasant leaders were hanged in the main square of the department capital.[77]

A century later, Peru's leaders looked again to highland villagers to save the nation. If the rondas end in the same way, without any real gain for peasants, they will be another parable of the persistence of savage inequalities in Peruvian and global society. The difficulty, perhaps impossibility, of any escape from hardship's grip was a favorite theme of

Peru's greatest poet, César Vallejo, nicknamed *El Indio* (The Indian), and a child of the Andes, who wrote "The Nine Monsters" while in Paris in the shadow of the Spanish Civil War: "Pain grasps us, brother men/from behind, in profile/and it crazes us in cinemas/nails us up on record players. . . . I can no more with so many pine boxes/so many minutes/so many lizards/and so many reversals, so much thirst for thirst."[78]

Yet much has also changed in Peru. Since the betrayal of the montoneros a century ago, this restless country has witnessed what anthropologist José Matos Mar calls *desborde popular* (popular overflow): the eruption of the "informal economy" and popular culture, the explosion of Lima into a labyrinthine megalopolis of over six million, the pervasive discontent with traditional political parties, and the breakup of the oligarchical state.[79] If Peru remains riven by exclusion and hierarchy, neither is it any longer what the nineteenth-century critic Manuel González Prada labeled a nation of "gentlemen and serfs." Although they may hold no grand promise of forward progress, the rondas fit with the stubborn refusal of Peru's majorities to accept a perennial role as history's passive spectators, or as second-class citizens in a nation that promises equality for all.

The future of the rondas will be written in the struggle within and against the desires for recognition and the forces of exclusion and marginalization. In the process, the "Andean" may be reborn, as it is in Puros. Or it may take less familiar paths. On one of my last days in Huanta, I visited a ronda-organized fish fry and soccer tournament in the cactus hills of the lower valley. People from Cangari-Viru Viru and many other resettlements and villages, including commandos like "Jeremiah" and "The Savage," raced and yelled as they played next to the rubble of an experimental farm burned by the Shining Path five years before. One of the gun-slinging ronderos explained in Quechua-accented Spanish that the fish came from a new artificial pond, and that a nearby resettlement wanted to turn the soccer field into a tourist complex with a hotel, volleyball courts, and canoeing. It is hard to imagine the success of a resort in mountains where guerrillas and soldiers still roam. But no one ever imagined that the rondas might forge peace from war in the first place, said the rondero with a sly laugh. Against the bustle of jokes and food and ballads of this day's Andean fiesta, and on the brink of an uncertain future, one can only hope for the sounds of more of the Borgesian "laughter [that] shatters the familiar landmarks of our thought . . . [and] ordered surfaces" to leave these women and men with something better.

Notes

1. Foucault (1971: xiv).
2. Two of the best studies of the Shining Path are Degregori (1990) and Gorriti (1990). For a fascinating look at the important role of women in the Shining

Path, see Kirk (1993b). Palmer, ed. (1992) collects some of the best work on the Maoists in English.

3. Benjamin (1968: 257).

4. Abimael Guzmán, "We are the Initiators" in Starn, Degregori, Kirk, eds. (1995: 461). This is a translation of the speech delivered by Guzmán on April 19, 1980, to call for the beginning of the armed struggle.

5. The figures for the numbers of village participants come from an unpublished survey from 1993 by the Instituto de Investigación y Defensa Nacional (INIDEN) in Lima. The name of the militias is a matter of confusion. Initially, they were mostly known as "Civil Auto Defense Committees," and this remains their name in the legal statutes that recognize them. Probably in an effort to improve the image of the then mostly forced organizations, however, army officers started to use the name of rondas campesinas, after the patrols begun by peasants in northern Peru to stop thievery and then resolve disputes and supervise small public works. For the purposes of simplicity, I use the words rondas campesinas and ronderos in this essay to refer to the patrols against the Shining Path. As part of its counterinsurgency strategy, the Peruvian government also attempted to form *rondas urbanas*, or urban patrols, in Lima, although these organizations have not grown in anywhere near the strength or proportions of their rural counterparts. Adding a further layer of complexity, there are also urban rondas independently organized only to fight crime, in both Lima and poor neighborhoods in the northern cities of Chiclayo, Trujillo, Sullana, and Piura. Despite their very different histories and missions, the rise of these different brands of self-defense organizations grows out of the broad context of the failure of the besieged Peruvian state to guarantee order in the 1980s and early 1990s.

6. José Coronel (1992, n.d.; Coronel and Loayza 1992) and Ponciano del Pino (1992, 1994) have done the best work on the rondas, and I am indebted to both of these Ayacucho-based scholars for their insights in our many conversations. Other sources on the *rondas* include Starn (1991, 1993), Starn, ed. (1993), and IDL (n.d.).

7. Silverblatt (1994: 290–91).

8. On a second visit in July 1994, villagers maintained the same watch system, but spoke of a feeling that threat of Shining Path attacks had lessened, if not disappeared.

9. "The walls and palisades with which Europe began to bristle were the symbol of a great anguish," wrote Bloch (1961: 39).

10. See Vargas Llosa (1983: 65–90). For useful discussions of Vargas Llosa and Uchuraccay, see Salcedo (1987) and Mayer (1991).

11. Vargas Llosa (1983: 69, 82).

12. Many soldiers and officers take war names to protect themselves from future Shining Path reprisals and prosecution for human rights violations.

13. Here and elsewhere I have changed names and places for security reasons. This and all subsequent translations from the Spanish are mine, unless otherwise indicated.

14. Andres Luna Vargas, interview, Lima, July 1989.

15. The quotes come from Burneo and Eyde (1986).

16. See Americas Watch (1986) on the Guatemalan patrols, as well as several of the articles in Carmack (1988).

17. Many Andean ethnic groups were ready to rebel against the Incas, and the empire was itself divided in the wake of the civil war of succession between Atahualpa and Huáscar. One of the best, and most accessible, histories of the conquest is Hemming (1970).

18. Stern (1982) offers a good introduction to the reducciones, and their role in Toledo's social engineering.

19. Flores Galindo (1987: 395).

20. Noel (1989) has written an interesting, and self-serving, memoir of his bloody years in Ayacucho.

21. See Balaguer (1993: 15).

22. See Manrique (1989).

23. See González (1982).

24. For an early view of the Shining Path as a peasant rebellion, see the otherwise insightful essay by McClintock (1984).

25. Chávez de Paz (1989) offers statistics on the social makeup of the Shining Path, based on judicial records.

26. The title of Wolf's (1969) fine book on peasant revolt.

27. Stern (1982: 30).

28. Most leaders of the Shining Path were known to villagers only by pseudonyms.

29. This information comes from my own interviews in the area in June 1993 and from Coronel (n.d.).

30. Interview in Cangari-Viru Viru, June 29, 1993.

31. Coronel (n.d.: 92, 45).

32. Interview in Cangari-Viru Viru, June 27, 1993.

33. The preceding president, Alan García, had handed over 200 rifles in 1988 to patrollers in the Apurímac, but Fujimori was the first to approve the largescale arming of the peasantry.

34. The right to arms appeared in Decreto Legislativo No. 757, reprinted in *El Peruano*, the Peruvian government's official newspaper, October 15, 1992, p. 134791.

35. The diaspora of migrants from some Andean villages, like Cabanaconde in Arequipa department, stretches from Lima to Europe and the United States, as wonderfully illustrated in a new film by anthropologists Paul Gelles and Wilton Martínez, *Transnational Fiesta*.

36. See Degregori (1985).

37. Simon Strong (1992: 47, 72).

38. For more on the northern *rondas*, see Gitlitz and Rojas (1983) and Starn (1992).

39. See, for instance, Coronel (n.d.), del Pino (1994), and Isbell (1992).

40. Urrutia (1993: 88).

41. Central Committee of the Communist Party of Peru (1989: 35).

42. A *chullo* is the wool cap often worn by peasants in high villages in the Andes.

43. Central Committee of the Communist Party of Peru (1989: 68, 80).

44. This quote comes from a Shining Path declaration of October 1989, which a news announcer in Huanta was forced to read over the radio under the threat of death.

45. Alvarez (n.d.: 23); cf. Fox and Hernández (1989).

46. See de la Cadena (1991).

47. Mossbrucker (1990) offers a useful analysis of the utopian strain of much of the scholarship on Andean communities.

48. See del Pino (1994) for more on the history of the rondas in the Apurímac Valley. IDL (1990) offers more on "Commander Huayhuaco," including his implication in major violations of human rights.

49. Decreto Legislativo No. 741, November 8, 1991, reprinted in *El Peruano*, the Peruvian government's official newspaper, November 12, 1991, p. 101687.

50. I borrow some of this phrasing from Ajani (1993: 5).

51. Galeano (1992: 282). Seligmann (1993) discusses the responses of Cuzco market women to Fujimori's austerity program.

52. My emphasis on heterogeneity should not be taken to imply that all earlier scholars of Latin American social movements ignored the problem of heterogeneity; see, e.g., Nash (1978) for an Andean case; and more generally, Wolf (1969).

53. Quoted in Starn, ed. (1993: 47, 43).

54. This story made *The New York Times*: "Peasant Farmers Said to Kill Rebels," March 14, 1990, section 1, p. 13.

55. For an account of the events in Paccha, see Amnesty International (1992: 25). Historian Nelson Manrique (1989: 167) makes the point about the brutality of peasant wars. Carlos Iván Degregori (1989a) takes issue with Manrique, and advances the case for the existence of a "punish but do not kill" ethic, in a response to Manrique. Although in disagreement with the essentializing thrust of both sides in this debate, I want to emphasize my broad admiration for the work of both of these scholars, who are among the most perceptive observers of contemporary Peru.

56. Interview on December 12, 1991.

57. This quote comes from Americas Watch (1991: 15), although I wish to stress my general admiration for their usually sharp-sighted work on behalf of human rights in Latin America.

58. Quoted in Starn, ed. (1993: 53).

59. Kirk (1991, 1993a) has done the best work on Peru's internal refugees.

60. Quoted in Starn, ed. (1993: 43).

61. Quoted in Degregori (1989b: 24).

62. Abu-Lughod (1990: 53).

63. Nietzsche (1990: 31, 32).

64. Quoted in Balaguer (1993: 15).

65. Moreiras (1990: 15).

66. Harvey (1989: 289).

67. Valcárcel (1950: 1).

68. Hall (1992: 22).

69. See, for instance, the overly enthusiastic claim of the normally perspicacious Celeste Olalquiaga (1992: 91) about Latin American cultural hybridity as "a directorial and spectorial delight."

70. I borrow this phrasing from the title of an article by Teresa Ebert (1992) and from George Yudicé (1992: 546).

71. See Shohat (1992) for a critique of postcolonial theory along these lines.

72. García Canclini (1990: 7).

73. Vargas Llosa (1983: 70).

74. Husson (1992) has published a fascinating history of Iquichan revolts of the nineteenth century.

75. José Carlos Mariátegui, *Mundial*, November 25, 1927, p. 21.

76. Olalquiaga (1992: 94). On a return visit in 1994, I found that sixty Puros families had indeed returned, part of a broad, and often painful, process of rebuilding dozens of villages in Iquicha, including Marcaraccay, Uchuraccay, Cunya, and Paccre.

77. Mallon (1983) details this history.

78. César Vallejo, "The Nine Monsters," translated by Robin Kirk in Starn, Degregori, and Kirk, eds. (1995).

79. "*Desborde popular*" is the title of an influential book by Matos Mar (1984).

References

Abu-Lughod, Lila. 1990. "The Romance of Resistance: Tracing Transformations of Power through Bedouin Women," *American Ethnologist* 17 (1): 41–55.

Ajani, Fouad. 1993. "The Summoning," *Foreign Affairs* (September–October): 2–9.

Álvarez, Sonia. n.d. "Theoretical Problems and Methodological Impasses in the Study of Contemporary Social Movements in Brazil and the Southern Cone: An Agenda for Future Research." Ms., Department of Politics, University of California, Santa Cruz.

Americas Watch. 1986. *Civil Patrols in Guatemala*. New York: Americas Watch.

———. 1991. *Into the Quagmire: Human Rights and U.S. Policy in Peru.* New York: Human Rights Watch.

Amnesty International. 1992. *Human Rights during the Government of Alberto Fujimori*. New York: Amnesty International.

Balaguer, Alejandro. 1993. *Rostros de la guerra/Faces of War*. Lima: Peru Reporting.

Benjamin, Walter. 1968. *Illuminations: Essays and Reflections*. New York: Harcourt, Brace, and World.

Bloch, Marc. 1961. *Feudal Society*, vol. 1. Translated by L. A. Mannion. Chicago: University of Chicago Press.

Burneo, José, and Marianne Eyde. 1986. *Rondas campesinas y defensa civil*. Lima: SER.

Carmack, Robert M., ed. 1988. *Harvest of Violence: The Maya Indian and the Guatemalan Crisis*. Norman: University of Oklahoma Press.

Central Committee of the Communist Party of Peru. 1989. "Interview of Chairman Gonzalo." Mimeo.

Chávez de Paz, Dennis. 1989. *Juventud y terrorismo. Características sociales de los condenados por terrorismo y otros delitos*. Lima: Instituto de Estudios Peruanos.

Coronel, José. 1996. "Violencia política y respuestas campesinas en Huanta." In Carlos Iván Degregori, ed., *Las rondas campesinas y la derrota de Sendero Luminoso*, 29–116. Lima: Instituto de Estudios Peruanos/Universidad Nacional de San Cristóbal de Huamanga.

———. n.d. "Comités de Defensa: Un proceso social abierto." *Ideéle*, No. 59–60: 113–15.

Coronel, José, and Carlos Loayza. 1992. "Violencia política: Formas de respuesta comunera en Ayacucho." In Carlos Iván Degregori et al., eds., *Perú: El problema agrario en debate/SEPIA IV*, 509–37. Lima: SEPIA.

Degregori, Carlos Iván. 1985. "Sendero Luminoso: I. Los hondos y mortales desencuentros" and "Sendero Luminoso: II. Luchas armada y utopía autoritaria." Working papers No. 4 and 6. Lima: Instituto de Estudios Peruanos.

———. 1989a. "Comentario a la Década de la violencia." *Márgenes* 3, No. 5–6: 186–90.

_____. 1989b. *Qué difícil es ser Dios. Ideología y violencia política en Sendero Luminoso.* Lima: El Zorro de Abajo.

_____. 1990. *Ayacucho 1969–1979: El surgimiento de Sendero Luminoso.* Lima: Instituto de Estudios Peruanos.

de la Cadena, Marisol. 1991. "Las mujeres son más indias: Etnicidad y género en una comunidad del Cusco." *Revista Andina* 9 (1): 7–29.

del Pino H., Ponciano. 1992. "Los campesinos en la guerra o como la gente comienza ponerse macho." In Carlos Iván Degregori et al., eds., *Perú: El problema agrario en debate/SEPIA IV*, 487–508. Lima: SEPIA.

_____. 1994. "Tiempos de guerra y de dioses. Sendero, ronderos y evangélicos." Ms., Instituto de Estudios Peruanos, Lima.

Ebert, Teresa. 1992. "Luddic Feminism, the Body, Performance, and Labor: Bringing Materialism Back into Feminist Cultural Studies," *Cultural Critique* (Winter): 5–50.

Flores Galindo, Alberto, ed. 1987. *Independencia y revolución 1780–1840*, 2 vols. Lima: Instituto Nacional de Cultura.

Foucault, Michel. 1971. *The Order of Things: An Archaeology of the Human Sciences.* New York: Pantheon.

Fox, Jonathan, and Luis Hernández. 1989. "Offsetting the Iron Law of Oligarchy," *Grassroots Development* 13 (2): 8–15.

Galeano, Eduardo. 1992. *We Say No: Chronicles, 1963–1991.* New York: Norton.

García Canclini, Nestor. 1990. *Culturas híbridas: Estrategias para entrar y salir de la modernidad.* Mexico City: Horizonte.

Gitlitz, John, and Telmo Rojas. 1983. "Peasant Vigilante Committees in Northern Peru," *Journal of Latin American Studies* 15 (1): 163–97.

González, Raúl. 1982. "Por los caminos de Sendero." *QueHacer* 19: 39–47.

Gorriti Ellenbogen, Gustavo. 1990. *Sendero: Historia de la guerra milenaria en el Perú*, vol. 1. Lima: Editorial Apoyo.

Hall, Stuart. 1992. "What Is This 'Black' in Black Popular Culture?" In Gina Dent, ed., *Black Popular Culture*, 21–33. Seattle: Bay Press.

Harvey, David. 1989. *The Condition of Postmodernity.* London: Basil Blackwell.

Hemming, John. 1970. *The Conquest of the Incas.* New York: Harcourt, Brace, Jovanovich.

Husson, Patrick. 1992. *De la guerra a la rebelión: Huanta, Siglo XIX.* Lima: Centro de Estudios Regionales "Bartolomé de las Casas."

IDL (Instituto de Defensa Legal). 1990. *Perú 1989. En la espiral de violencia.* Lima: IDL.

_____. n.d. *El papel de la organización social campesina en la estrategia campesina.* Lima: IDL.

Isbell, Billie Jean. 1992. "Shining Path and Peasant Responses in Rural Ayacucho." In David Scott Palmer, ed., *The Shining Path of Peru*, 59–81. New York: St. Martin's Press.

Kirk, Robin. 1991. *The Decade of Chaqwa: Peru's Internal Refugees.* Washington, DC: U.S. Committee for Refugees.

_____. 1993a. *To Build Anew: An Update on Peru's Internally Displaced People*. Washington, DC: U.S. Committee for Refugees.

_____. 1993b. *Grabado en piedra. Las mujeres de Sendero Luminoso*. Lima: Instituto de Estudios Peruanos.

McClintock, Cynthia. 1984. "Why Peasants Rebel: The Case of Peru's Sendero Luminoso," *World Politics* 27 (1): 48–84.

Mallon, Florencia E. 1983. *The Defense of Community in Peru's Central Highlands: Peasant Struggle and Capitalist Transition, 1860–1940*. Princeton: Princeton University Press.

Manrique, Nelson. 1989. "La década de la violencia." *Márgenes* 3 (5–6) (Lima): 137–82.

Matos Mar, José. 1984. *Desborde popular y crisis del estado*. Lima: Instituto de Estudios Peruanos.

Mayer, Enrique. 1991. "Peru in Deep Trouble: Mario Vargas Llosa's 'Inquest in the Andes' Reexamined," *Cultural Anthropology* 6 (4): 466–504.

Moreiras, Alberto. 1990. "Transculturación y pérdida de sentimiento." *Nuevo Texto Crítico* 6:15–33.

Mossbrucker, Harold. 1990. *El concepto de la comunidad: Un enfoque crítico*. Lima: Instituto de Estudios Peruanos.

Nash, June. *We Eat the Mines and the Mines Eat Us*. New York: Columbia University Press.

Nietzsche, Friedrich. 1990. *Beyond Good and Evil*. Translated by Michael Tanner. London: Penguin.

Noel Moral, Roberto. 1989. *Ayacucho: Testimonio de un soldado*. Lima: Publinor.

Olalquiaga, Celeste. 1992. *Megalopolis: Contemporary Cultural Sensibilities*. Minneapolis: University of Minnesota Press.

Palmer, David Scott, ed. 1992. *The Shining Path of Peru*. New York: St. Martin's Press.

Salcedo, José María. 1987. "El caso Uchuraccay, cuatro años después." *QueHacer* 45: 14–15.

Seligmann, Linda J. 1993. "Between Worlds of Exchange: Ethnicity among Peruvian Market Women," *Cultural Anthropology* 8 (2): 187–213.

Shohat, Ella. 1992. "Notes on the 'Post-Colonial,' " *Social Text* 31–32: 99–113.

Silverblatt, Irene. 1994. "Becoming 'Indian' in the Central Andes of 17th Century Peru." In Gyan Prakash, ed., *After Colonialism: Colonial Histories, Postcolonial Displacements*, 272–94. Princeton: Princeton University Press.

Starn, Orin. 1991. "Sendero, soldados y ronderos en el Mantaro." *QueHacer* 74: 60–68.

_____. 1992. " 'I Dreamed of Foxes and Hawks': Reflections on Peasant Protest, New Social Movements and the Rondas Campesinas of Northern Peru." In Arturo Escobar and Sonia Alvarez, *The Making of Social Movements in Latin America: Identity, Strategy, Democracy*, 89–111. Boulder: Westview Press.

_____. 1993b. "La resistencia en Huanta." *QueHacer* 84: 34–41.

_____, ed. 1993. *Hablan los ronderos: La búsqueda por la paz en los Andes.* Lima: Instituto de Estudios Peruanos.

Starn, Orin, Carlos Iván Degregori, and Robin Kirk, eds. 1995. *The Peru Reader: History, Culture, Politics.* Durham: Duke University Press.

Stern, Steve J. 1982. *Peru's Indian Peoples and the Challenge of Spanish Conquest: Huamanga to 1640.* Madison: University of Wisconsin Press.

Strong, Simon. 1992. *Shining Path: Terror and Revolution in Peru.* New York: Times Books.

Urrutia, Jaime. 1993. "Ayacucho: Un escenario pos-Gonzalo, ¿Ya?" *Ideéle* 59–60: 8–90.

_____. 1950. "Introduction." In Pierre Verger, *Indians of Peru.* New York: Pantheon.

Vargas Llosa, Mario. 1983. "The Story of a Massacre," *Granta* 9: 62–83.

Wolf, Eric. 1969. *Peasant Wars of the 20th Century.* New York: Harper and Row.

Yúdice, George. 1992. "Postmodernism on the Periphery," *South Atlantic Quarterly* 92 (3): 543–56.

8

Pan-Maya Activism in Guatemala

Kay B. Warren

One of the great horror stories of the late twentieth century has been the virtual ethnocide of the Maya villagers in Guatemala during the 1980s. The Guatemalan army, in an attempt to destroy a guerrilla movement, massacred many Maya and forced others into army-run settlements where they often were not given enough to eat. The villagers, as in Peru, were compelled to patrol their areas against the guerrillas. Anybody who dissented from the army's policies was considered a subversive. Death squads took care of union leaders and other organizers, including those of the Maya movement, when they dared to speak out against abuses.

Since the peace accord between the guerrillas and the Guatemalan government in late 1996, the situation has improved somewhat. But, as anthropologist Kay Warren makes clear here, the Maya have been deeply scarred by the campaigns that wiped out tens of thousands of their brethren. The way in which they are beginning to organize is rather different from the other indigenous groups examined in this volume. Perhaps only Colombia, with its increasing violence in the countryside, will have similar types of organizations. However, in Guatemala (unlike Colombia) the Maya are the majority of the population, thus making this case an especially poignant one.

Kay B. Warren is a professor of anthropology at Harvard University. She has written extensively on both Peru and Guatemala.

> There are Mayas who argue these studies do
> more harm than good for the movement.
> —*Demetrio Cojtí Cuxil (1997, 133)*

Despite the hegemonic image Ladino culture enjoys in national affairs, alternative realities erupt from time to time to defy its terms,

From Kay B. Warren, *Indigenous Movements and Their Critics: Pan-Maya Activism in Guatemala* (Princeton: Princeton University Press, 1998), 194–206. Reprinted by permission of Princeton University Press.

even on the highest level. While addressing the Guatemalan National Congress in 1975 about Ladino land seizures that had victimized Maya peasants, Representative Fernando Tezahuic Tohón (one of only two Maya representatives in Congress at that point) was said to have suddenly lapsed into his Maya language. He was immediately called to order for not speaking in the official national language, Spanish. The incident was reported in the national press and is still referred to years later. Pan-Maya activist Enrique Sam Colop interprets this as a moment when the representative, speaking about an issue that affected him deeply, switched unconsciously to his maternal language in order to express himself freely. This was not simply a tactical move or protest. For Mayanists, the unintentional "failure to observe order" (*falta al orden*) and the anger it evoked in Congress reveal the arbitrary and imposed nature of the official system (1983, 66).

In their writings, Mayanists suggest that the national order is fated to crack and fissure only to expose other underlying realities: how little is actually shared, how much is unintelligible to those in power, how fragile the claim is to a singular nationality, and how social critiques claim audiences in other than the official language. Thus, the belligerent call to order—a dramatic show of control—only revealed a much more fundamental lack of control. As Alberto Melucci (1989) would suggest, remembering the event in this vein pushes the discourse of power to its limits and demonstrates the self-contradictory character of state rationality. Once the instability and arbitrariness of existing arrangements is unmasked, Mayanists argue it is imperative that the government and wider public recognize the national stature of the country's cultural pluralism. Given that Mayas make up a substantial percentage of the national population and that indigenous rights were propelled to center stage in the 1996 peace accords, these issues are likely to gain greater attention in the next decade. As Cojtí Cuxil has announced: "Guatemala is a multinational society. . . . That is to say, 'Guatemalan culture' cannot be other than a confederation of cultures and languages in which each preserves its originality" (1991, 6, 84).

History, of course, provides complex protagonists, and so it turns out that Tezahuic Tohón is most often remembered in silence as a warning rather than a hero. In 1976 he attempted to create the Indigenous Party of Guatemala and become "the maximal leader of the indigenous people," only to be forced—after hostile accusations in the press and Congress that he was promoting racism and class conflict—to repackage the political party as non-discriminatory and nationalist. The renamed Front for National Integration was compelled to retool its nascent indigenous agenda and forge alliances with existing parties as Tezahuic Tohón sought votes to extend its base past the core of several hundred activists. In what are portrayed as desperate attempts to consolidate power within the raw hegemony of insider party politics, Tezahuic Tohón courted parties across the spectrum only to end up joining the right-wing alliance supporting General Lucas García for president. This futile alliance generated few votes and no momentum or enduring party structure. In hindsight, it was also a terrible political misstep, as Lucas García soon became one of the chief architects of state terrorism directed toward the Maya highlands in the early 1980s.[1]

This whispered story of the dangers of Guatemalan democracy and the complex vulnerability of those who seek political power haunts Mayanists who acknowledge the formidable obstacles to entering party politics on the national level despite the Maya numerical majority in many highland communities. It illustrates why a movement that holds presidential candidate forums and is proud of the election of Maya mayors and congressional representatives and the formation of civic committees to promote local candidates has nevertheless been extremely cautious about organizing politically as long as other paths to influence prove effective and parties resist change.

At the heart of Pan-Maya activism is the project of rendering "national culture" explicitly problematic. Most officials in the country's legal and educational systems have not shared this concern; for them, national culture remains obviously synonymous with urban Ladino culture. According to Sam Colop (1983, 61), however, this self-satisfaction only masks a submerged identity crisis:

> "National culture" is the set of habits that Ladinos practice, a sum of North American-Hispanic elements that do not diminish it yet render it dependent. Jean-Loup Herbert says of this culture: They look endlessly for a definition of national culture: *mestizo,* Hispanic-American, Iberian-American, Latin American, or modern— empty terms that reflect the alienated search of a minority. Paradoxically they hope for and predict the disappearance of indigenous culture into this historic nothingness: [According to Joaquin Noval,] "integration does not require that all indigenous people are transformed into Ladinos, but this will probably be their destiny."

Sam Colop's quotations of Ladino skepticism deconstruct the rightful authority and authoritativeness of existing constructions of "national culture" to represent the country.[2] It is clear to Mayanists how Ladinos have been able to reproduce the illusion of a hegemonic national culture— through their monopoly of the schools, church, mass media, and political structures.

History continues to be on the mind of these activists. Movement intellectuals and students have studied the sixteenth-century chronicles— Spanish and Maya—of the foreign invasion of what later came to be Guatemala. They have been quick to demonstrate the tactical and debilitating use of these documentary sources in official histories that portray Maya culture as timeless and marginalize indigenous Guatemalans from the development of the modern state. Pan-Mayanists have also produced powerful testimonial histories of the recent civil war. A preoccupation with genesis crosscuts these projects: a concern with the pre-Columbian sources of Maya culture and the colonial and contemporary sources of Guatemala's ethnic formation through which indigenous populations have been designated as the devalued "other."

Another issue for Pan-Mayanism has been the exploration of the powerful fiction of the unitary, all-powerful state—or, in Michael Taussig's (1993) terminology, state fetishism—in a situation of tremendous state violence. Sam Colop's analysis of Spanish chronicles and their use in official history shows how Guatemalan nationalism is strategically constituted as standing above ethnicity; Montejo's testimonial ethnography demythologizes the state as a singular protagonist.

With a focus on the logics of racism, this activist research continually runs the risk of elevating the indigenous "self" by categorically denouncing the Spanish/Ladino "other" as a racist, thus creating a variant of reverse orientalism. Yet, in a different move, Maya intellectuals have also read indigenous narratives of struggle and resistance across the grain to examine the underside of state fetishism—the painful complicity of some Mayas, as soldiers and civil patrollers, with military forces that brutally oppressed other Mayas. These observers ask in realist ethnographic terms: How precisely does a terrorist state exert its coercive powers over individuals, some who internalize violence and come to enjoy it and others who in the worst of circumstances find an exit or discover small ways to draw a line even when overt resistance is impossible? . . . Mayas both inside and outside the Maya movement have felt compelled to produce culture that expresses the existential dilemmas they faced during the heightened uncertainties and ambiguities of the counterinsurgency war.

These issues will not disappear with the peace accords. From all reports, the military, even as it downsizes and disbands civil patrols, is currently organizing new structures of surveillance. Many Guatemalans feared that demobilized soldiers, police, and guerrillas would only find violent lines of work that exploit their combat training. They were right. Unless employment and land issues are effectively addressed in the peace implementation process, robberies, kidnappings, murders, and extortion are likely to escalate still further. In the past, rising anxiety has sometimes led people in unexpected quarters to call for authoritarian regimes to reestablish order in civil society or for renewed militarization (which may involve U.S. intervention) to deal with increased drug-related violence and corruption.

Current analyses of language and politics have important implications for models of national political organization. Mayanists and others are proposing models for democratic organization that range from territorial autonomy to administrative regionalization to class-based and transethnic political blocs acting within existing forms of participatory democracy. For Mayanists, the emerging metaphor is "nation" as contrasted with "state." Sam Colop (1983, 35) defines nation in the following terms:

> Nation is a state of social consciousness, a psychological phenomenon. It is collective loyalty that unites a society with its collective past and involves it in common aspirations. It is cultural identification, sentiment, and a common means of communication: language. We do not include the term race[3] because this biological terminology has been surpassed. This means that a legislated or objective standard does not make a nation. Rather, we insist that it is the psychological or intellectual self-conception of the human group to which we are referring.

A nation, in this view, becomes synonymous with a people or community, which echoes UN rights discourse and the Spanish word *pueblo*.

On the one hand, Mayanists differentiate between "state," a sovereign instrument of administration and control over a territory, and "nation," which does not always have juridic or political power or even territorial expression (Cojtí Cuxil 1991, 4; Sam Colop 1983, 36). Jews were recognized as a nation before the state of Israel, Enrique Sam Colop reminds us. This, of course, is a telling example of dispersion and reunification. Elements of nation emerge from the *"hilo invisible de la etnia"* (the invisible thread of ethnicity), which involves identification with a group having a common history, its own culture, a collective memory, religion, ways of dress, and future aspirations—in short, a deeply felt essence no one else shares. In a Barthian way (1969), one can change in innumerable ways—shifting dress, religion, language, work, and the region where one lives—without losing the essence, the thread of common consciousness. Mayanists argue that constitutions and statutes do not really have the capacity to argue against this essence, for theirs is another nature: as political texts they are vulnerable and ephemeral, as Guatemalan history certainly shows. A common judicial system does not unify distinct nations into a singularity because this imposed abstract uniformity fails to relate to the cultural reality of the indigenous majority (Sam Colop 1983, 37–39; Cojtí Cuxil 1991, 11, 20, 36–39).

In imagining a multinational state, Cojtí Cuxil (1991, 68–71) suggests a new role for Maya languages, as indicators of regionalized cultural identities, or nationalities, which would serve as the basis for territorial subdivisions and self-government. As such they would become the basis of political mobilization to break with existing models of internal colonialism, which subdivide the country into departments without attention to the ways language and history have shaped the landscape.[4]

This federalist vision is where Mayanists differed from the *popular* Left in the early 1990s. At the Second Continental Meeting for Indigenous, Black, and Popular Resistance, the national goal was to bring Guatemalans together on the basis of class and work affiliations for a transethnic movement of Ladinos and Mayas. Through working papers distributed at the conference and ongoing work groups on "indigenous and mass unity," the Left stressed a language of cultural respect and autonomy for indigenous peoples of the Americas. Yet, the idea that autonomy might be expressed in administrative regionalization in Guatemala was troubling to the *popular* leadership. On the whole, Mayanists judged the *popular* model as calling for their assimilation into national society, much as the Guatemalan state has acted in educational policy. *Popular* organizers were seen as externalizing injustice by focusing their critiques on U.S. imperialism and colonialism—and more recently on global "neoliberalism"—rather than giving high priority to patterns of Guatemalan racism, internal colonialism, and cultural distinctiveness.

As this analysis has argued, Mayanists and Maya activists from the Left were brought together more successfully during the peace process through the Assembly of Civil Society and the COPMAGUA forums. The result was a striking coalitional consensus on the importance of "identity and rights of indigenous peoples," which became a separate section of the accords, signed by government and guerrilla representatives. As offshoots of the COPMAGUA process continue to meet to plan agendas for the implementation of the accords, it will be interesting to follow the next stage of consensus building and strategies to influence the National Congress.

The process will be highly charged on all sides. After emerging from a 1996 meeting, one Mayanist complained that coalitions dominated by URNG guerilla allies were still creating documents peppered with "*lucha, lucha, lucha*" ([class] struggle, struggle, struggle) and that he felt ostracized for raising the issue of new political languages—including crossclass alliances—to replace old paradigms. Strong Ladino backlash in the face of indigenous organizing has caused public intellectuals such as Marta Elena Casaus Arzú to call for a rethinking of the Ladino stakes in prevailing definitions of nation and state, which marginalize indigenous citizens. Rightist parties, especially Rios Montt's allies in the Guatemalan Republican Front (FRG), will continue to block reforms using strategies developed during their furious, though ultimately unsuccessful, opposition to Guatemala's endorsement of the ILO 169 accords on indigenous rights, which they sidelined for years in the legislature and the courts.

Cojtí Cuxil (1991, 12–13, 70–76) and other leaders will continue to work toward an image of Guatemala as a federation of nations, each with its own government, territory, laws, and means for cultural development. Public administration would, in this vision, speak the language of those governed, not the other way around; state government would routinely translate documents into regional languages. Representatives from national subunits—Maya and Ladino—would make up the overarching government of the state.

While the 1996 Peace Accords brought recognition of Maya culture, so far the issue of alternative state structures has fallen outside the scope of actual reforms. Thus, Cojtí Cuxil's early condemnation of national politics still holds:

> We have to admit that until now the problem of nationalities has not been resolved by any revolution or counterrevolution, by any reform or counterreform, by any independence or annexation, by a coup or countercoup. (1991, 13)[5]

The problem remains more than recognizing different nationalities or assuming that an abstract language of rights will easily transcend diversity. Rather, it involves conceiving a formula "to federate diverse nationalities [and] articulate diverse national identities democratically" (Cojtí Cuxil 1991, 13). In his view, to govern without wider legitimacy is to risk cycles of violence, as those who govern seek to impose their system and those who want to evade domination push for a more radical decentralization. In early writings, Mayanists cited Lebanon during its civil war,[6] although the world abounds with more timely examples that argue their point. Without a concern for the multinational character of the country, Mayanists hold that neoliberal regional development plans that seek only decentralization are bound to be insufficient (Cojtí Cuxil 1991, 13, 15).

Mayanists have used comparative examples to make their case for the viability and necessity of national reform. First, they show the range of European societies—all high status and democratic, such as Belgium and Spain—that have achieved what some would dismiss as an apocalyptic goal for Guatemala. Latin American examples, such as Peru during its reformist period, are included to establish that multicultural reforms have been attempted in New World countries with substantial indigenous populations. Second, they point out that peoples caught in much more dramatic diasporas have reunified through the thread of a common consciousness to create viable nation-states. Finally, they argue that suppressed ethnicities do not disappear when the larger system mutes them. The failure to negotiate *pluricultural* alternatives has torn other states apart. Pan-Maya comparative politics shows another dimension of nations as "imagined communities"[7]: other systems, perceived as counterparts, can be evoked as political leverage to demonstrate the feasibility of imagined alternatives and the dangers of failing to address the existing social order. The threat is as real as it is oblique.

How does one measure the success or influence of Pan-Mayanism in Guatemala? Mayanists have not organized their own political party. They have avoided the term "activist" for their participants and "political" for their organizations. Rather than seeking to demonstrate their strength through mass demonstrations, they have organized all sorts of conferences, meetings, workshops, educational programs, and editorial campaigns.

The goal of these efforts has been to incorporate new generations of Maya professionals, elementary school teachers, councils of elders, and working adults into their discursive community. The decision to stress "cultural" issues—language, education, religion, community leadership, and ecologically sensitive "development" strategies—reflects the Pan-Maya analysis of cultural difference, Guatemalan racism, and state violence. The ruthlessness of the counterinsurgency war during the late 1970s and 1980s, which severely punished any activism deemed political, shaped Pan-Mayanism in important ways.

Institutionally, Mayanists have founded a vast array of research and educational organizations, linked by national networks, such as COMG [Consejo de Organizaciones Mayas de Guatemala] and its successors, which keep groups in touch with each other. Many of these organizations have local representatives and agents, some have community committees throughout the highlands. Perhaps the most visibly successful program has been the network of private Maya schools. In the 1980s, Maya leaders began to critique the national school system as marginalizing impoverished agriculturalists, some of whom are monolingual in indigenous languages and many of whom are illiterate in Spanish, which serves as the medium of instruction for their children in school. In the subsequent decade, Mayanists have been acting on their critiques by creating alternative schools, textbooks, national educational alliances, and images of nation with more than one official language. There are now several hundred private Maya elementary schools and adult education programs, supported by a variety of foreign funders.

Beyond their successes with Maya schools and centers for research and cultural programming, Pan-Mayanism has had a wider, though much more difficult to measure, effect on Guatemalan society. Like the powerful continuing effects of feminism in the "post-feminist" United States, Pan-Mayanism has promulgated new languages to personalize identity politics, understand inequality, and organize across communities. Cultural innovations—such as the linking of human, civil, and cultural rights— have had a diffuse yet striking effect on the terms of debate in national and local politics. Just as Mayanists adopted and expanded the rights language used by the *popular* movement to include cultural rights, so groups with very distinctive politics have over time found themselves adopting aspects of the Pan-Maya analysis of cultural diversity, although they are highly ambivalent about ethnic organizing per se. The clashing interplay of movements and critics is evident in such shifts in political language.

In debates over the legitimacy and the social vision of Pan-Mayanism, Maya public intellectuals have selectively marshalled essentialist arguments about the deep stability of Maya culture under siege and the foundational wound of racism in marginalizing indigenous peoples. Their critics have countered with tactical post-modernist deconstructions to denaturalize Maya culture, reveal the hybridity of current cultural practices, and highlight moments when Maya class mobility has trumped racism. The dynamic tension between modes of argument—in practice, all sides use foundational and deconstructionist rhetorics—has proved difficult to control. For instance, critic Mario Roberto Morales's spoof of "Ladino identity," originally designed as a foil to ridicule Maya identity politics, helped fuel serious self-questioning among progressive Ladinos about their sense of identity and taken-for-granted entitlement to national culture. For Mayanists, their vital sense of cultural difference has never been able to displace the urgency of widespread poverty that crosscuts, yet is reinforced by, fierce ethnic discrimination.

These cultural transformations have been accompanied by the emergence of a new class of indigenous professionals, who, given Guatemala's ethnic formation, might have passed as Ladinos in past decades or disappeared from the national scene in diasporas of Guatemalan refugees, yet now assert their Mayaness. I have argued that while anthropology has important conceptual and ethnographic contributions to make to the study of hybrid class formation, the field seems hobbled by the way class issues have been framed in the past, especially in works on rural Latin America. In many ways there has been an unexamined ambivalence about class mobility for the rural poor. Perhaps this is a consequence of classical historical materialist frameworks, which, given Latin America's rural poverty, justifiably focused on exposing structural exploitation yet, in the process, produced reductive views of class identity. Yet, dismissive or cynical judgments of mobility reappear in more recent non-Marxist works. The irony, as Mayanists have pointed out, is that most U.S. analysts are middle-class intellectuals with urban and rural working-class roots in their parents' or grandparents' generations. . . .

Many Mayanists are members of new parallel middle classes in rural and urban spheres, which have complex relations with their Ladino counterparts. Thus, one extraordinarily important effect of the movement has been its service as a conduit for novel class-ethnic blends in a society slow to open doors to indigenous employees. Given Pan-Mayanism's leadership, composed in some cases of professionals who pulled themselves back from the brink of passing—by becoming active in Maya organizations and gaining fluency in their hometown's Maya language, sometimes as adults—it is interesting that the movement has not chosen to work with migrants who have passed into Ladino society over the last generation or two. Rather, in a move that reveals another important source of contemporary Maya culture, Pan-Mayanism has focused on forging cross-class alliances with rural middle and agricultural classes in the highland communities where Maya languages are commonly spoken. Here the political contours of Pan-Mayanism's selective definition of communities of shared discourse become evident.

As this analysis has argued, the rural interplay of class, ethnicity, and Pan-Mayanism needs to be examined from multiple points of view. While anthropologists such as Carol Smith (1992) argue that Maya university students forged the movement through debates with their neo-Marxist peers, this analysis has found a wider array of rural as well as urban sources for Pan-Maya activism. It is important to recognize the longer tradition of indigenous intellectuals in rural communities—from the *k'amöl b'ey* archives of traditional knowledge and the *ajq'ij* shaman-priests to catechists and development experts—whose leadership is informed by Maya leadership norms, historical generations, and waves of community organizing by international groups. In San Andrés, local intellectuals have long seen their work in traditionalist saint societies and in sacramental Catholic groups as involving social criticism and activism for the indigenous community. Arjun Appadurai's (1996, 18) insight applies here. Rather than being primordial, the localism of Maya communities is itself a historical product that reflects and inflects the dynamics of the global.

Today, the relation of Mayanists to local intellectuals is played out in the sometimes clashing, sometimes coalitional involvements of generations of activists in local affairs. Pan-Mayanism continues to generate some leaders—such as Alfonso Ixim—who, though active in national organizations, most value the perspective of localized communities, and others—such as No'j Ixim—who advocate pan-community standardization yet maintain close ties to their hometowns. To the extent that decentralized rural schools actually incorporate traditionalist or neotraditionalist elders with localized cultural commitments, these creative and sometimes highly politicized tensions will continue. More likely, the standardized Maya culture and linguistics taught on the high-school level will impress families when it reaffirms generalized translocal values and will be treated as just another form of esoteric knowledge—another academic discipline, like calculus or chemistry—when it strays from recognized norms.

The capacity of the local community of San Andrés to withstand the intrusion of powerful organizations, even when they appear poised to overrun the municipal center, is legendary and subject to a good measure of local pride. In some instances, as with the 1950s establishment of Catholic Action, young adults in the community used the new organization to address the tensions between generations, yet they also reworked the national organization's anticommunist ideology to reflect local concerns about poverty and ethnic tensions. Responding to the establishment of a conservative, extremely hierarchical Opus Dei seminary in the early 1990s, the Catholic community easily buffered itself from external control by selectively channeling outsider participation in local affairs. Soon enough the seminarians relocated to another venue, and the residential complex became the regional Catholic girls' school.

That Maya schools are meeting important educational needs and that teachers are engaging in very creative teaching of young children is clear from my classroom observations in San Andrés. The school, which offers subsidized meals, reaches the children of poor families as well as working adults who can afford small tuition payments to study at night. Teaching in Maya languages at the post-elementary level, however, is a greater challenge, given that the civil war and the availability of work have pulled many adults (teachers and students) away from their home regions. Maya secondary schools will be under much greater competitive pressure to respond to parents' assessments of skills that will give their children highly valued advantages in the wider job market. I suspect that the schools will receive the same treatment as other imports in this tactically syncretic and resilient rural culture.

For both national and local intellectuals, John Watanabe's (forthcoming, 4) insight holds:

> Rather than objectifying culture as essential traits that endure or erode, anthropologists have come to treat Maya cultures in Guatemala as strategic self-expressions of Maya identity, motivated—and thus presumably more appropriately authenticated—by Maya propensities and possibilities in the present rather than by pre-Hispanic primordialisms.

There are ongoing tensions and debates in the political process of authenticating Maya culture rather than an easy emergence of standardized forms through the movement. Mayanists stand on both sides of these divides with locally anchored intellectuals not infrequently at odds with transcommunity activists on issues of language and dialect loyalty, though both groups agree on other issues. Norms of community consultation and consensus decision making have brought the two halves of the movement together at critical junctures, such as in commission meetings designed to make policy recommendations about accord implementation.

Foreign funding of peace accord initiatives will have a great impact on the movement over the next five years. Mayanists are directing attention to the transnational patterns of World Bank and Inter-American Development Bank support for the reconstruction of civil society. At meetings on democracy and development in March 1998, Cojtí Cuxil questioned whether international donors plan to respect and support Maya culture. Or will funding serve to recreate ethnic hierarchies in which Creoles become the project directors and Mayas the beneficiaries of democratization funding? The paradigm shift he hopes for would be a decolonizing one in which protagonists are routinely Mayas, projects make active use of indigenous culture, Mayas would have decision-making power and encourage direct consultation on local preferences, and the aid process could be used to realize the autonomous potential of indigenous culture.

In practice, projects arising from the indigenous accords have favored standardized strategies to train experts in a range of innovative fields and provided temporary employment opportunities for bilingual profession-als in the urban and rural middle classes. Standardized elementary-school materials are published by Maya presses in a range of indigenous lan-guages. International funding has raised and transformed the stakes for the credentialing of intellectuals at the same time that access to high school and college has been expanded. But the wider accords have also favored decentralized strategies to cultivate democratic participation and deal with socioeconomic needs.

In this situation, Pan-Mayanism will experience conflicting tensions and continuing challenges to its development as a movement. To continue its success, Mayanists will have to generate effective cross-class and cross-generation connections at the very moment when stratification within Maya communities is growing and marked in novel ways. The movement will have to continue its national networking across organizations yet ar-ticulate with the country's very different regional economies. Most im-portantly, Pan-Mayanism will have to find ways of appealing to geographically mobile Mayas, including restless youths, refugees, former soldiers, and urban migrants. If Michael Kearney (1996) is right, the eth-nic appeal has great potential for these groups. In the event that Pan-Mayanism does not expand its outreach, other groups will make their appeals in the name of Maya culture.

The accord process has made it very clear that funding models are not designed by Mayanists but rather by the international community and increasingly by groups like the World Bank, which has less experience with indigenous issues. In 1997, $1.9 billion was pledged to Guatemala in reconstruction assistance through the Inter-American Development Bank and the World Bank (Ruthrauff 1997; Ruthrauff and Carlson 1997). While the movement has benefited greatly from foreign support in the past, it will not be given high priority in programs that focus on other aspects of the accords. At issue in the future will be income-generating activities from well-established organizations such as the Maya publisher Cholsamaj and new initiatives such as the founding of a Maya university.

There are various possible futures for the Maya movement. Pan-Mayanism may find a way to ride the global wave of decentralized gov-ernment services and successfully promote regional cultural autonomy in education and self-administration. In the process, the movement may widen its base by recruiting educated youths active in local bread-and-butter issues and rural politics. A federalist solution to multiculturalism and self-determination would reconfigure the Guatemalan state and generate novel institutions to represent linguistic regions in local and national affairs in which Mayanists would play a central role. Mayanists would become in-stitution builders and take an active role in designing a Maya university, public school system, consensus decision-making bodies to represent local communities in wider affairs, an intercultural court system, and regionalized development projects.

Alternatively, the movement will continue to produce urban-trained and rurally affiliated professionals for existing organizations that deal with indigenous issues. This specialization would fuel the three-decade expansion of the bicultural Maya-identified middle class, consolidate routes for mobility across generations in rural families, and give Maya elites a greater voice in national affairs. As we know from the work of Florencia Mallon (1995), James Ferguson (1994), Claudio Lomnitz-Adler (1992), and Steven Feierman (1990), however, there are great risks in bureaucratic reforms driven from the center. In the worst-case scenario, the creation of centralized bureaucratic power structures in the name of reform and decentralization will foster tactical political alliances to constrain alternatives, remove important social issues from the realm of political debate, and generate images of rural life that further naturalize inequalities. More optimistically, after a peace process in which social issues were repoliticized, Maya public intellectuals will continue to cultivate media access in order to publicize their running critiques of national policy and confront the moral consequences of the growing disparity between the life chances of middle income and impoverished Mayas. Similar preoccupations have been powerfully expressed in the writings of Henry Louis Gates and Cornel West (1996) for the urban African-American professional class in the United States.

Still another possible future for the movement is the generative, cultural one of authoring novel discourses of identity and citizenship for the country as a whole. Even in the event that Pan-Mayanism does not expand far beyond its current national network of highly committed advocates, the movement's centers and coalitions will continue to circulate innovative ideas—such as the multiculturalism of Guatemalan society, the revitalization of Maya language and culture, the interlocking agenda of cultural rights, and the rethinking of national education—that other political actors will absorb and appropriate. There is little doubt that the movement has already contributed to a paradigm shift in the way the international community and many indigenous and Ladino Guatemalans think about the country. Political groups on the Right and the Left are now forced to articulate their stands on a range of Maya initiatives that were unheard of or ridiculed in the early 1970s.

In their own ways, each of these imagined outcomes underscores the power of indigenous rights—as a social movement and a critical discourse—to raise important issues for emerging democracies at this historical moment. As Deborah Yashar (1996) argues, this complex power comes from the fundamental tensions in post-Cold War democracy, neoliberal economic policy, and groups marginalized by the hypocritical winds of change. In the next decade, after the efflorescence and likely decline of international funding, Pan-Maya research centers may find ways to become self-sustaining and independent through entrepreneurial activities that marshall Maya cultural capital (in multilingual publications, training centers, continuing education activities, holistic health and development programs, and consulting for the organizational legacies of the peace accords) through specialized international support, and through joint economic endeavors with other indigenous groups in the Americas. Or the movement may be supplanted by new organizations with related agendas, wider membership, different coalitional possibilities, and more direct influence in the Congress and political parties. As individuals decide where to put their energies in the future, the compelling issues for these activists will include the consequences of maintaining or losing control over their central philosophy and political vision, the profound heterogeneity of the Maya *pueblo*, the ways different political interests recast Maya culture for their own political aspirations, and the necessity of finding new ways to work with Ladinos.

As of 1998, members of prominent Pan-Maya organizations eagerly anticipate the formation of exclusively Maya-speaking workplaces within their urban organizations—with Kaqchikel or K'ichee' as their lingua franca—while they have begun to employ sympathetic Ladinos for the first time. One can see these moves as paradoxical responses to political pressures and hostile critics or as inventive next steps in coalition building to mainstream the movement. The internal politics of these moves are just as complex as their intercultural politics. Clearly, Pan-Mayanism's ongoing history is much more absorbing to follow than to predict.

Notes

1. See Falla (1978b), Arias (1990), and de Paz (1993). Falla saw this failure as proof that Mayas would not be able to organize on the basis of ethnic or cultural identity as opposed to revolutionary class identity in solidarity with Ladino workers.

2. Cojtí Cuxil takes this a step further by personalizing the identity crisis as one characteristic of Ladinos (1991, 4–10). This is a particular kind of reverse orientalism, given that its goal is to deconstruct naturalizations of the Ladino as dominator by showing the volatility of the category in history and lack of persuasiveness of the term for the population in question. If cultural identity involves self-conception and Ladinos resist this, then their control seems much less categorical and given. Cojtí Cuxil argues that there is a particular signature to Ladino cultural domination that flows from their insecurity.

3. On race, see also Cojtí Cuxil (1991a, 6, 17–21, 26–27).

4. Actually, only some existing departmental divisions conform roughly to cultural and linguistic regionality. Despite Tax's (1937) elevation of the *municipio* as the basic unit of cultural identity, there is a great deal of indigenous multiculturalism within municipal divisions, which undoubtedly has a long history. See Carmack (1995) and Brintnall (1979).

5. In this and other central phrasings, Cojtí Cuxil employs the Maya aesthetic of parallel phrasing, much like the *k'amöl b'ey* does in ritual discourses.

6. This is an ironic choice, given that Lebanon's discord resulted in part from an inclusive but rigid system of ethnic representation.

7. While Anderson's (1991) language is useful, the culturalist analysis represents an important critique of his top-down model.

References

Anderson, Benedict. 1991. *Imagined Communities: Reflections on the Origin and Spread of Nationalism*. London: Verso.

Appadurai, Arjun. 1996. *Modernity at Large: Cultural Dimensions of Globalization*. Minneapolis: University of Minnesota Press.

Arias, Arturo. 1990. "Changing Indian Identity: Guatemala's Violent Transition to Modernity." In *Guatemalan Indians and the State, 1540–1988*, ed. Carol Smith, 230–57. Austin: University of Texas Press.

Barth, Fredrik, ed. 1969. *Ethnic Groups and Boundaries*. Boston: Little, Brown.

Brintnall, Douglas E. 1979. *Revolt against the Dead: The Modernization of a Mayan Community in the Highlands of Guatemala*. New York: Gordon and Breach.

Carmack, Robert. 1995. *Rebels of Highland Guatemala: The Quiche-Mayas of Momostenango*. Norman: University of Oklahoma Press.

Casaus Arzú, Marta Elena. 1992. *Guatemala: Linaje y Racismo*. San José: FLACSO.

Cojtí Cuxil, Demetrio. 1991. *Configuración del Pensamiento Político del Pueblo Maya*. Quetzaltenango, Guatemala: Asociación de Escritores Mayances de Guatemala.

_____. (Waqi' Q'anil). 1997. *Ri Maya' Moloj pa Iximulew: El Movimiento Maya (en Guatemala)*. Guatemala: Editorial Cholsamaj.

de Paz, Marco Antonio. 1993. *Maya' Amaaq'xuq Junamilaal; Pueblo Maya y Democracia*. Guatemala: Seminario Permanente de Estudios Mayas and Editorial Cholsamaj.

Falla, Ricardo. 1978. "El Movimiento Indígena." *Estudios Centroamericanos* 33, nos. 356–57 (Junio–Julio): 437–61.

Feierman, Steven. 1990. *Peasant Intellectuals: Anthropology and History in Tanzania*. Madison: University of Wisconsin Press.

Ferguson, James. 1994. *The Anti-Politics Machine: "Development," Depoliticization, and Bureaucratic Power in Lesotho*. Minneapolis: University of Minnesota Press.

Gates, Henry Louis, Jr., and Cornel West. 1996. *The Future of the Race*. New York: Alfred Knopf.

Kearney, Michael. 1996. *Reconceptualizing the Peasantry: Anthropology in Global Perspective*. Boulder: Westview Press.

Lomnitz-Adler, Claudio. 1992. *Exits from the Labyrinth: Culture and Ideology in the Mexican National Space*. Berkeley: University of California Press.

Mallon, Florencia. 1995. *Peasant and Nation: The Making of Postcolonial Mexico and Peru.* Berkeley: University of California Press.

Melucci, Alberto. 1989. *Nomads of the Present: Social Movements and Individual Needs in Contemporary Society.* Edited by John Keane and Paul Mier. London: Hutchinson Radius.

Montejo, Victor. 1987. *Testimony: Death of a Guatemalan Village.* Willimantic, Conn.: Curbstone Press.

Ruthrauff, John. 1997. "The Guatemala Peace Process and the Role of the World Bank and Interamerican Development Bank." Paper presented at the Conference on Democracy and Development, Rafael Landívar University, Guatemala.

Ruthrauff, John, and Teresa Carlson. 1997. *Una Guía al Banco Interamericano de Desarrollo y al Banco Mundial: Estrategias para Guatemala.* Guatemala: Centro para la Educación Democrática.

Sam Colop, Luis Enrique. 1983. "Hacia una Propuesta de Ley de Educación Bilingüe." Thesis for the Licenciatura en Ciencias Jurídicas y Sociales, Universidad Rafael Landívar, Guatemala.

Smith, Carol, ed. 1992. "The Second 'Encuentro Continental.' " *Guatemala Scholars Network News*, April, 1–3.

Taussig, Michael. 1993. *Mimesis and Alterity: A Particular History of the Senses.* New York: Routledge.

Tax, Sol. 1937. "The Municipios of the Midwestern Highland of Guatemala." *American Anthropologist* 39: 423–44.

Watanabe, John. Forthcoming. "Mayas and Anthropologists in the Highlands of Guatemala since the 1960s." In *Ethnology*, vol. 6 of *Supplement to the Handbook of Middle American Indians*, ed. John Monaghan. Victoria Bricker, gen. ed. Austin: University of Texas Press.

Yashar, Deborah. 1996. "Indigenous Protest and Democracy in Latin America." In *Constructing Democratic Governance: Latin America and the Caribbean in the 1990s, Themes and Issues*, ed. Jorge Domínguez and Abraham Lowenthal, 87–105. Baltimore: Johns Hopkins University Press.

IV

Indigenous Leaders Speak Out

9

Marta Silva Vito Guaraní

This speech, delivered in May 1994 before the U.S. House of Representatives, in a nutshell gives the all-too-familiar litany of problems for indigenous peoples throughout the Americas. This is not to say that these abuses are not real, but the themes of ecological degradation, deeply unfair power relations in the countryside, and the horrendous consequences of indigenous displacement to urban slums are common among many native peoples. In this case, the Guaraní who live in the Pantanal region of Brazil (on the western border with Bolivia and Paraguay) represent an extreme case where there is not much left to be saved. What is interesting here is the way in which Marta Silva, the president of the Kaguateca Association for Displaced Indians—Marçal de Souza, characterizes several ethnic groups in western Brazil she knows and describes how each has fared.

I have come before this tribunal to speak about the life of the Indians who live in the state of Mato Grosso do Sul, in a region known as the Pantanal. There are nearly 60,000 Indians, of the Guaraní, Nhandeva, Kaiowá, Ofaié-Xavante, Guató, Kadiwéu, Quinikinawa, Quaxi, and other nations.

They are courageous and brave Indians, who were able to survive the violent attacks of our enemies—white men who in their ambition of land have evicted us. They kill and degrade us. If today the world knows about the beautiful Pantanal (Wetland) of Mato Grosso—one of the last ecological reserves on the planet—it is because we Indians defend and preserve it. Much Indian blood has run, and still runs, on the ground of that land. Millions of Indians were killed, and the majority of the different nations were decimated. But there are still many survivors.

The Ofaié-Xavante, the people with lips of honey, are gentle people who have spent the last 100 years being kicked out of one place or another. Today, they live on the Paraná River. The government has now taken them from their lands, because it will be flooded in order to build a factory. The Guató also live there, one of the last Canoeiro tribes left in the

From Marta Silva Vito Guaraní, "A Pantanal Indian Speaks Out," Amanakaia Amazon Network.

world. They were the first inhabitants of the Pantanal. Today, they live on the border of the Paraguay River, in the city of Corumbá, and some on Insau Island, where they wish to return and live their culture. Their lands are in the process of demarcation on this island. The Kadiwéu live in Mato Grosso. They are known for their warrior spirit and for the beauty of their pottery decorated with natural paints. The Terene, who were able to survive from their gardens and plantings, live in Mato Grosso. They also have problems with the invasion of their lands.

Now I want to speak of my people: the Guaraní Nhandeva and Kaiowá. There are statistics which show that we are the poorest and most abandoned peoples in Brazil. We are people with an ancient culture, descendants of the people from the Sun. There are Guaraní in all of Brazil, especially in the southern part of the country. The Guaraní are a great indigenous nation, which has been able to survive the Conquest, perhaps by their nomadic life. For the Guaraní, the core of resistance is religion. But today there are many Protestant churches that come to our communities with the same discourse as the Jesuits who came during the "discovery" of Brazil. They are killing our religion, killing our culture. Without a cultural identity, our people wander the highways and streets of the cities, drinking, begging, and being ridiculed by the white society. I am the niece of Marçal de Souza, who was murdered in 1983 by gunmen hired by rich landowners. They wanted him to shut up, because he was denouncing to Brazil and the world the disrespect with which we are treated in our own country. In Brazil, the murder of Indians doesn't shock anymore—not the politicians or the government or the civil population. There is a minority concerned with indigenous people and for this, we need to sensitize the whole world. And that is what we are doing now.

At the government level, FUNAI (National Indian Foundation) is in charge of Indian issues. We also have a chapter in the Brazilian Constitution. But if we continue dying, suffering, and living in misery, if we are marginalized, we must ask: Why the chapter of the Constitution? Why FUNAI?

The lands of my people were occupied by large landowners, who have lands that go as far as the eye can see, full of well-treated and well-fed cattle. On my land, cattle are worth more than Indians. Many Indians in Mato Grosso do Sul are leaving their communities and moving to urban centers. They go to live in the slums, and little by little they start losing their cultural identity and become "nobodies." In the villages they live surrounded by gunmen and by the ranchers' cattle. The cattle stomp on their gardens and tractors knock down their houses. The rivers are dirty with the waste from the large farms in the region: pesticides, mercury, etc. They finished with our forest, they are finishing with what is left of our savannahs. They killed our birds and our animals. And they say that we are no longer Indians because we wear clothes. . . . Over seven thousand Indians are working in the charcoal factories and the sugarcane processing plants. They live in a state of slavery. This is the integration that white society offers us. But we Indians, the first owners of this land, cannot accept this humiliating and inhuman integration!

For this reason, young Guaraní are killing themselves; they are searching for the end, hanging themselves. The women from the community of Jaguapiré told me that they will kill their children and kill themselves afterwards if they try to take their land away again. I cannot cross my arms before the massacre of my people. It is for them that I am here to tell the world that the Indians of Brazil do not see land as private property. Land is important for peoples to survive culturally and in their humanity. To populate an area is to give human value to a place, to complete a stage in our evolution—therefore taking away the [land] means to kill the people. For this, it is necessary to demarcate the indigenous land in Brazil. It is necessary to secure the land for our survival.

Land is culture and culture is life for us. Brazil needs to stop being the nation which least respects its native peoples on the face of this earth. The true history of the Brazilian Indian remains to be told. We have resisted for 400 years. We are not enemies, we want to live in peace in this country, with enough land for all: white, black, and yellow. Along with me, all the Indians are dreaming of this moment. Marçal de Souza, Angelo Krata, Simão Bororoo, and so many other anonymous heroes shared this dream with us.

10

Davi Kopenawa Yanomami

Anthropologist Napoleon Chagnon first studied the Yanomami, one of the most famous of the Amazon peoples, and characterized them as the "Fierce People" who are constantly at war over resources. In 2001, Patrick Tierney, in Darkness in El Dorado, *asserted that Chagnon had misrepresented them.*

Be that as it may, in the late 1980s gold was discovered in Yanomami territory, which straddles the border between Venezuela and Brazil. As a result, thousands of miners entered the region. Many Yanomami who refused to work in the mining operations or who resisted encroachment were killed. Also, disease as well as pollution caused by the use of highly toxic mercury to refine the gold brought about many deaths. Although the situation has improved somewhat over the past few years, the struggle between outsiders and the Yanomami continues to this day. As Davi Kopenawa Yanomami points out in this interview in Multinational Monitor *in 1992, the Brazilian army's emphasis on security and the economic development of border regions continue to trouble relations between the Brazilian state and the Yanomami, even with the creation of the Yanomami Reserve. Davi Kopenawa was one of the indigenous "stars" of the Rio Earth Summit, a man in a feather headdress who visually represented the image of the Amazon Indian.*

Why did you choose to attend the Rio Earth Summit?

DKY: I know that the authorities and many people came here because the planet is sick and they are trying to find out how to cure it. The people who come from many places, from the other side of the big lake, all came here to learn about how we [the Yanomami and other indigenous people] live.

I want to speak giving the message from Omai. Omai is the creator of the Yanomami who also has created all the *shaboris* that are the shamans. The shaboris are the ones that have the knowledge, and they sent two of us to deliver their message. The message is to stop destruction, to stop taking out minerals from under the ground, to stop taking out the steel

From an interview with David Kopenawa Yanomami, Center for World Indigenous Studies, Fourth World Documentation Project Archive.

with which all the metal utensils are made, and to stop building roads [through forests].

We feel that a lot of riches have already been taken out of the indigenous lands, and a lot of these riches are getting old and useless, and it would be much better if the Brazilian government would give these riches to the poor in Brazil. Our work is to protect nature, the wind, the mountains, the forest, the animals, and this is what we want to teach you people.

What has been the effect of gold mining on the Yanomami people and their land?

DKY: In the years 1986 and 1987, the gold miners, the small-time gold diggers known as *garimpeiros*, invaded our territory. In the very beginning of the invasion, in 1987, the garimpeiros killed four Yanomami.

They have now opened up airstrips to be able to settle down in the area, to bring in food, to bring in their tools and to start mining. There were between 40,000 to 50,000 invaders on our lands.

After some months of staying on our territory, they started to transmit malaria to us. That means that the garimpeiros were already sick. Mosquitos bit the garimpeiros and then bit us. That is how we got the disease.

The garimpeiros also brought in other diseases. There are complications of pneumonia, sometimes associated with malaria; tuberculosis; skin diseases that often are associated with other diseases and, especially in children, that can be fatal; there was an epidemic of yellow fever in the area; hepatitis.

How many of the Yanomami have been affected by these diseases?

DKY: Some 15 percent of the Yanomami have died in the last three years. Last year, in 1991, the National Health Foundation registered 175 deaths, of which 110 died of malaria. That is very underestimated. One can assume there were four times as many people who died last year.

The diseases were all brought by the garimpeiros?

DKY: Many of these diseases were not registered before the invasion in the Yanomami area. Malaria existed only in the outskirts of the Yanomami area. However, with the arrival of the garimpeiros, it became the main reason for the deaths.

What steps are being taken to confront this spread of disease?

DKY: The Brazilian government has set up a health project run by the National Indian Foundation of Health, which is trying to eradicate malaria. However, it is very difficult to do this and they have not been able to do it yet.

We also have our own project. We are at the present time working in an area of about a thousand Indians, and we have already taken doctors and nurses to a number of areas throughout our territory, and we are now opening a new site. This project has been helping us a lot.

What is your reaction to President Collor's [Fernando Collor de Mello] recent legal demarcation of your land?

DKY: News of the demarcation was very, very good news for us. We have been fighting for thirty years for this. President Collor has set aside a special budget for FUNAI, the National Indian Foundation, to be able to do this work and they finished the demarcation recently.

Is the demarcation sufficient?

DKY: I don't believe it's really guaranteed. I don't believe that the demarcation and the ratifying of the law are enough because we have a lot of enemies. There are the military, there are the governor and other politicians who are getting payrolls. There are also big Brazilian, American, German, and Japanese mining companies that have a big interest in trying to change this law and to enter our territory.

What else should be done to protect your land?

DKY: Although FUNAI has set up Indian posts that are supposed to protect our lands, it will be very difficult to operate them because FUNAI has no money. We the Yanomami also have a rule. We have to look out, we have to watch where the garimpeiros are entering. It is a preoccupation that we have and that the Commission for the Creation of the Yanomami Park has, so that through this vigilance we can detect where the new invasions are occurring.

Have you experienced any racism at the Earth Summit?

DKY: We feel that there are many white people who don't like the truth and that they don't like it when we tell the truth about things. This is how discrimination starts.

How does racism affect the lives of the Yanomami?

DKY: The Portuguese [and their descendants] have done cruel things to our people, and the fact that many Yanomamis have died with the invasion of the garimpeiros is proof of it. These people want to get rid of the Indians; they pay off people to kill the Indians. They have lawyers who will defend them and get them off without having to be punished.

In Roraima there is really a big problem of discrimination against Indian populations. In the city of Roraima, the white people often refer to Indian populations as *bishus*, which means animals. The white people say that they know everything, that they know how to make machines, to make radios, that they have technology and that the Indians are lazy, that we only eat and sleep and don't produce, and that we are animals.

These are the people who want to cut down the forest and sell the wood to Japan and other countries. They are the ones who are interested in minerals to make rings and necklaces. And they are destroying our lands.

The Brazilians want to destroy the Amazon because they're very worried that the foreigners will come and take everything away. They want to be the first to make use of it. Our enemies say that the people who work with us [foreign nongovernmental organizations] are interested in working with us because they are really interested in taking our riches.

What has been your reaction to the Earth Summit?

DKY: We have asked the shaman to get in touch with his teacher, an elder shaman, and tell him that this conference is taking place, and tell him that he should do some special shamanism so that the Americans should agree with what's going on here. They are asking the help of the older ones, who are the elders and teachers, so they should give more force to them here, and speak so that they will be able to communicate with President [George H. W.] Bush, and convince him to go along with the other countries to save the universe. We don't want to hurt him. We want to ask him to respect us. And we want to ask him to sign the [biodiversity] treaty together with the other nations and to return our rights to life.

President Collor should also agree with preserving the planet. If he doesn't, then we are going to get together all of the shamans of Brazil and we are going to do a very strong shamanism.

President Bush thinks that he is the owner of the world but the shamans are the ones who have the knowledge. He is not the First World. We are the First World.

11

Luis Macas

Luis Macas, a lawyer, is one of the most influential indigenous persons in Ecuador. He has served as president of CONAIE, the Ecuadorian pan-indigenous organization. Although he is a Quechua speaker from the Andean highlands, Macas (as well as his fellow Ecuadorian Nina Pacari—see Chapter 12) sees the implications of skewed economic development on native peoples not only within Ecuador but also on a global scale. He is also able to see how these worldwide phenomena affect local processes among his constituents in the various indigenous groups that make up CONAIE. This 1994 interview with Macas in Multinational Monitor *provides a good introduction to the ideas and programs of CONAIE.*

Macas was also heavily involved in the January 2000 movement that resulted in the overthrow of the elected president, Jamil Mahuad. Unfortunately for him and for CONAIE, his participation did little good for indigenous peoples, as Vice President Jorge Noboa took over and in the end implemented the same policies, including "dollarizing" the economy (the U.S. dollar is now the legal tender in Ecuador). Also, as of mid-2001, a U.S. judge has again thrown out the case brought by the indigenous peoples against Texaco and Maxxus Oil.

Why was CONAIE formed?

LM: CONAIE was formed in November 1986 to carry on the struggles of the indigenous peoples' movement in Ecuador, including the fight to recoup our lands and to rescue our language and culture. Above all, it was formed to search for unity among all the indigenous nations through these common struggles, where before they had fought for their rights in isolation. CONAIE fights for the rights of human beings and for the life of the natural world, and works for a future of justice, equality, respect, liberty, peace, and solidarity. It is an autonomous organization forged from the grassroots through a democratic process of active participation.

What are some of the major issues facing indigenous peoples in Ecuador?

LM: The problems facing indigenous peoples are deeply connected to the issue of land ownership. When the colonizers arrived, they cleared

From an interview with Luis Macas, Center for World Indigenous Studies, Fourth World Documentation Project Archive.

out the Indians. Today, land is concentrated in the hands of the few, and many of our people don't have any land.

In the Amazon region, there is a crisis caused by the presence of oil and mining companies and their violations of indigenous peoples' rights. The displacement of people from their homes has made it impossible for indigenous people to meet basic living conditions.

The oil companies have not only caused the decomposition of our communities and the decomposition of our culture but also the destruction of the ecology. The fight for land is thus extended to the struggle for maintaining the ecology.

The Seventh Licensing Round [in which the government grants land concessions to oil companies] now taking place will affect 85 percent of the Amazon region in Ecuador, including many territories of indigenous peoples. Yet this process includes no input from indigenous peoples. My concern is rooted in the twenty years of experience we've had with Texaco, which has shown us that vertical decision making cannot adequately deal with our concerns.

Land ownership is also the central issue in the highlands, and it is an issue that must be resolved through negotiations. What often happens is the government tells the community that they should try to buy their land from landowners who then put a very high price on this land.

In the general uprising in 1990, many indigenous people in the highlands gained recognition of their rights to extricate themselves from feudal oppression and to acquire communal land title. But there is still much work to be done so that these people will have just conditions to be able to live a secure life on their land.

For example, agro-business companies who cultivate flowers for export are continuously pressuring our people to leave their lands. We have criticized these companies because large-scale extensive cultivation of flowers does not feed people. The profits of these companies merely enrich individual businessmen.

We believe agriculture should not be oriented this way. Instead, it should be geared toward self-sufficiency, to feed our people first, instead of being oriented toward export.

In the coastal area the principal problem is the cutting of the forests and the tricking of community leaders into allowing this to occur. The lumber companies are trying to get concessions of large areas to cut down the forests. The Chachi people, for example, who live in one of the last forest reserves in the western region, are constantly being pressured to lease their lands to lumber companies.

Commercial shrimp farmers have also destroyed indigenous lands in the coastal region, as well as having wiped out the few remaining mangrove forests along the coast.

These are the historic problems of Amazon indigenous peoples. But I think that they are broader and more complex given the neoliberal economic approach in Ecuador today. We are living in a process of structural adjustment in which the rise in prices for necessities affects all Ecuadorians, but the situation is even more serious for those most affected by structural adjustment—indigenous peoples who don't have any insurance, salary, or other protection.

The policies of structural adjustment wear the mask of modernization. But this modernization is really just privatization of government agencies and our natural resources. It's a way to hand them over to private interests. The struggle we're involved in is to avoid the impacts of structural adjustment, as manifested in the policies of privatization, multinational corporations, and the upward adjustment of prices by the Ecuadorian government.

Strategically, there are two main directions in which we work: to fight for our rights as indigenous peoples and to help work for proposals for political change, together with other sectors of society. Therefore, we have made concrete political proposals not only for indigenous peoples, but for all of Ecuadorian society.

What has been the role of the World Bank and the International Monetary Fund in promoting the neoliberal approach?

LM: I think that the government follows the directives of the World Bank and the IMF very closely, and these are policies that impact indigenous peoples throughout Latin America. The Ecuadorian government has to accept the conditions of the IMF and World Bank in order to obtain new credit. And it doesn't matter if this negatively affects a great majority of Ecuadorians. What matters is that they do what is necessary to obtain credit. These are policies imposed from outside, but they create problems inside our country.

It's really part of a global problem that is very complicated. But we are questioning the priorities of multilateral banks and government agencies and will encourage them to intervene and affect the situation in Ecuador. We want multilateral development banks to see the impact of projects that are carried out in Ecuador. Loans for the modernization of the oil sector, for example, directly affect indigenous peoples by encouraging hazardous oil development on their lands.

What are CONAIE's main demands to the government?

LM: A permanent demand to the government is that they genuinely legalize the ownership of indigenous lands in the Amazon. This would also serve as a way to preserve the environment. Despite the fact that indigenous lands are legalized—with written land title—the government still hands over the rights to take oil out of these lands to multinationals, claiming government ownership of what is under the land.

We are also asking for a complete investigation of what has happened until now with oil development, not only in terms of ecological impacts but also what has happened to our peoples, because what we are really talking about is the extinction of a people.

It is the position of CONAIE and other organizations representing indigenous peoples of the Amazon that the Seventh Licensing Round should be postponed and a moratorium on oil development be put into effect until there are measures to protect the people of the Amazon.

How has the government responded to your demands?

LM: The government has vacillated. They have never satisfied the aspirations of indigenous peoples. They have never engaged in a serious dialogue, so we have not had answers to our concerns. Moreover, the government has tried to manage and distort information both in Ecuador and in the international media by creating entities in order to control the indigenous movement. They claim to be "helping" indigenous peoples, but in reality, they are doing nothing to help. For example, without any discussion with indigenous organizations, the government recently created a Secretariat of Indigenous Affairs. For all the problems of the indigenous peoples to be reduced to just one office is absurd. Even when we are going through structural adjustment cutbacks, the government is creating these new bureaucratic entities. This is both contradictory and cynical.

What has been the effect of Texaco's operations in the Ecuadorian rainforest?

LM: In terms of environmental impact, this is one of the greatest disasters that has taken place in the Ecuadorian Amazon, It is well known that the resources—the biodiversity—cannot be recuperated. There is no way to bring this back; it is now a biological desert.

Besides provoking a disappearance of species, there has also been a decomposition of communities in the Amazon. Texaco poisoned the places where people lived and worked and threw away its wastes in a totally irresponsible way.

Texaco is extracting a resource that brings tremendous wealth, but in the places where it has been extracted there is only poverty and slums that are not fit for human habitation.

Indigenous and environmental groups are now seeking to hold Texaco accountable in the U.S. courts. We have chosen the United States to air our concerns since that is where Texaco makes its decisions. There is no violation of Ecuadorian sovereignty, since the principal headquarters of Texaco is in the United States. Yet there has been a very violent reaction on the part of the Ecuadorian government to try to move this case to Ecuador. But from a legal and the political perspective it is appropriate to hear the case in the United States.

CONAIE will continue to press the Texaco case because among the plaintiffs are the Cofán peoples, who are members of CONAIE.

What are the other elements of your campaign against the company?

LM: Indigenous and environmental organizations have managed to make people in Ecuador aware of the necessity to defend the environment and also national sovereignty, because it runs against our national interest to hand over a vast area—for example, 5 million acres under the new Licensing Round—to multinationals. But also, importantly, an international network with ecological and human rights groups has been created in support of the human rights of indigenous people who are affected directly by oil development.

Fundamentally, we have tried to work for solidarity both inside and outside of the country. The response has been very positive and has led to a broad-based and concrete campaign against Texaco. When dealing with a multinational, it is important to look for help on an international level, and we've been able to find it. A great interest in solidarity organizations, with environmental groups on the national and international levels, has meant that there has been a lot of help provided.

Our objective is to put pressure on oil companies in the United States, since the companies that are in Ecuador are U.S. companies. We want to make people in the United States aware that in Ecuador there are indigenous people who want to set a different course and have some say in what's going on. This campaign has had a lot of success and we hope it will be more fruitful in the future.

What is the role of the Ecuadorian government in oil development?

LM: Unfortunately, the national government has tried to transfer all aspects of the operation, exploration, exploitation, and even the administrative part of oil development to foreign companies. The role of the government has been no more than to hand over extensive territories for prospecting and all the other steps of oil development. There has been no legislation or rules that would enable the government to exercise control over environmental impacts that are caused, and there are no instruments that force the companies to comply with anything that would control the social and ecological impacts.

Does Petroecuador, the state-owned oil company, act more responsibly than the multinationals?

LM: Petroecuador took charge of Texaco's operations. I do not believe that Petroecuador will impose policies for what can really be termed a true "development" of oil resources for the benefit of Ecuadorians. Working with the World Bank, the principal objective of Petroecuador has been to privatize the mechanisms of oil development into the hands of private companies.

How has the military treated indigenous people in Ecuador?

LM: Until now, the military has said that the indigenous struggle is against the law of national security, so indigenous peoples have remained under constant threat. The military has worked to guarantee the security of the companies and they watch over and guard the companies' operations.

They say they care about national security, but obviously, the moment that they allow a company to fence off an extensive territory, they are handing over our sovereignty to foreign interests. When we protest this, the military says it is we who are threatening national security.

Can you describe the role of multinationals in the agrarian sector?

LM: There is currently a plan that they call "modernization" in the agricultural sector, which is being processed by the Inter-American Development Bank. The plan's goal is to create a system which is run by agro-industry that would encourage agricultural production for export, disregarding the basic food needs of the Ecuadorian people.

What is your alternative vision?

LM: CONAIE's agrarian reform proposal now in the Ecuadorian Congress is derived from the way that indigenous people see this question. It's meant to benefit not only the indigenous people but the entire agricultural sector. The first aspect is a restructuring of land ownership. It's impossible to talk about agricultural development when land is in the hands of the very few.

The second chapter deals with making production more dynamic and sustainable. The goal is not only to try to meet the needs of the farmer and his community, but the internal needs of all of Ecuador. This part of the law is directed at encouraging sustainable development of the Amazon, but it would also be applied in the coastal region.

The last part deals with the democratization of government institutions overseeing the agrarian sector in order to increase the participation of indigenous peoples and farmers, because now there is no democratic participation in these institutions. It is all a personal decision of the president.

There's been a backlash of sorts against the indigenous movement in Ecuador. Can you describe the backlash and where its roots lie?

LM: There are various sectors that are involved in this reaction. They include the government, which has always tried to defame the aspirations of the indigenous movement, as well as the Agricultural Chamber of Commerce, the large landowners, the armed forces, and the political interests of the right that have always fought against the indigenous movement. But now the public as a whole are understanding our problem. They are understanding that it is a national problem, not only an indigenous one.

12

Nina Pacari

Nina Pacari has become one of the most important and articulate indigenous leaders in modern Ecuador. The first Indian lawyer in the country, she is a co-founder of the Pachakutik Party, which promotes Indianist programs, and a deputy in the National Congress. She is also one of the principal organizers of CONAIE, the pan-Indian association that encompasses all important Ecuadorian native peoples. CONAIE has been instrumental in a number of uprisings from 1990 onward, at times bringing the government to its knees. Although the struggle continues, CONAIE perhaps reached the apex of its power in January 2000 when, with the army, it helped overthrow the administration of Jamil Mahuad, a deeply unpopular president (see Chapter 4).

It is clear from this interview that while Pacari has not given up extralegal means to promote her Indianist program, she is deeply pragmatic and believes it is possible to change attitudes and power structures through electoral means. Pacari also admits to the internal divisions that face CONAIE. Interesting here is her rejection of the use of class analysis (that is, Marxist strains) in the drive toward Indian rights. Her main focus is on making Ecuador a "plurinational" state that accepts the wide differences between the native peoples, the whites (who have traditionally run the country), and the significant population of African descent.

NP: In ten years we have come a long way. We have mayors in city halls, prefects in the provincial councils, and deputies in the National Congress. That means that now it is our turn to govern. That's why we can't continue with accusatory rhetoric. However, since the problems of state structure and the exercise of power have not been resolved, we will continue to demand the recognition of a plurinational state.

What is the difference between a national state and a plurinational state?

NP: The indigenous peoples are not grouped around particular interests. Our process of historical struggle and our claims are now much more global and national. Since the beginning of the '90s we have had as our

From José Steinsleger, "Ecuador: Entrevista a Nina Pacari, diputada indígena," Servicio de Información Indígena. Translated here by Erick D. Langer.

plank the construction of a plurinational state because we believe in horizontal power, shared and distinct from an absence of identity as was understood in terms of class struggle in the '60s. The struggle has to do with the state structure and the exercise of power.

Does this imply a modification of the notion of power?

NP: No. [It means] a modification in the strategies of struggle. In the proposal for a plurinational state there was always implied the concept of power, but a distinct power, a horizontal one, shared, more democratic, with space for decisions and the redistribution of resources on equitable terms on the level of gender and cultural participation.

How does the rebellion of January 21 [2000] enter into the context of demands for a plurinational state?

NP: Essentially, the action of January 21 was an action of popular sovereignty. Nonetheless, although one of the key points of the rebellion was the fight against corruption, there were problems. Although the indigenous peoples were the only sector that up to the moment was completely transparent not only on an individual but also on a collective level, I think that we should be careful not to commit errors that condemn us doubly, bringing us in danger of falling apart.

Does this mean that the protagonists of the rebellion were manipulated?

NP: I don't think there was manipulation. On the 21st of January a number of different aspects came together. In principle, let's say that before the corruption of the Mahuad government, nobody was undaunted. The levels of corruption were so high that not even the president's own party supported him.

Instead of the corruption, the social problems, and the danger of national disintegration, Mahuad only thought of the bankers. All wanted to get rid of him, but nobody wanted to show his face. The indigenous mobilization and the social movements converged with the position of the Armed Forces and the politicians [who watched] from afar, seeing how things evolved.

As a member of CONAIE, what did your party think of the indigenous rebellion?

NP: In CONAIE we had posited a plurinational state with a plurinational government. A triumvirate was not the expression of that position. What failed was the coherence viewed in terms of a process of construction [of the state]. On January 21 there was a taking of the government. In the indigenous movement, what is under debate is how do we become the government, whether through elections or through the taking of power.

Would it be correct to say that the Ecuadorian indigenous movement represents the social sector that is the best guarantee to prevent the fragmentation of the national state?

NP: It's on the mark to say that we question the character of the state. Because of that, on the municipal level we have assumed local governance. The democratic experience of the indigenous people in localities such as Guamote and Cotacachi is extremely important in comparison to, for example, the authoritarian municipal government of Guayaquil. They are distinct forms in style and content and are seen as a model for the country. And this process is being done by the indigenous mayors.

Are the Indigenous Parliaments alternatives to the Legislative branch?

NP: There is a lack of serious debate. Congress should channel the debate and bring together the different proposals to see how we can create a regimen of autonomy that permits us to organize ourselves and see us as a country.

What forces are opposed to the autonomy of indigenous peoples?

NP: In Ecuadorian society there is a recognition of diversity, of plurality in discourse, but the bankers, the business lobbies, and the groups with economic power oppose this because they fear they will lose their privileges.

In the interior of the indigenous movement, what obstacles do you observe?

NP: The diversity within the indigenous movements also contains different interests. We haven't advanced in how to manage these conflicts via a dialogue, consensus, and debate. There is an institutional weakness and a lack of leadership. The danger is not so much the lack of credibility of the traditional politicians but that we do not need politicians.

You speak of "traditional politics" but you have been elected Congresswoman of a party that obeys the rules of the electoral game. Are you a traditional politician?

NP: The Ecuadorian indigenous movement has been clear: we have not abandoned the extra-institutional struggle. But when we followed the institutional struggle through elections or, better said, with established rules, we see that it is difficult to transcend [the old ways] in respect to the new styles of acting politically. The ethical side of the matter is essential. It is important that the legislating style does not consist of a formulation by the elite and of four experts, but that it be part of a process.

What do you think about people who assert that the indigenous movement is archaic or fundamentalist?

NP: We are not homogenous. We also have fundamentalist ideologies and racist behavior that causes negative effects. Some people talk about class struggle that comes from analysis of the '70s and '80s; we don't dialogue well with the government, and those who go to the dialogue are lackeys of the government. If we are in Congress we are perceived as being all the same; people do not see the differences between us.

How do the fundamentalist tendencies manifest themselves?

NP: There are sectors on the Left that do not understand indigenous society and its right to assert its concepts and its analysis. I do not deny that in the indigenous movement the extremes are absent; for example, those who propose the recuperation of the Inca empire or that we are ancient cultures, etc. It's true; we come from ancient cultures. But we are like all other cultures, and as every other society we have the right to be creative, to modernize.

Identity is uniformity? Why be an Indian?

NP: In the indigenous movement there is no real uniformity. Among the indigenous peoples of Ecuador there exist various nationalities. That is undeniable. That is why we see ourselves as indigenous. We believe that we have an identity. But I believe that we should not keep on saying that we are "indigenous peoples" without overcoming the homogenizing reductionism and develop ourselves as much as we can as the collective identities that we have as the Shuar, Chachi, or Quechua people. And it is this multiplicity and multiculturalism that begins to become visible from the way we use language.

13

Felipe Quispe Huanca

Felipe Quispe, known as "El Mallku" (The Chief), one of the most radical leaders of the Bolivian peasant movement, is attempting to create an Aymara political hegemony in his country. He was a co-founder of the Guerrilla Army Túpac Katari (EGTK) in the early 1990s and was jailed when captured in 1992. After his release, he became the president of the CSUTCB, the largest union of peasant workers. Quispe was the most important leader in the 2000 "Water War" in which the people of Cochabamba fought the privatization and sale to a foreign corporation of the municipal water works. He became one of the main power brokers during the Banzer administration (1997–2001), and his union's capacity to shut down the country through blockades has made him a man much feared in government circles.

Below is a speech, "Oppressed but Not Defeated," that provides some indications of the way Quispe thinks and what he wants. Note that he is clearly widely read; his references range from Aymara sayings to Machiavelli. Note also how he jumps from racist literature in the colonial period to the nineteenth century and then tars all whites in the twenty-first century with the same brush. His views of Aymara cultural hegemony and historical importance are interesting and might explain why he does not have much of a support base in the south or east of the country, where there are few Aymaras.

I will not just speak of the Aymaras, but also of the Quechuas, just as it's important to talk of the Guaranís.[1] Quechua is an exact copy of Aymara in many words; for example, breast is *ñuñu*, knee is *qunquri*, neck is *kunka* in both languages. Because of this, our ancestors, or our grandfathers, said *q'ichu aru*, a Quechua word, not *quichua* or *qhichwa*, they said *q'ichu aru*. The Spaniards, hearing *q'ichu aru*, write "Quechua," the word that in Aymara is pronounced *q'ichu*.

From Felipe Quispe Huanca, "Oprimidos pero no vencidos y el potencial contestatario de la lengua Aymara," *Aruskipasipxañasataki: El siglo XXI y el futuro del pueblo Aymara*, ed. Waskar Ari Chachaki (La Paz: Editorial Amuyañataki, 2001), 97–101. Translated here by Erick D. Langer.

We can say more; let us talk, breathe, and think well in Aymara, and in Aymara also we will shout; that is what is right for us. This is what in truth we all must do today and we must live in Aymara. They say that the brothers in the large nations are making their own original languages come alive. In India there are Brahmans, the major chiefs; here there are *gringo*[2] bosses whom you can't touch, you can't breathe on, nor look at directly. In turn they, without knowing, in five years they were supposed to have learned things and with this knowledge they run the state. And we can run our own, brothers and sisters; can't we do it too?

Speaking about that, let us speak a little bit in Spanish. They call our lands "territory." And I will speak from my own thoughts, I will not speak from books because, brothers, you have not gone to the university, in these times nobody has; for the college graduates we can speak in Spanish and we can deal with theories and scientific terms, but today we will speak simply in our Aymara language so that we may understand. That's why I will speak in Aymara. Please excuse me, perhaps some of you do not understand Aymara anymore. I like speaking in Aymara because I am Aymara. I also understand Quechua and, as the union leader, I can speak other languages as well because a leader needs to be well educated.

In these moments we think: Why is there Samaypata?[3] which is Santa Cruz. The name Samaypata is Aymara (it means "resting in the heights"). In Argentina they speak of Catamarca, but the Spanish chroniclers are wrong. In Aymara, *Qata marka* means "salt village," brothers and sisters, so that we start from there and we know that the name *Qata marka* is Aymara. In Chile, Atacama is *Jatamarka* in Aymara, which means "the place of the original people." Roberto Choque[4] has spoken of the Chachapoyas, of the Huancas; *Chachapoya* is Aymara as well. On the other hand there is the term *Kitu*, that is what one hears many times, it is *K'itu*[5] . . . but that must have been that way since the Aymara period *K'itu*, from there it must have been [of] the Aymaras; year by year we must have lost it [for] ourselves. But we continue to exist. In truth, there must have been the Pukina and Uru languages; there have been all types of languages that have been lost. Who has made us lose them? We are the guilty ones or those who come from abroad like *tumaykus siwiq'aras* who spend our money poorly. In Quechua they say *qhasi uju*; they also say *yawar ch'unqu*, they are the ones who suck blood every day. Those are the ones who made us lose them.

I want to speak a bit about the chronicles; they have been written by priests. One of them is a writer of Bolivian history, José Manuel Cortés,[6] who affirms: "the Indian is vigilant over his own things; he keeps them, and what is not his he eats until he explodes." Afterward, in those times, for example, they say: "the Indian watches over his possessions like a lady over her servant, and he uses his woman like a slave." They also say that the Indian is very good in his love for God, that the Indian dies and does not fear God, that the Indian sleeps without a care; thus, in those times they wrote with hate. Bautista,[7] for example, writes: "this Indian with the face of stone." This is how, with humiliation, they have always referred to us. Reading these things is enough to make us mad. Other authors say: "they only live like a dog who is preoccupied with eating and finding a mate; they only think about those two things."

I now will say, brothers, why they wrote about us, what is the reason. Bartolomé de Las Casas[8] with other Spaniards fought in the sixteenth century. One of them said: "these Incas don't have any spirit," and another said: "they don't have a human soul, because if they had a soul, they would have accepted God." That is how they saw us among themselves. Others asserted that "the Indian is a little superior to the llama." They thought those thoughts then, until today they continue to see us in the same way. We aren't seen as human beings, we are not remembered as persons, only they go forward [progress].

And what will we do now? As we have said, we will speak in Aymara. As Aymaras, what will we do in the Confederación Sindical Única de Trabajadores Campesinos de Bolivia? What is being done? It is now different; that's why I say that the union is going downhill, the union doesn't work as a union anymore. Before, in the '50s, in '52,[9] and when Gualberto Villarroel in '45 brought about the First Indian Congress, in those moments it must have worked; today there are already various laws and also we now speak Aymara mixed [with Spanish]. In this way, they also mix up the laws, and that's why the CSUTCB has changed its thoughts and its ideology. You must have heard on the radio or on television that the union isn't anymore tied to class analysis or to the peasantry; that's why the Central Obrera Boliviana[10] isn't for us and the people don't respond anymore. It's that they have fought only class warfare. The fight for land and territory, what we have plowed and moved, that isn't good anymore for them. Under the ground, there might be gold and silver and other metals, and at the most profound depths there might be petroleum and water. They don't want to recognize that this is ours.[11] Today, our enemies have decreed the Water Law, but as a union we can't say anything. According to the union, we are peasants and not Indians anymore, we aren't the aboriginal people anymore. Thus, these laws challenge the CSUTCB to see if we are united or tied like a shoe; but within us there exist Communist influences, there are brothers who think like Communists.

Now we have changed in the Confederación. Those who manage the political aspects, those who think aren't on our side; many are missing, and that is why we are not moving forward, that's why we in truth need to prepare ourselves. They say in Spanish, "the Indians aren't prepared," maybe that's true; but it's been many years since the Agrarian Reform was decreed,[12] and from that moment onward what has been recognized? From that moment onward we already knew Spanish, but in Spanish the radio stations speak as they wish, comrades, there's much mixture and they are making Aymara disappear. Who? The radio stations, those who are on television, the teachers. I remember 1952, I went to school and the teacher said that it's not allowed to speak in Aymara, so how couldn't we begin to forget Aymara? Neither can we learn to speak Spanish easily, you can't just learn it. The same teachers and the same people in charge of education are those who have let us get to this point. But we can say something else; when the Spaniards arrived and even at independence, still Aymara was spoken well, even the clothing was ours and was well utilized. Now we wear other clothes that aren't as good. In the country-side we put a doll dressed in used Western clothes like a person in the fields to scare away the birds. We can say that we today are dressed like scarecrows.

The schools have been one of the principal guilty parties why Aymara is not pronounced well, but today we still speak Aymara; if now we try to live more our language, that's where the enemy cuts us off. Some of us have read Nicholas Macchiavelo [*sic*], who said that the first thing that must be done is to "cut the culture" to get people to submit. The gringos have read Macchiavelo, just as have Jaime Paz Zamora, Banzer, and Sánchez de Lozada, among others.[13]

Macchiavelo taught that one must cut out languages first, brothers, that's why we are already cut, that's why in school we start with Aymara and we finish with Spanish. Who is at fault? We ourselves are and some-times even myself. We aren't conscious of this. What does consciousness mean? It's a big thought with all heart. Let's not be like the evangelists who sell a gringo God, and afterward they dance in the streets. We must lift ourselves up; from now on, we must mobilize. Let's think in Aymara and let's speak in Aymara. Who among us speaks to the children in the mother language of education? The children now only speak in Spanish. We are Aymaras and only in that way should we speak in *Kollasuyu*.[14] If not, we are lost.

Notes

1. Quechua, the other major Andean language in Bolivia besides Aymara, was the imperial language of the Incas and is spoken mostly in the southwest. Guaraní, the third most spoken indigenous language in Bolivia, is heard mainly among peoples of the Andean foothills and in the semitropical lowlands. It is not consid-ered an Andean language but comes originally from Brazil and Paraguay.

2. *Gringo* is a derogatory term for "white man."

3. Samaypata is the location of an Inca fortress on the eastern edge of the Andes.

4. Choque, also of Aymara origin, is a prominent Bolivian historian.

5. Quispe is referring to Quito, the capital of Ecuador.

6. Cortés wrote an influential textbook in the midnineteenth century.

7. Quispe is referring to Bautista Saavedra, the president of Bolivia (1921–25) and a leading *indigenista*.

8. The famous sixteenth-century friar who defended the Indians against exploitation.

9. 1952 was the year of the Bolivian National Revolution, which led to significant land reforms.

10. The COB is the umbrella labor organization for Bolivia.

11. The Bolivian state reserves all rights to subsurface deposits.

12. This occurred in 1953.

13. These three are all former recent presidents of Bolivia.

14. *Kollasuyu* was the Inca designation for the territory where most of the Aymara speakers lived in pre-Conquest times.

14

R. Marhikewun

The Mapuche people of Chile have had a long, conflictive history with the state. They were one of the last large agricultural groups to be conquered and did not fully submit until the 1880s, when the Chilean government turned its battle-hardened troops from the War of the Pacific (1879–1883) to invade the Araucania, the region between the Bío-Bío River and Puerto Montt. The Mapuche were alloted small reservations on marginal lands. Under Salvador Allende's Socialist government (1970–1973), the indigenous people were able to regain some of their territory through land invasions that the government then sanctioned. However, under the brutal dictatorship of General Augusto Pinochet (1973–1990), all land reverted to the white owners.

Since the return to partial democracy, the Mapuche have organized and have become a potent political force in the southern part of the country (see Chapter 2). However, especially in the south, the practices of the dictatorship have not completely disappeared. Large landowners there have dominated local societies and at times have used violence to gain their ends. In particular, the construction of a series of dams threatens the few territories that the Mapuche still possess. Here one of their own people, R. Marhikewun, a British-based journalist writing in 1998 for the Mapuche International Link, comments on the Chilean government's anti-Mapuche policy.

The Chilean government had hardened its repressive policy against the Mapuche with police raids in several parts of the country and the detention of ten Mapuche youths—two of whom had to be hospitalized because of the brutal action of police force. The Indigenous Law is under siege to accommodate multinational corporations; land disputes are multiplying and the Lumako case arises again, with the government wielding the threat of applying the Internal State Security Law.

On the issue of territorial rights and the preservation of indigenous cultures: our peoples have been waiting generations for a change of attitude from the Chilean society and its authorities. The lack of perspective

From R. Marhikewun, "Chilean Government Hardens Its Anti-Mapuche Policy," Mapuche International Link.

and of political will to define a clear and transparent political project on the matter is causing a polarization which, if it continues, will lead us (as expressed in a Mapulink communiqué) to the edge of a cliff; and this is a dangerous tendency which should not be exacerbated, in the interests of Chileans and Mapuche alike. Therefore urgent and just measures should be taken by the government in order to face constructively the conflicts arising from the unfortunate state in which we find ourselves. The Frei administration's intransigence, its lack of credibility, and its inability to generate initiatives, coupled with its frequent blunders on indigenous affairs, have contributed to worsen the situation, as happened in the administration's handling of the situation of the hydroelectric power stations. One should also take into account the innumerable land disputes and the dismissal, in little more than a year, of two Mapuche directors of CONADI (National Corporation for Indigenous Development) for dissenting from the government's policy and for defending the application of the Indigenous Law, all being the result of the government's hostile attitude. To complete the picture, Mapuche students have now been targeted and, as in the worst times of the dictatorship, they have been threatened with the application of the Internal State Security Law.

Those people who speak of national unity and historical reconciliation, while forgetting that we the Mapuche also have feelings, are simply engaging in demagogical calls void of all sincerity, and must be ignored. It's necessary for Chilean society as a whole to face reality thoughtfully and to make an effort to find lasting solutions for coexistence. Chilean authorities must look into their hearts and recognize that the benefits they enjoy are derived directly or indirectly from the land and the resources taken from the Mapuche nation. The authorities and political parties must accompany their talk with concrete action, because the Mapuche have had it with empty speeches, with promises, and with projects that are announced with big headlines but never carried out. Electoral tactics—now used not only for elections by those who hold or aspire to hold the State's political and institutional power—will no longer sway our people. The lesson we can derive from the recent past is that despite the efforts to destroy us economically and culturally by stealing our resources and land and by the application of assimilationist policies aimed at eroding our identity as a nation, the Mapuche have not lost our consciousness of being a people; on the contrary, we have maintained intact, through generations, our spirit of kinship and solidarity. In fact, every time a community has suffered an act of aggression, it becomes a concern of the entire Mapuche people. In early August of this year, when Bernardita Calfuqueo was brutally beaten by Rolando Flores, mayor of Lumako (of the rightist Renovación Nacional Party), for denouncing racial discrimination and demanding respect for her rights as a professional, it hurt us as if she were a close family member. We are also very clear on the fact that our people are no longer willing to tolerate the kind of overbearing and degrading government treatment that has remained unchanged from the times of the Conquest. Times have changed, and now there exists the consciousness that we also have a right to justice and the right to be treated in a civilized way, despite the fact that the justice system has continually disappointed us.

The Current Situation

In relation to the latest developments, it's good to ask ourselves why the Mapuche have started again to reoccupy disputed land in several parts of the Araucania region. Perhaps the statements by the peasants who took over the Santa Rosa de Colpi estate, Traiguén, may shed light on the reasons for this kind of action. They stated that they were "tired of waiting for the verdict from the Chilean justice system, which in any case would never find in our favor" (*El Austral*, Sept. 9, 1998). This shows that the land recuperation actions are but the result of the profound frustration felt by our people with regard to the authorities and of the loss of confidence in the Chilean justice system. Justice is done automatically when it comes to defend the interests of large landowners and usurpers; it is always aided by the police and deployed to punish with brute force those Mapuche who demand justice. This sad scenario was seen once more in Concepción on October 8, where uniformed and plainclothes police acted against young Mapuche and *winka* (non-Mapuche Chilean) students during a peaceful demonstration at the headquarters of CORMA [Corporación de la Madera, a logging business association]. José Llanquileo (19) and Juan Pichicura (24) were wounded and had to be taken to the Concepción Regional Hospital. Abuses of power, racist slurs, and torture perpetrated by the Chilean police against the Mapuche are never investigated, nor are the perpetrators reprimanded, as happened in the case of Juan Carlos Reinao (22); because of its brutality, the case was widely reported in Chile and abroad. One of the students detained still remains in the Temuko public jail: Aníbal Salazar Huillacura (25), who was turned over to the Temuko court, where he was questioned by Judge Víctor Reyes, who is in charge of the case [NT: Chilean judges investigate, prosecute, and rule on cases in their charge].

Domestic and international public opinion have known about the glaring abuses derived from the controversial project to build a dam and hydroelectric power station on the Upper Bío Bío River, an example of which are the tactics employed by the Spanish company ENDESA to "persuade" local inhabitants to abandon their lands. The abuses denounced by the Mapuche-Pewenche are many, and include harassment, pressure tactics, and all kinds of deceits, all aimed to force the Pewenche to abandon their ancestral lands and to accept the promises to exchange them for ownership of plots in mountainous zones which stay covered by snow the greatest part of the year. Domingo Namuncura is a former director of CONADI who was booted by the government for supporting the rights of the Pewenche and affirming the Indigenous Law, and he clarifies the situation in an interview for the daily *La Tercera* (August 28, 1998): "after interviewing fifty-nine Pewenche who had agreed to the land exchange, one arrived at the conclusion that forty of them were not happy and that their previous consent was due to the way in which the deal's concepts were presented to them, and also to a clear sense of resignation [for what they saw as unavoidable]."

The Pewenche have said that the company assured them they had no choice, and that the project would be carried out despite their unwillingness; they were told that if they did not sign the agreements they would lose everything, since—according to them—the project had been approved by the President of the Republic. The President repeatedly underscored this last point to the press in several declarations where he expressed being in favor of the construction of the dams. Further substantiation of his position was provided by the subsequent revelation that President Eduardo Frei himself is one of the project's shareholders.

We do not want to create the impression that the situation of other indigenous peoples of the world is better than ours; nevertheless, let's look in particular to the United States, whose total indigenous population is, in relative terms, less than that of the Mapuche in relation to Chile. Many of these nations [in the United States] have had their treaties recognized; they make use of their right to self-determination; they have their own governments, education, and health systems, their own customs and tax systems, their own police. In addition, they have been compensated for the lands that could not be returned to them, and even more: some receive rental payments for use of the land still occupied by the non-indigenous. And this happens in the most powerful country on the planet. Why? Because there is respect for the rule of law, and the governments have had the political wisdom to honor the agreements signed by the State; because they have created policies to encourage integration and historical reconciliation, and also because there exists the certainty that it is possible for peoples of different cultures to share the same land in a civilized and harmonious manner, with mutual respect. Similar situations can be seen with the indigenous of Canada, the aborigines of Australia, the Maori of New Zealand, and the Sami of Scandinavia, just to name some.

Chilean laws themselves have started to be used to fight for the recuperation of Mapuche lands that were illegally confiscated by the State. Mapuche lawyer José Lincoqueo has said repeatedly that as far as land tenure disputes go, "judgement is against the State of Chile," because the

State is guilty of illegal confiscation of our territory, and the matter should be adjudicated in this framework. In fact, on June 11, 1997, Mr. Lincoqueo sued the State of Chile at the 13th Civil Court in Santiago, representing the Mapuche-Pewenche community of Paillao Colcuma in the municipality of Tirúa, Arauco province, for the restitution of 26,000 metric hectares of land usurped by logging companies, among them the Forestal Mininco. His arguments are founded in the historical records and reinforced by the terms of the Parliament of Negrete held between the Mapuche nation and the Spanish Crown in 1803, before the creation of the State of Chile. On the side of the Chilean government the suit has been joined by the State Defense Council and Forestal Mininco. This case is unprecedented in the annals of Chilean judicature; the results are yet to be known—the verdict will certainly mark the start of a new stage in the long struggle of the Mapuche people for the recuperation of their ancestral territory.

The Mapuche Are Not Alone

Our Mapuche people are part of an important segment of humankind; according to UN figures, indigenous peoples number more than 300 million. According to UNPO (Unrepresented Nations and Peoples Organization), we are more than 600 million. Whatever the figure and the status conferred on them (some peoples, like the Mapuche, are not recognized by their national constitutions and therefore are technically non-existent), the truth is that these peoples are a reality, and they continue to speak out from all corners of the planet. They are the peoples that fight for the noblest of ideals, for values and principles that are universally recognized and on which Christian Western civilization is founded; they struggle for justice, freedom, the right to live on ancestral lands; they are the ones who fight against racism and intolerance and in favor of the recognition of cultural diversity. They are the peoples who are in the forefront of the battle against the depredating incursions of the transnational companies; they are the ones who defend the tropical forests, the rain forests of the Amazon, the Philippines, or Indonesia.

Their contribution to civilization was recognized at the Rio de Janeiro Summit of 1992, as declared in its Agenda 21, as they are the ones that for generations have developed a sustainable life system in harmony with the land and with Nature. This is a pressing concern for all those who wish to preserve ecological balance and diversity and to ensure the future of the planet and its inhabitants.

The Mapuche, just like other indigenous peoples of the world, are not alone. The indigenous peoples of Chile and Argentina are receiving growing support from all social and political groups, including Chileans and Mapuche living abroad. Numerous people believe in the need to create a more equitable and truly democratic society; we refer especially to those people who fight along with the indigenous to preserve the environment and the ecosystems endangered by the acts of the multinationals; those who question the economic order and the uncontrolled proliferation of [development] projects justified in the name of a supposed "common good" or "national interest" detrimental to the interests and the rights of the indigenous peoples and to legality itself. We refer to those who protest and raise their voices alongside the Mapuche-Pewenche against the construction of the dams in the Upper Bío Bío.

This growing current of Chilean voices received an important recognition from the international community when, on October 7, 1998, it was awarded the Alternative Nobel Prize (Right Livelihood Award). This prize was given to Juan Pablo Orrego, president of GABB (Action Group for the Bío Bío), in recognition for his contribution to the country and to humankind with his defense of the environment. This international recognition also stresses the righteousness of his struggle and does away with the propaganda that sought to put down his positions and dismiss them as "ecoterrorist" or "extremist." The activities of this group—and others similar to it—constitute undoubtedly a significant appeal for a national awareness about the problem of the environment and for a constructive debate within society. At the same time they serve as warnings about the adverse effects on the indigenous communities and on the environment that accompany the implementation of certain development projects now under way in Chile.

It is also encouraging to see that a growing number of Chileans admit that there is a historical debt to be paid to the indigenous peoples, which the State must see to. There are also those who make efforts to create the conditions necessary to construct a multicultural and multiethnic Chile, which are solid bases to enhance the process of democratization of Chilean society and to create the coordinates for a true historical reconciliation with the original inhabitants of the country.

To conclude, and in relation to the repressive wave unleashed by the government: our Mapuche people and its organizations, along with those Chileans who struggle to build a more just and equitable country for all, must join forces, must respond and explore forms of defense that are active but nonviolent, with the aim of changing the anti-indigenous ways of the current government and so prevent an indigenous outburst, which would have unpredictable consequences for the stability of the country.

Selected Bibliography

Arias, Arturo, ed. *The Rigoberta Menchú Controversy*. Minneapolis: University of Minnesota Press, 2001.

Collier, George A., et al. *Basta! Land and the Zapatista Rebellion in Chiapas*. Rev. ed. Berkeley: LPC, 1999.

Garfield, Seth. *Indigenous Struggle at the Heart of Brazil: State Policy, Frontier Expansion, and the Xavante Indians, 1937–1988*. Durham: Duke University Press, 2001.

Joyce, Christopher. *Earthly Goods: Medicine-Hunting in the Rainforest*. Boston: Little, Brown, and Co., 1994.

Katz, Friedrich, ed. *Riot, Rebellion, and Revolution: Rural Social Conflict in Mexico*. Princeton: Princeton University Press, 1988.

Kicza, John E., ed. *The Indian in Latin American History: Resistance, Resilience, and Acculturation*. Wilmington, DE: Scholarly Resources, 1993.

Lucas, Kintto. *We Will Not Dance on Our Grandparents' Tomb: Indigenous Uprisings in Ecuador*. London: Catholic Institute for International Relations, 2000.

McDonald, Theodore, Jr. *Ethnicity and Culture amidst New "Neighbors": The Runa of Ecuador's Amazon Region*. New York: Allyn and Bacon, 1998.

Menchú, Rigoberta. *I, Rigoberta Menchú: An Indian Woman in Guatemala*. London: Verso Books, 1987.

Rabben, Linda. *Unnatural Selection: The Yanomami, the Kayapó, and the Onslaught of Civilization*. Seattle: University of Washington Press, 1998.

Ramos, Alcida Rita. *Indigenism: Ethnic Politics in Brazil*. Madison: University of Wisconsin Press, 1998.

Stern, Steve J., ed. *Resistance, Rebellion, and Consciousness in the Andean Peasant World, 18th to 20th Centuries*. Madison: University of Wisconsin Press, 1987.

Stoll, David. *Rigoberta Menchú and the Story of All Poor Guatemalans*. New York: Westview Press, 2000.

Tierney, Patrick. *Darkness in El Dorado: How Scientists and Journalists Devastated the Amazon*. New York: W. W. Norton, 2000.

Urban, Greg, and Joel Sherzer, eds. *Nation-States and Indians in Latin America*. Austin: University of Texas Press, 1991.

Van Cott, Donna Lee, ed. *Indigenous Peoples and Democracy in Latin America*. New York: St. Martin's Press, 1994.

Warren, Kay B. *Indigenous Movements and Their Critics: Pan-Maya Activism in Guatemala*. Princeton: Princeton University Press, 1998.

Zamosc, Leon. *The Agrarian Question and the Peasant Movement in Colombia: Struggles of the National Peasant Association, 1967–1981.* Cambridge: Cambridge University Press, 1986.